MOSCOW
FLYER

MOSCOW FLYER

JESSICA HARRINGTON
WITH DONN McCLEAN

Published in 2005 by Highdown,
an imprint of Raceform Ltd
Compton, Newbury, Berkshire, RG20 6NL
Raceform Ltd is a wholly-owned subsidiary of Trinity Mirror plc

A CIP catalogue record for this book is available from the British Library.

ISBN 1-905156-18-9

Cover designed by Tracey Scarlett

Interiors designed by Fiona Pike

Printed in Great Britain by William Clowes Ltd, Beccles, Suffolk

RACING POST

Sunday, December 5, 2004   *WWW.RACINGPOST.CO.UK*   £1.40

Issue No. 5,396

Moscow marvel

**Moscow Flyer raises the roof at
Sandown with brilliant Tingle
Creek success, pages 2-4**

CONTENTS

Acknowledgements

I am greatly indebted to Brough Scott for planting the germ of the idea of this book in the first instance. His continued support and advice throughout have been invaluable. To Jonathan Taylor and all at Highdown for their professionalism and attention to detail. To Donn McClean for his unfailing patience. To Johnny and my children for putting up with me for the last few months. And, of course, to Moscow Flyer. I hope that he will approve.

CHAPTER ONE

STILL TINGLING

I hate waiting. I hate hanging around. I don't care if it's for taxis or for people or for horses, I just don't do the waiting thing very well. It was a huge relief, therefore, when the time came to go and collect the saddle. At least from then on I would be doing rather than waiting.

Tingle Creek Chase day, Sandown, 4 December 2004. This was to be a defining day in Moscow Flyer's career. The day when we would know if we still had a Champion Chase horse on our hands.

Moscow Flyer was ten years old, almost eleven. Champion chaser in 2003, he had lost his crown when he lost his jockey at Cheltenham in March 2004. Azertyuiop was the new champion. There were those who believed that Azertyuiop would have beaten Moscow that day anyway, even if Moscow and Barry Geraghty had not parted company at the fourth-last fence. I wasn't one of them.

Azertyuiop was there at Sandown, present and correct. The

reigning champion, haughty and bullish. The seven-year-old in the prime of his years. He was there to put this issue beyond doubt. To prove that he was, without question, the fastest horse in the world over two miles and thirteen fences. No excuses would be accepted this time.

And Well Chief was there. The young pretender. The five-year-old who had won the Arkle Challenge Trophy at Cheltenham that March. I had thought that his trainer Martin Pipe might shirk the challenge. That he wouldn't want his young horse to take on the two-headed monster that was Azertyuiop and Moscow Flyer at this stage in his career. I was wrong. Martin Pipe is not one for shirking issues.

As I walked from the weigh room to the saddling boxes with Moscow's saddle in my arms, I thought that this could be the end of a magnificent journey. It was probably unrealistic to expect that Moscow Flyer, at his age, would have the speed necessary to win a Tingle Creek Chase. And this was no ordinary Tingle Creek Chase. The consensus was that these three horses were the most talented two-mile chasers we had seen in a generation. Moscow could run his heart out and still finish third.

As I neared the saddling boxes, I thought of all that he had done, all his achievements. I suppose you do that when you think that the end is nigh. His career flashed before my eyes. Before he ever started jumping fences, Moscow Flyer had been an extremely talented hurdler. Top class. He was the only horse Charlie Swan feared when he rode Istabraq. Moscow's record over fences was quite incredible: twenty races, fifteen wins, five non-completions. No horse had ever beaten him when he had managed to remain upright with his jockey in situ. Among those fifteen wins were seven in Grade 1 contests. You just couldn't go any higher in National Hunt racing and remain beneath the stratosphere.

Remarkably, since his first race over fences, he had failed to complete on every fourth run. Three wins, then a fall. Every time. He had won his previous three races before the 2004 Tingle Creek Chase. If the sequence was to be maintained, he was due a fall.

But deep in my guts I knew that he was well. Strange to relate that, at the age of ten, I felt he was better than he had been at any stage of his career. He had come in from his summer holiday bouncing like a spring lamb. He had won his prep race at Navan as impressively as he had ever won a prep race, and his training since then had been flawless. I had never known him to be in better form. Neither had Eamonn Leigh.

Eamonn was with Moscow when I got to the saddling boxes. That was not a total surprise. In fact, it is highly unusual to see Moscow Flyer without seeing Eamonn Leigh. When Moscow is on the gallops at home, Eamonn is on his back. When Moscow is in the back of the horsebox on his way to the races, Eamonn is in the front seat. When Moscow is walking around the parade ring at a race meeting, Eamonn is the one at his head. And when Moscow is out in his field during the summer, Eamonn is either out in the field with him or watching him from his kitchen window.

Moscow was difficult to saddle that day. He squashed both me and Eamonn against the walls of the box a couple of times. 'Galway' – Sam Murphy's regular box driver – was holding his head as we tried to get the saddle on. I don't know if he was feeling the pressure. If he was feeling anything like I was feeling, his heart was doing overtime. Eamonn and I didn't talk much as we worked. All the talking was done.

I walked down towards the parade ring with Moscow and Eamonn. When Moscow got to the top of the hill, just before you come down into the parade ring, he stopped. Not for too long, but just for long enough to enable him to have a look at the crowds packed four deep the whole way round, hoping to catch a glimpse. It wasn't that he was not used to crowds. God knows he had had his fill at Cheltenham and Aintree and Punchestown and Sandown before. It was as if he was savouring the moment. Appreciating the adulation. Delighting in the attention, and milking every minute.

Brian Kearney was in the parade ring with his wife Patricia when we got there. Brian is the man who will be able to tell his great grandchildren that he owned the legendary racehorse that was

Moscow Flyer. His first racehorse. That he hadn't even met the trainer before he asked her to buy him a horse, and that she actually bid on, and failed to get, two other horses before she ended up buying Moscow Flyer for him. It is quite an extraordinary tale that will fill many an evening in front of the fire with a pipe and a pair of slippers.

Brian and I had discussed the possible implications of this race many times. We had talked about what we would do if he got beaten, if he didn't still have the speed to beat these youngsters over two miles. We'd have to step him up in distance, we figured. The King George, we reckoned, over three miles. It would be a big step, but he had stayed two and a half miles well at Aintree the previous season, and his pedigree suggested that he had every chance of staying three. But if he were to go and win the Tingle Creek; if he were to go and beat Azertyuiop and Well Chief and regain the mantle of fastest two-mile chaser in the world; if he were to prove that he still had all that speed, at the age of ten . . . Well, we would just deal with that happy, happy scenario if it arose.

The bookmakers didn't think that it would. They usually know about these things. Their livelihoods depend on their knowledge. They were shouting odds-on about Azertyuiop and 2–1 about Moscow Flyer. It was the first time since the 2002 Tingle Creek Chase that Moscow had not been favourite for a race in which he was competing. Fortunately, Moscow didn't know that.

Barry Geraghty knew it, but he didn't care. In fact, he didn't agree. Barry had ridden Moscow in nineteen of his twenty steeplechase races and eleven of his twelve hurdle races. What Barry didn't know about Moscow Flyer, the racehorse, was either not worth knowing or untrue. Barry was the man who had guided Moscow Flyer, the green and gormless novice, over the obstacles, off the sports pages and straight on to the front pages. Moscow was the horse who had picked up Barry Geraghty, the talented young rider who could go places, put him on his back and carried him to superstardom. Together they made a formidable team.

Barry's confidence as he nodded his hellos in the parade ring bordered on arrogance. But it was reassuring. His whole demeanour was reassuring. I always leave tactics up to Barry. He knows how to ride the horse in a race much better than anybody else does. And he told us what he would do. He'd be travelling well coming out of the back straight. He'd take it up before the third last, the Pond Fence, and look around. They'd expect him to kick on after looking around, but he wouldn't. He'd jump the fence, look around again, and then kick for home. It would catch them unawares. I nodded and said, 'Whatever you think.' I still don't know what the plan would have been if he hadn't been travelling well.

I legged Barry up, wished him luck and headed off to the owners' and trainers' stand with Brian and Patricia. We got to the stand just in time to see Moscow and Barry cantering down to the start. My daughters Emma and Kate were with me. Kate was sitting on the steps, closing her eyes and covering her ears. Couldn't bear to look, couldn't bear to listen.

And as I stood there on the stand, a strange thing happened. My nervousness seemed to dissolve in the air. Soon they would be off, and soon it would be over. Then we would know. We would know whether or not we still had a champion chaser on our hands. The waiting was all but over. There was nothing more I could do. A calmness descended. The starter called them in and they were off.

The two-mile start at Sandown is up to your right-hand side. They run down the straight, jump two fences – a plain fence and an open ditch – pass the winning post, turn right-handed and go off to complete a circuit of the track. Moscow jumped off well in second place, just on the outside of Cenkos. I was glad that Cenkos was in the race, as he was a front-runner and would set a decent pace. Barry would find it easy to settle Moscow in behind him. It's quite a short run from the start to the first fence, but Barry got Moscow settled nicely and he jumped it well. He actually jumped it a little big if anything, but I was happy that he was over the first. I wished that I was as well settled as he appeared to be. He jumped the open ditch well too, and galloped up past the winning post for the first time just about two lengths off Cenkos towards the outside. Azertyuiop sat in third place on the inside, just about two lengths behind Moscow. Well Chief looked on from fifth place. I hadn't seen the young horse jump the first two – there had to be a doubt about his jumping as he was so inexperienced – but he seemed to be travelling nicely, so I could only assume that he had jumped them well.

The third fence is on the side of the course as they run away from you. This fence always worries me as it is slightly downhill and the ground runs away a little bit on the landing side. Moscow got in a little tight to this one. That is exactly what you don't want to be doing at a downhill fence. If you get it a little tight and clip the top of the fence, suddenly you are landing steeply on a downhill slope. There's only one possible outcome then. I held my breath. I saw him land and almost closed my eyes in anticipation of Barry's backside disappearing over the fence on to the ground. It didn't. He did lose a little momentum, allowing Azertyuiop to nose up his inside, but it was nothing serious.

They turned down the back straight and faced up to the seven fences that stand to attention in a line there. Plain, plain, open ditch, water, then the three Railway Fences. It is probably a great thrill for a jockey to turn at the top of the back straight and see these big black obstacles waiting for him, but for an onlooking trainer I can assure you it is not.

No change over the first two. They all jumped them well. Barry saw a stride at the open ditch, kicked Moscow in the belly, and he flew it. They raced in Indian file down to the water jump, at intervals of two lengths – Cenkos, Moscow, Azertyuiop, Well Chief. They could have been in formation.

The water jump is a strange one. We don't have them in Ireland and we don't school Moscow over one. He never seems to have a problem with them, but I am always a little worried when he approaches one. Probably because it would be a real sucker punch if he were to make a mistake at a water jump – the smallest obstacle on a steeplechase track – and hinder his chances as a result. No need to worry here, though. He met it in his stride and jumped out over it nicely.

Barry Geraghty is a thinking man's jockey. Directly after the third Railway Fence at Sandown, you turn right-handed out of the back straight. The three fences are so close together that it is unlikely you will be able to switch position between fences at Tingle Creek pace and maintain your balance. Consequently, you have to pick your position going to the first of them. Jump the first one on the inside, and you should be turning the corner on the inside.

On the approach, Cenkos began to drift towards the middle of the track and Barry took Moscow to the inside. Saving ground. Moscow met the first in his stride, got in tight to the second, and pinged the third. Cenkos got the third one wrong and suddenly Moscow was in front. I was startled by the crowd's reaction. As soon as Moscow's white noseband struck the front, a huge cheer went up from the grandstand. A tingle went up my spine, and I shuddered. I couldn't help myself. I had to join them. Go on, Moscow! Go on, Moscow!

But we weren't even near the end-game yet. Barry took a slight tug and the others concertinaed up behind him, Azertyuiop in his slipstream and Well Chief just behind him. Cenkos was still there on the outside, but Richard Johnson was flat to the boards on him. It was developing into the tripartite battle everybody had envisaged.

Out of the back straight and on to the third last, this was turning from a horse race into a game of chess. None of the three jockeys had moved a muscle. Then Barry looked around. I had forgotten that he was going to do it. It was a long, leering look. Come and catch me. But, just as he had told us, he didn't do anything else. Just had a look.

Ruby Walsh moved Azertyuiop to the outside going into the wings of the Pond Fence. Timmy Murphy got after Well Chief. Barry just sat still so that he could measure his fence. He wasn't meeting it on a good stride. Come back here. Just pop it.

He did. Ears pricked. Moscow quickly got his hind legs under him and accelerated away from the fence. Going around the home turn Barry had another glance. A protracted one. And kicked. Can you not catch me?

Moscow was at least a length and a half up on Azertyuiop going to the second last. Just jump it. Barry asked for a long one. One, two, up! Moscow flew it. I couldn't hear myself think. I couldn't hear myself scream. This was it. Two lengths clear over the second last, and this horse doesn't stop. Not here. Not up this hill.

Between the last two, Barry asked Moscow for everything he had. Moscow responded. Azertyuiop and Well Chief were flat out now and making little impression. If anything, Moscow was going away. Just jump the last.

Foot perfect. Barry sat down to drive his willing partner up the hill to the line. Nothing between them and the winning post now but green grass and a deafening roar. Was Moscow Flyer still the fastest horse in the world over two miles and thirteen fences? This old stager? Did he really still have the ability to beat the reigning champion chaser and the Arkle winner? Had he genuinely retained enough speed? At the age of ten? Did he really beat them on merit? No excuses? Did he? Really?

Barry allowed himself the luxury of a salute to the grandstand fully three strides from the line. In fairness, he had earned the right. If Moscow hadn't needed all his limbs to remain upright, I'm sure he would have saluted as well.

I was ecstatic. So many thoughts, so many emotions. There were elated people everywhere. Brian was euphoric. Emma was in tears. Kate was in tears. I'm sure I was in tears. We had our horse back. We had our champion. He had proved the doubters wrong. He had beaten the reigning champion. He had beaten the young pretender. And he had beaten them on merit. It had been as true a race as anyone could have wished for. No mistakes, no excuses. He was simply the fastest horse in the race.

Perhaps this journey wasn't at an end yet. This voyage that began in May 1994 in a stable out the back of Eddie Joyce's house in

Meelick, County Clare. This expedition that embraced me when the hammer finally fell on Lot 432 at the Tattersalls Ireland Derby Sale in June 1998. Perhaps there was a little more mileage in this one yet.

Just a little.

CHAPTER TWO

DERBY SALE 1998

If you are an Irish National Hunt trainer, you go to the Tattersalls Ireland Derby Sale. It is a given. That's where some of the best young Irish National Hunt horses are sold. As we prepared for the drive from Moone in County Kildare to Fairyhouse in County Meath on 26 June 1998, we could never have known the real extent of the journey on which we were about to embark.

We had an order from a new owner, Brian Kearney, to buy a horse for him for not more than 20,000 guineas. That was going to be the main business of the day. It wasn't going to be easy. The good ones don't come cheaply at the Derby Sale.

The first thing that strikes you about the Tattersalls Ireland sales complex is the serenity of the place. As you drive slowly up the laneway – you have to drive slowly because of the chassis-shattering ramps – to the Old Fairyhouse Stud, the copper beech trees enshroud you on either side and marshal you towards your destination. In reality, however, our destination was a long way off.

When Richard Tattersall founded the first ever bloodstock auction house in 1766, he didn't know that it would grow to become probably the most powerful bloodstock sales company in the world today. Tattersalls bought a 44 per cent stake in the old Ballsbridge International sales company in Dublin in 1979. Ironically, it was there that Moscow Flyer's grandam was sold in 1976. Tattersalls bought out the company in 1985 and moved to the Old Fairyhouse Stud, just across the road from Fairyhouse racecourse in Ratoath. That became Tattersalls Ireland. They claim that their Derby Sale is the premier sale for National Hunt horses in the world today. In fairness, they are probably right.

The sale is confined to untried, unbroken three- and four-year-old geldings and fillies. The average price paid for each horse over the course of the two-day sale is around €40,000, although €300,000 was paid for a Saddlers' Hall gelding out of a Strong Gale mare in 2004. Interestingly, a Moscow Society filly out of Mellick Lady made €215,000 in 2002. Quite a lot of money, you would have thought, for a horse that might not even be able to raise a gallop.

The thing that excites you most about buying at the Derby Sale is also the thing that strikes the fear of God in you. Nobody knows how good these horses are. They have not been broken – never had a saddle on – so you know that they have not been tried over five furlongs against something slow, or popped over a few schooling fences out in the back field. So the seller doesn't know how good his horse is, but neither does the prospective buyer. He could be anything, and he could be nothing. You simply don't know. You just do your best to maximise your chances of buying a good one. Poise and balance. Pedigree and conformation. How a horse is bred and how well he is put together. It's a bit like going to a car sale and not being allowed to test-drive the car you are going to buy. Imagine buying a car and not receiving the keys until the car is delivered to your home. You can check out the bodywork, study the spec, have a look under the bonnet and kick the tyres, but you can't drive it until you have paid for it.

But that's also the beauty of it. You can buy a lottery ticket for little money and wait to see if your numbers come up. In the foyer of the sales complex in 1998 there was a photo of One Man winning the Champion Chase – bought at the Derby Sale for 4,000 guineas. Another one of Cool Dawn winning the Gold Cup – bought for 8,500 guineas. The numbers came up for John Hales and Dido Harding, that's for sure. It would not be long before they would have to put up another picture in the foyer.

And everybody is there. Jonjo O'Neill, Nigel Twiston-Davies, Arthur Moore, Noel Meade, Willie Mullins. All there in their jeans and boots looking to pick up the next Cheltenham contender. You have to be there just in case. If you are not there, then quite literally you are not at the races. These young horses are the stars of the future. The Champion Hurdle winners. The Champion Chase winners. The Gold Cup winners. The trick is to be able to spot the 2002 Cheltenham winner in June 1998.

There were so many horses we wanted to buy. So many smashing-looking horses. And all the top stallions were represented: Strong Gale, Roselier, Phardante, Montelimar, Be My Native, Glacial Storm, Good Thyne, King's Ride, Supreme Leader, Un Desperado. It's the child-in-the-sweet-shop syndrome. But you can only buy whatever your mum will allow you to buy. Johnny doesn't allow me to buy on spec without an order any more. Actually, I could buy on spec, but I would have to hide the horse.

We bought two cheap horses early in the sale – one early on the first day and one early on the second day – but our main focus was the order we had from Brian Kearney. Brian was a new owner – I hadn't even met him before the sale – who had been introduced to us by a friend of his son's, Arthur Craigie, who had a horse with us. We were anxious to get him something good. It is important that new owners have a positive first experience of racehorse ownership. Too many are lost to racing because someone has tried to make a quick shilling out of them.

We were greatly restricted by our budget, though. While 20,000 guineas is not an insubstantial sum of money – a guinea is equivalent to £1.05, the theory being that the auction house gets the five pence in the pound – it was only a little higher than the average cost of a horse at the 1998 Derby Sale. Therefore we were limited in the type of horse we could even look at. There is a very fine balance to be struck here. As we thumbed through the catalogue, we couldn't pick anything that was so well bred that it would be out of our price range, yet it needed to have some sort of pedigree in order to stand a chance of being able to race. Much more important, however, was how it looked. That is why it was imperative that we got to see as many horses in the sale as possible.

Jim Mernagh and Johnny Harrington, my husband, go back a long way. Right to the height of Johnny's Curragh Bloodstock Agency days. Jim owns Coolamurry Stud and does a great job of consigning horses at the National Hunt sales. Jim knew what Johnny looked for in a horse and he had often come up with suitable horses for him in the past. This year, Jim was annoying Johnny about one horse in particular. Lot 432, a four-year-old Moscow Society gelding out of a Duky mare. 'He's a smasher. You have to come down and have a look at him.' It wasn't even down as being sold by Jim's Coolamurry Stud. The consignor was Ballymorris Stud – the property of Mr John P. Ryan. It turned out that Mr Ryan is the father-in-law of the breeder, Eddie Joyce, but Jim was looking after him on his behalf, and he had prepared him for the sale all right. Johnny told Jim that he would come down later and have a look at him. Jim seemed happy enough with that.

We looked at the page. Lot 432. We looked for black type. If a horse wins or is placed in a graded or listed race, that horse is printed in bold in a sales catalogue. Hence the term 'black type'. You had to go a long way down Lot 432's page to find any. Bramble Tudor and Ivy Green were top class, but they were both under the fourth dam – in human terms the great great grandmother. We were unenthused.

We bid on two horses for Brian Kearney on the first day of the sale. Nice horses with very acceptable pedigrees. But when the bidding went above 20,000, we had to stop and let them go. They were the owner's instructions: don't go above 20,000.

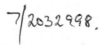

Going into the second and final day of the sale, we still hadn't filled our order. We really didn't want to go home without a horse for Brian, but it was proving difficult. The nice horses were making nice money. It looked like you were going to need more than twenty grand in order to compete.

Johnny met Jim again. 'You haven't been over to see my horse yet,' said Jim. 'I'm telling you, you need to see this horse.' You get an awful lot of that at the sales. Vendors telling you that you need to come and see their horses. If you went with all of them, you'd spend your day doing what vendors wanted you to do and not what you wanted to do yourself. But Jim was persistent.

'I don't know, Jim,' said Johnny. 'Moscow Society isn't going so well. And he's out of a Duky mare. I'm not sure. His book is a bit thin.'

'Johnny,' said Jim, almost hurt. You can insult a man directly to his face, but never insult his horse. 'I'm not selling you a book. I'm selling you a horse.'

'OK then. I'll be over to see him later.'

Jim wasn't about to allow him away with that. 'Look, come on and see him now. You'll be making your plans for the day and if you don't come over now you probably won't come over at all.'

Jim knew Johnny well all right.

Johnny relented. In fairness to Jim, he did seem to be very anxious that Johnny should see this one. More so than usual. Johnny respected Jim's judgement and he knew that Jim had a fair idea of the characteristics he valued in a horse. Moreover, Jim's consignment was in Barn A, which is right beside the actual sales ring. The handiest thing to do was to go and see him with Jim immediately. At the very least, it would get Jim off his back.

An inquisitive head peered over the half-door of Box 32 as Johnny arrived. Ears pricked. An unusual white blaze on his face. Almost as if someone had put a blob of white paint on his forehead, right above his eyes, and the paint had trickled down the middle of his face all the way to the end of his nose.

It's not easy for these horses. Still immature, they have been taken from their home and dropped into this completely alien

environment. Over the course of these few days, they are constantly hauled in and out of their boxes. Walked and trotted. Poked and prodded. It is remarkable that the vast majority of them behave so well.

Johnny liked this fellow even before Jim had him taken out of his box. He liked the head that peered over the door. He liked his step – positive and assured. This could be our horse. Johnny immediately found me and we went to look at him together. I was quite excited going over to see him as Johnny did really appear to like this one.

He caught my eye immediately. The first thing that struck me about the horse was how well balanced he was, how well he moved. You couldn't knock him off balance. He was a very correct horse, and well proportioned. I liked the way his head sat on his neck. How his neck went into his body. Nice deep chest. How his legs were just right for his body. He wasn't over big; everything was where it should have been. He had plenty of scope and it was easy to imagine him jumping a fence.

We went back to see him a couple of times that day. Each time we saw him, we liked him more. You can get a little horse-sick at these sales. You see so many of them. Although you take notes, you can sometimes forget what it was that made you really like one. It's always a good idea to go back and see them again. Just to be sure. The more we went back to Box 32, Barn A, the surer we got.

Jim Mernagh kept telling us that he would be a cheap horse. Johnny began to shuffle from one foot to the other, which was a sure sign that he liked this one and was excited about the prospect of having him home with us. 'He'll be a cheap horse all right,' Jim kept saying. 'He's coming up late in the sale.'

I don't know if we would have gone to see him had Jim not continually accosted Johnny, but there is a good chance that we wouldn't have. His pedigree was very light on top and he didn't have a huge amount to recommend him before we saw him. It just goes to show you that at these sales, especially the National Hunt sales, it pays to go and have a look at every horse. Or at least to have someone look at them on your behalf. It might have been the case that we would have seen him being led around before going into the actual ring. But it might not have been. The way it worked out, we got to see him properly and we got to like him a lot. This was the one we wanted. Our only fear was that he would go above twenty grand. If he did, we would have to leave him behind.

About half an hour before a horse is due in the sales ring at Fairyhouse, he is led around the ring outside. It's just like a small parade ring, except that instead of a saddle, each horse has two small stickers on either side of its quarters displaying its lot number. This is where people who haven't seen the horse in his box can have a look, or where prospective buyers can conduct one final examination. Some very astute judges can be found leaning over the rails here looking for a nice horse that might be going cheaply.

We went out to look one last time. Just to be sure to be sure. We saw nothing to change our minds. The same balance. The same poise. The same well-proportioned animal with the same self-assured step. Even at six o'clock in the evening on the final day of the sale, after being pulled in and out of his box for the last two days, he was showing no signs of awkwardness or tiredness.

The Moscow Society gelding was led into the covered area. The last halting ground before entering the sales ring. We took up our places in the main auditorium. The sales area at Fairyhouse is quite compact. There is tiered seating three-quarters of the way around the sales ring, from the auctioneer's podium round to where the horses enter and exit the ring. The other quarter, on the auctioneer's left-hand side, is a standing area officially designated for bidders. In reality, though, you can find bidders all over the auditorium. They can be standing at the acorn where the horses enter the ring or sitting in the seats straight in front of you. Johnny and I usually stand in the bidders' section, but for this one we sat in the seats to the auctioneer's right.

Just as we were taking our seats, auctioneer David Pim was bringing the gavel down on a four-year-old filly by Strong Gale out of the Deep Run mare Ailwee Dawn.

'Forty-eight thousand,' said David. 'Thank you very much, madam.'

It is often difficult to see who the buyer is when the gavel drops. The trick is to watch the spotter and watch where he or she goes with the docket. This docket was taken directly over to Henrietta Knight, who signed it unflinchingly. That filly would later be named Hurricane Dawn and would win two novice hurdle races for Henrietta and her owner Martin Broughton.

There was no fanfare when Lot 432 entered the ring, no trumpet blast. Just an announcement: 'Lot 432 from Ballymorris Stud is a bay gelding by Moscow Society out of Meelick Lady. A veterinary certificate from Mr Justin Brown has been issued which states that, in his opinion, this gelding shows no clinically discoverable signs of disease, injury or physical abnormality likely to prejudice this animal's use for racing. Mr Joe O'Sullivan of the veterinary panel agrees, and further notes scar, back left-hind fetlock, and outside right-hind pastern which, in my opinion, are of no significance.'

My heart began to beat a little faster than normal. Just a little. I always get excited before I bid on a horse, but this was a slightly unusual feeling. I guess I was nervous in case we didn't get this one. It may have been the fact that there were only 48 lots left in the sale after this fellow and we had no real fall-back position for our new owner. Or it may have been that, deep in my heart, I knew that this one had the potential to be something special.

David Pim turned on his microphone.

'Here he is. Lovely horse by Moscow Society, who has done so well in recent times. Start me for him where you like, out of a Duky mare, out of a mare by No Argument. Give me twenty thousand for him. Twenty? Well put him in ten, then. Ten? Ten for him. Put him in ten. Five bid.'

The first bid was in before the horse had completed a circuit of the sales ring. He let out a whinny at the precise moment that the auctioneer said 'five bid'. It was as if he knew he was in demand. I had a look around the auditorium as I was anxious to see who was bidding. These early bids are often difficult to spot.

'Five thousand guineas the Moscow Society. They all win by this fellow. Six thousand, seven bid, eight thousand I have. Eight thousand guineas bid for him now, close to him, the Moscow Society.'

Johnny looked towards the auctioneer's rostrum and lifted his catalogue slightly. Subtle as you like. But David Pim was watching out for it. He was probably aware that Johnny and I had been down to see this horse a number of times. And even if he wasn't, he would have seen us coming into the auditorium. He spotted Johnny's sleight of catalogue. To the untrained eye it was a fairly innocuous motion, just a fellow moving the book that happened to be in his hand. But to David Pim, it was a bid of 10,000 guineas.

'Ten thousand bid. Ten thousand guineas bid for him now beside me here. At ten thousand. This is a really nice horse. At ten thousand guineas.'

People will tell you that they are not influenced by the auctioneer, that they have valued a horse at a certain price and they won't go beyond it. But I have no doubt that a good auctioneer can often get you to go one or even two bids more than you had intended. David Pim is a good auctioneer, and this fellow was zinging.

'Twelve bid. Twelve thousand guineas bid for him now. At twelve. At twelve thousand. At twelve thousand guineas bid for him now.'

I looked around the ring to try to see who had bid twelve grand. It's difficult after the first bid from a new bidder has been taken. Subsequent bids are even more subtle. The auctioneer and the spotters are watching you and the slightest twitch will see you spend another thousand or two.

Johnny nodded his head. If you were asking him a question and he gave a response like that, you would wonder if he were answering in the affirmative or not. David knew that he was.

'Fourteen. Fourteen bid for him now. Now, sir, look at me. At fourteen. This is the one I want. He's there all right. He's on the market and I sell him below in the cap.'

This may seem like another piece of auctioneer-ramble, but it is significant. Once the auctioneer says that he is on the market, it means that the reserve the seller has placed on him has been reached and surpassed. Often this can spark an auction into life. If the reserve is not reached, the horse is led out of the ring unsold and you can go and negotiate privately with the vendor, if that is your desire. But once a horse is on the market, he will have a new owner when the gavel drops. If you want him, you have to bid now.

The bid of fourteen grand was Johnny's. He in the cap. I braced myself for an onslaught of bids. The bay gelding moved nonchalantly around the ring below us, oblivious to the somersaults my heart was doing. He was ours at fourteen grand. For now, anyway.

'Fifteen bid.'

My heart sank.

'Fifteen thousand guineas bid for him now. The good-looking son of Moscow Society. At fifteen thousand. He's on the market. Make no mistake. I sell him at fifteen thousand guineas. Any more across for him? You're out down below.'

That was us down below. We were out. We still had another 5,000 in us, but he was going so fast that it was looking bad. This fellow could make thirty grand. I had probably been unrealistic thinking that we would be able to pick him up for less than twenty. He was such a good-looking horse, and even though he was late in the sale, those who wanted him had obviously stuck around. The more I began to think that he would sail away out of our price range, the more I wanted him.

'At fifteen thousand. They all win by this fellow. Out of a Duky mare. The family of Bramble Tudor and Ivy Green. At fifteen.'

Stop reminding them, David! They can read the catalogue if they really want to know.

'Sixteen. Sixteen I'm bid again. Fresh blood.'

Disaster. Fresh blood is rarely a good thing when you are trying to buy. A new bidder. And it is definitely not a good thing when you only have four grand left in you. Moreover, we were now on the wrong leg. We would bid seventeen, he'd bid eighteen, we'd bid nineteen, he'd bid twenty and we'd be out. At least if we had bid the sixteen we would have been the ones to land on twenty.

I followed the auctioneer's eyes down to the gangway where the horses enter and exit the ring. There was a number of people there, as there always is, but the one who caught my attention was Bryan Murphy. Bryan owns the excellent Dunraven Arms Hotel in Adare in partnership with his brother Louis. He is a great National Hunt man – the annual Irish National Hunt awards are held every year in the Dunraven Arms – and he runs a highly successful racing and breeding operation himself. We have spent many an enjoyable evening in the Dunraven Arms at the awards, or just stopping off for something to eat on our way back from Killarney or Listowel. This fellow was exactly the type of horse Bryan would buy. Not over big, just nice and compact, and well put together.

I concluded that the 16,000 was Bryan's bid because of the Moscow Society connection. Bryan had bought and sold one of the stallion's very first success stories, Mighty Moss, who was beaten only a length by Istabraq in the 1997 Sun Alliance Hurdle. Amateur rider Fred Hutsby wasn't allowed to claim his 7lb allowance because it was a championship race. There are still those who say that Mighty Moss would have beaten Istabraq that day had he been ridden by a professional. Personally, I'm not so sure.

I thought about the possibility of going above twenty, if that was what would be required to buy Lot 432. If Brian Kearney wanted him for 25 or 30, he could have him. If he didn't, we'd have him ourselves, or try to sell him to one of our current owners. Although Johnny generally doesn't allow me to buy on spec, we both really liked this fellow. Maybe he would make an exception.

'At sixteen, and I sell in the gangway. At sixteen thousand. You're all gone below me here. At sixteen thousand. You're gone in the cap. You're gone beside me. I sell him this time.'

David looked down at Johnny. Almost apologetically. One more bid and you might have him. There's really not a lot I can do.

And just before David broke his gaze, Johnny nodded. It was a subtle yet confident nod. He knew that the eyes of the auditorium were on him. Or at least the eyes of our rival bidders. It was a nod that said there was plenty more in us. Bidding against us is a fruitless exercise. We're going to have this horse. David lit up.

'Seventeen bid. Seventeen. Seventeen here beside me in the seats. At seventeen thousand, I sell the Moscow Society. At seventeen thousand guineas. Done with him?'

I looked down at Bryan Murphy. He was looking at his catalogue. He looked from his catalogue to the horse as he was being led around the ring and back to his catalogue again. He read the same information as he and we had been reading all day. No black type until you get to the fourth dam. He closed his catalogue and looked straight ahead of him into the distance.

The auctioneer lifted the gavel in his right hand. We were approaching the end-game, but we were not over the line yet. Not by a long chalk. The gavel could hover for an eternity. It frequently did. Depending on the determination of our rivals, there could be a few more bids left in this one yet. My heart began to beat faster as I willed it to fall.

'Last call.'

There didn't appear to be anything more coming from Bryan. Drop the hammer. Quickly!

'He's sold this time.'

Crash! The gavel hit the counter with a suddenness that shocked me and left me needing a second or two for the realisation to dawn. He was ours. The Moscow Society gelding was ours for 17,000 guineas. Well within our budget. And a new owner coming into the yard. Johnny looked at me and smiled. We'll have some craic with this fellow.

'To Mr Johnny Harrington. Thank you very much indeed.'

Bryan Murphy turned and walked slowly out of the sales ring. That's the way it goes. Sometimes you get them, sometimes you don't. He wouldn't usually go to much more than 20,000 for a horse at the Derby Sale anyway. He was buying for himself, and as he saw it, we were probably buying for an owner with deep pockets.

He didn't know that we would have had to concede at 20,000. If he had, he might well have pushed us there. He told Jim Mernagh later, before Moscow ever set foot on a racecourse, that he should have gone a few more bids. That he really liked this horse and was sorry that he didn't have him home with him. Jim still pulls Bryan's leg about it every time he sees him.

Johnny and I went for a drink with Jim and Eddie Joyce in the bar at Fairyhouse that evening. It was our first time meeting Eddie, who had bred the Moscow Society gelding out of his mare Meelick Lady. This was the first horse he had ever sold at public auction and he was beside himself. Jim was saying that he'd thought the horse would make a bit more than 17,000, but Eddie seemed delighted with the price.

The news was being shown on the television in the corner. The SDLP was emerging as the front-runner in the Assembly elections in the North, according to exit polls. Ireland's new television station, TV3, would be launched in the autumn. Dublin's new light rail system, Luas, was delayed again. Michael Flatley had danced his last dance. Teenage sensation Michael Owen would start for England that evening in their World Cup clash with Colombia. David Batty was out, and David Beckham would partner Paul Ince in the centre of midfield. Sam Torrance led the French Open field. Christy Roche would ride Campo Catino and not Risk Material in the Irish Derby on Sunday.

There was no mention of the purchase of Lot 432 at Fairyhouse. No mention of the good-looking Moscow Society gelding out of Meelick Lady. No mention of his poise or his balance, or of his prospects of scaling the dizziest heights. All in good time, I thought.

When I looked away from the television, I noticed that Eddie was watching me. He could have been reading my thoughts. He smiled, and raised his glass.

'Good health, Jessica,' he said. 'The very best of luck with him.'

CHAPTER THREE

THE BEGINNING

As you drive from Galway to Limerick, just before you get to the outskirts of Limerick city, you will see a small signpost for Meelick on your left-hand side. Go down that road for about two miles and you will come into the adjoining parishes of Meelick and Cratloe. There isn't much to either. A couple of shops, a school, a church, a couple of pubs. But it is not difficult to find someone in any one of the pubs to talk about Moscow Flyer, if you are so inclined. Or in one of the shops. Or, indeed, in the church, if you are happy to speak quietly. Meelick's place in National Hunt folklore is assured. For it was here, at Eddie Joyce's Summer Hill Stud, that Moscow Flyer came into the world.

Moscow Flyer's fourth dam was Hedge Law, who was the first mare the Mernagh family ever had at Coolamurry Stud back in the 1950s. She bred Bramble Tudor, who won the Cotswold Chase (the present-day Arkle Trophy), and Ivy Green, who won a Galway

Hurdle and finished second in a Champion Hurdle. She also fell at the final flight in a Champion Hurdle. The late Pat Taaffe always maintained that she would have won that one had she not come down. Hedge Law was also the dam of Indicate, who won five times herself and bred Artic Ale, who won a Topham Trophy, and Vamble, grandam of John Hughes Trophy winner Bells Life and John Hughes and Becher Chase winner Indian Tonic.

But the most significant of Hedge Law's offspring so far as the Moscow Flyer story is concerned was Brambling, who won for her buyer Lord Joyce, before he sold her back to the Mernagh family at the end of her racing days. Brambling was the dam of Quiet Life, who would ultimately be Moscow Flyer's grandam. It was because of this ancestry tracing back to the old Coolamurry family that, when Eddie Joyce needed someone to prepare his unbroken four-year-old for the Derby Sale in 1998, it was to Jim Mernagh that he turned.

Jim's family bred Quiet Life. Jim remembers her as a gorgeous-looking mare and maintains that it was from her that Moscow Flyer inherited his good looks. Jim brought her to the old Ballsbridge Sales as a three-year-old in 1976 – he led her up himself – where she was purchased by Tommy Wade. Tommy's father was a horse dealer, and Tommy grew up riding ponies. He started riding working ponies when he was four years old. He ended up going down the show-jumping route, essentially because he was too heavy to race ride, although he did ride a few point-to-point winners. But he loved show-jumping, and he was good at it.

Mention Tommy Wade to anybody with a passing interest in horses or show-jumping these days and they will immediately think of his famous horse Dundrum. But it was through an unlikely turn of events that Dundrum even got to see an arena. Indeed, it was through an unlikely turn of events that he was ever allowed out from the harness at the front of his cart.

Dundrum was pulling carts when he was three. He wasn't very good at it. He used to frustrate the hell out of his owner, Paddy Hennessy, who now owns a couple of racehorses himself. One day,

Dundrum ran away with the cart and crashed into a line of cars. That was the final act. Paddy went down to the Wades' that evening to ask Tommy's father if he had a horse they could put under a cart instead of this feisty little three-year-old. Tommy himself had just bought a horse at Kilrush fair. He was only sixteen at the time, and had saved for ages to get the £30 to buy him. He had thought that the horse would make a show-jumper, but he just wasn't good enough. So Tommy told Paddy to take his horse and see how he would go. As it turned out, the horse was as quiet as a lamb and perfect for a cart. Tommy got his £30 back, and Paddy asked him if he would take his wild pony and see if he could do anything with him. From the first time that Tommy popped Dundrum over a pole, he knew he was going to make some kind of jumper, though he could never have known just what kind.

Dundrum was only 14.2 hands at the time as a three-year-old. He grew to be $15.1^1/_2$ hands, which was still very small. But size didn't matter to this fellow. He won his first championship at the Dublin Show as a five-year-old and never looked back. Dundrum was on two winning Aga Khan Cup teams in Dublin, he won the King George V Gold Cup at White City, and he won Grand Prix in Amsterdam, Brussels, Ostend and just about everywhere else. In fact, he won just about everything that he could win. Tommy says he was the best he ever sat on.

Tommy started to train racehorses when he was 28. He had to give up show-jumping after he hurt his back. Actually, he had had a bad back since he fell off a racehorse on the gallops at home when he was fourteen. It was an even tougher sport then than it is now – no back protectors or helmets – and his father simply told him to get up. That he was grand. Unless you were missing a limb, you got back up on your horse. Tommy's family, you see, were all top hurlers. Tommy himself played minor hurling for Tipperary. His father was on the Tipperary senior team, and one of his uncles played for Dublin. With hurling, as with horses, you stayed in the game as long as you were conscious.

Even when Tommy was at the very top as a show-jumper, his

back gave him problems. Nobody knew about it except himself and his mother. He used to wear a brace on his back when he jumped which he got from Harvey Smith, who had the same problem. Not many people knew that either.

So Tommy was training racehorses when he went to the Ballsbridge Sales in 1976. That sale was the equivalent of the Derby Sale today. Tommy had his eye on Jim Mernagh's mare, whom he thought had the best pedigree in the catalogue. He liked the Brambling/Bramble Tudor/Ivy Green lineage. Her sire, No Argument, wasn't a bad sire, but he wasn't fashionable at the time. Tommy, though, was happy to suffer the sire in order to be able to buy into the dam line.

He rarely bought mares. He didn't like training them. And this one was a lunatic at the sale. He remembers that Jim Mernagh himself was having trouble leading her up. Tommy figured that this would put a lot of people off, and he might get her cheaply. He did. Well, relatively cheaply. He signed the docket at 900 guineas, which was just about average for the sale. He didn't have an owner for her at the time, but he figured that he would find one quickly enough.

Tommy had been good friends with Dermot Joyce, Eddie Joyce's uncle, for years. Dermot was paralysed from the waist down since the time as a young man when a cart went over his legs. But it didn't stop him getting around, and it didn't stop him going to race meetings or greyhound tracks. Eddie used to drive him whenever he could. He walked with the aid of two sticks in his younger days and was ultimately confined to a wheelchair.

Dermot and Tommy had had a lot of dogs together and a lot of good gambles. Eddie remembers two young dogs in particular, Derk Glin and Derk Grove, which Dermot thought would be very good. The best place to get money on a dog in those days – as it probably is today – was Shelbourne Park in Dublin, and the best man to get the money on for you was Tommy Wade. Dermot drove up the road from Limerick to Dublin with the two dogs and his nephew Eddie. Eddie was earning £4 a week working for Dermot.

He had saved up £30 to put on the dogs, and he gave it to Tommy on the quiet. When his uncle asked him how much he was having on – 'A tenner, are you?' – Eddie just nodded and examined his shoes. They backed the first dog from 3–1 to even money, and he won doing handsprings. They backed the second dog down to 6–4, and he got up to win by a head. Eddie is not sure how much was taken out of the betting ring in total at Shelbourne Park that night, but he knows that he went home with £160. Forty weeks' wages.

Dermot had already had a horse in training with Tommy. Up Treaty had won a few point-to-points, but he wasn't that good and they'd sold him on. When Tommy came home from Ballsbridge with the No Argument mare, he had it half in his head that Dermot would be the man for her. Dermot and his brother Jim, Eddie's father, used to call down to Tommy's most Sunday afternoons, just to have a chat, mainly about dogs and a little about horses. The Sunday after the sale, Tommy showed them the No Argument mare. Dermot liked her, and she was his for 900 guineas.

She was a quirky mare. Difficult to break and wholly uncooperative. Tommy had a few very good point-to-pointers at the time, Mustang Prince and Von Trappe among them. Tommy was riding the former, probably the best hunter chaser in the country at the time, in a good piece of work one morning. He told Pat Kelly, who was riding the mare, to settle her in behind and just to follow him for the mile-and-six-furlong gallop. 'She'll probably try to pull up after a mile, but try to stay up.'

After a mile, Tommy looked to his left to see Pat and the mare tanking along upsides. Tommy couldn't believe it.

'Go easy with her, Pat!' Tommy shouted. 'Go easy!'

'She's flying, boss!' came the exhilarated response.

She never looked back from that day. Something had clicked in her mind. They named her Quiet Life and won two point-to-points with her. Tommy was sure that wherever she ran, she'd win her bumper. That was before they brought her to Wexford, and she sweated up badly beforehand. After finishing down the field there, Tommy figured that there was no need to run her in another bumper. She had been such a good jumper between the flags that she might as well go straight over hurdles.

After a sighter at Roscommon, she won her maiden hurdle at Thurles before going to Roscommon for a valuable novices' chase. The race was worth about £10,000 and was restricted to horses who had never run in a chase. Of course it attracted a lot of the top hurdlers in the country, but with Quiet Life's point-to-point experience and jumping ability, she wasn't going to be far away.

Tommy and Dermot backed her from 20–1 to 5–1. She was running away going to the last, missed it completely, got going again and got up on the line to win by a head. Dermot and Tommy had had about £5,000 on her between them. A friend of Tommy's had the money on: £50 here at 20–1, £200 there at 16–1, and all the way down. He averaged 9–1 to the £5,000. When Tommy told Dermot that he only got 9–1 to his money, he wasn't overly impressed.

'But she opened at 20–1 on the course,' was Dermot's response.

'You try getting five grand on at 20–1,' said Tommy, 'see how far you get.'

'Sure there were fellows here from Limerick were on at 20–1.'

Tommy saw red. 'And who the hell told the fellows from Limerick about the horse?'

Silence.

'They probably took the price on all of us,' Tommy continued. 'Well, you can come down here tomorrow and take your fucking mare out of the place. I don't want to have anything to do with her again. Or you.'

'Ah now, Tommy,' said Dermot, 'I don't want to be falling out with you over this. Sure it's great. Nine to one is great.'

Crisis averted. Quiet Life won three races under Rules and two point-to-points during her racing career. When she was finished racing, Dermot gave her to his nephew Eddie as a present.

Eddie had land and was doing some farming, but the breeding of thoroughbred horses wasn't high on his list of priorities at the time. He had had ponies about the place, and his family had always had horses, but thoroughbred breeding was not high on his to-do list. He might have got into it even if his uncle had not given him the mare, as Clare is a daughter of Dr Jack Ryan of Ballymorris Stud, and her family is steeped in breeding. But this was a great kick-start all the same.

Myelife was Quiet Life's first foal, by Le Bavard. The Burkes' riding school was the big riding establishment in Newmarket-on-Fergus at the time, and Eddie gave the young mare to Kevin and Vincent Burke to train. She ran first time up in a point-to-point in Dromoland. A quiet run. As Eddie was walking out the gate, Tom Costello stopped him.

'I'll buy that mare off you,' he said.

'No you won't, Tom, but I'll tell you what you can do. You can train her for me.'

These days, you think Cheltenham Gold Cup and you think Tom Costello. It's almost automatic. But you won't find his name on the racecard or anything. He doesn't train them or ride them. But he can spot them, usually as foals or yearlings. And when he spots one, he rarely leaves it behind him.

Even back then, Tom was a national – fast becoming an international – institution. He had bought and sold Midnight Court, who had won the Gold Cup in 1978. The 1987 winner The Thinker had also benefited from the experience at the Fenloe academy. More Gold Cup winners would follow: Cool Ground, Imperial Call, Cool Dawn and, of course, Best Mate. And never, in the aftermath of any of those wins, did you see Tom Costello dancing around Cheltenham's winner's enclosure. He is still the best-known quiet man in the business.

Tom buys 60 or 70 foals every year, most of them privately. He'll have 400 or 500 horses on his farm at any one time. He travels to all corners of the country seeking the right raw material. He seems to have this wonderful, uncanny gift for knowing what a foal will look like six or seven years thence. Size is everything. They can't be too big or too small, and they have to be capable of carrying twelve stone when they race. That's the key. Pedigree is secondary. It's much more important for Tom that he is buying a nice horse rather than a good pedigree. You can't teach that. It is not coincidental that, every year, a significant proportion of the Gold Cup field are Costello graduates.

Back at the Costello ranch at Fenloe, there is a strict regime through which the foals are marshalled. Nothing is left to chance. They are broken at two and popped over a pole. They are ridden again at three and jumped riderless in an indoor school. Poles on one side and a plastic chase fence on the other. It was in this indoor school that Jim Lewis first saw Best Mate arch his back. As soon as they turn four, the For Sale sign goes up. Ask the price and Tom will quote you as high as you like. It is not just a horse you are buying; you are also buying the education. It's like employing a highly qualified university graduate: you pay more than if you are employing a school leaver. The Costello university is Harvard for horses.

Tom's training fees weren't cheap, but Eddie Joyce didn't have a problem with that as he knew he was good. You knew that your horse was getting the best treatment.

Eddie had an agreement with Tom that he didn't want to know when they were having the money down. He gave his few pounds to Tom and told him to have him on when the time was right. He still talks about the day when Myelife ran at Carrigtwohill. Eddie and Tom were relieving themselves together behind a truck on the side of the road.

'We're sparking today, Eddie!' said Tom as they lit up the side of the truck.

And they were. The money was down, and Myelife won as she liked.

Two years later they went back to Carrigtwohill with Myelife's full sister, Your Life. There was a good strong market there and the bookmakers would take a bet. They figured that they would be in trouble if they opened the mare up at 6–1 or more. They'd take no notice at 3–1 and a better average could be had. And so it came to pass. Your Life went in and they partied again.

The full sisters Myelife and Your Life, both by Le Bavard out of Quiet Life, both bred by Eddie Joyce and both trained by Tom Costello, went on to win the Gain Mares' Final in 1990 and 1992 respectively. Tom told Eddie when he thought they had had enough racing. 'Go and breed from them, Eddie. They're from a great old jumping family.'

He did. Your Life bred Lifes a Flyer, whom I bought at the Derby Sale in 2000 and who won a couple of races for Andrew Doyle, and Thisisyourlife, who is currently in training with Henry Daly. Your Life is nineteen years old now and still lives down in Meelick behind Eddie Joyce's house. She is due a foal by Moscow Society early in 2006.

In 1987, Quiet Life was covered by The Parson, who was standing at Hugh Williams' Ballyvolane Stud just down the road in Bruff. Hugh and his wife Ginnie have been great friends of ours for years, since long before Moscow Flyer was even thought of. The Parson sired many top-class National Hunt horses including Danoli, Very Promising, Large Action, Trapper John and Monsieur Le Cure. Unfortunately, Quiet Life lost the foal by him. By the time she did, The Parson had died.

Hugh had a new stallion at Ballyvolane called Duky, whom he had bought in Holland and about whom Eddie didn't know too much. Nevertheless, Eddie had a mare there and Hugh owed him a covering. So Quiet Life was covered by Duky, and eleven months later Meelick Lady was born. She was all set to go racing when she got a spasm in her hip. She never would have been suitable for the track, so Eddie decided to send her directly to the breeding shed.

By the time Meelick Lady was five years old, Hugh had acquired a new stallion at Ballyvolane. Moscow Society was an American-bred stallion by Nijinsky who had been trained by Henry Cecil to finish second in the 1988 Queen's Vase, where he broke down. Hugh had been on the lookout for some time for a replacement for The Parson. One evening in June 1989 he received a phone call from George Harris, an American-based bloodstock agent, telling him that there was a Sheikh Mohammed-owned horse whose racing career had been ended by injury and who might suit his needs. Hugh went over to Warren Place to see him and liked what he saw. Anthony Stroud, Sheikh Mohammed's racing manager, quoted the price. 'You'll pay me that or else you won't have him.' There was no negotiation. Hugh liked the horse a lot and wanted him. I don't know what he paid for him, but Hugh says it was a lot at the time. Stroud didn't beat about the bush. Of course, in hindsight, he was a bargain.

Hugh had a little mare by Duky called Luvaduk. She was only small, but Hugh decided that he would cover her with Moscow Society, just to get his new stallion started. It was late in the year and there was little to lose. She produced a filly who took after her mother in terms of size. Hugh named the little filly Muscovy Duck and sent her to be trained by local man Austin Leahy when she was a three-year-old. But she had sore shins, and Michael Hourigan had a swimming pool, so it made sense to move her to Hourigan's. Austin didn't mind. Hugh figured she probably wouldn't turn out to be that good anyway. On the contrary. After a month Michael contacted Hugh to tell him that, sore shins or not, this little filly could go a bit. She proceeded to win twice, and was placed fourteen times on the Flat and over hurdles in three seasons of racing.

It was a great start for Moscow Society. He was somewhat unusual as a stallion in that his first crop numbered one – Muscovy Duck. That was it. Hugh was delighted that his new stallion had produced something so good out of a mare with a limited pedigree. Muscovy Duck's ability was also the first indication of an unlikely appropriate cross – Moscow Society with a Duky mare. Eddie Joyce didn't know this when he brought Meelick Lady to visit Moscow Society. The cross also surfaced later on through Rouble, Kopeck and Society Brief, all by Moscow Society out of the Duky mare Cashla.

The difficulty with any new stallion, but especially with one that hasn't been among the very top echelons as a racehorse, is that it takes time for him to establish himself. So significant is the time lag that a National Hunt stallion is often not acclaimed as a success until after his death. Hugh Williams didn't have much money to spend on marketing his new stallion, and as a result Moscow Society's books of mares were limited during his first few seasons. Forty mares at most. £300 for a colt foal, £100 for a filly. Of course a stallion's best marketing tools are his progeny. But, for a National Hunt stallion, they don't set foot on a racecourse until a minimum of four years after he has gone to stud. In the interim he is reliant on the quality of his foals and word of mouth.

In 1991, Hugh covered a Menelek mare of his, Corrielek, with Moscow Society. Tommy Wade bought the resulting colt foal as a two-year-old for not very much money, and sold him on to Tom Conroy before he raced. Hugh didn't see the foal again until he went to see him sluice in on his debut in a bumper at Listowel. Named Moscow Express, he contested 81 races in total, winning 26 of them, including a 20-runner Flat handicap up The Curragh, the Grade 2 Morris Oil Chase at Clonmel, where he had Micko's Dream and our own Ferbet Junior behind him, the Powers Gold Label at Fairyhouse, where he had Florida Pearl and Dorans Pride behind him off level weights, and of course the 1999 Galway Plate. He was the best advertisement for Moscow Society they could possibly have had.

Moscow Society lives these days at Ballyvolane Stud with two sheep. Twenty years of age in 2005, he is still covering mares. Indeed, Eddie Joyce has a two-year-old filly out of Meelick Lady whom he is intent on sending to Moscow Society next year. Hugh put one of the sheep in with the stallion to keep him company about eight years ago. He didn't know for how long sheep lived, so he put another one in three years ago to take the first one's place. Just in case. The first one is still thriving, so they all live happily together.

In the spring of 1993, Eddie Joyce asked his father-in-law, Dr Jack Ryan, to go to Ballyvolane Stud and choose a mate for Meelick Lady. There was no choice to be made. Dr Ryan loved Moscow Society. He had seen him at Ascot when he had run in the Queen's Vase over two miles, and maintains that he would have won had he not broken down. He was by Nijinsky, and Dr Ryan thought that Nijinsky had been the best racehorse of the last 50 years. A big, robust horse with plenty of speed and stamina – precisely the qualities National Hunt horses need.

A couple of days later, Dr Ryan was taking Meelick Lady in the horsebox to Ballyvolane to visit Moscow Society when, suddenly, a tractor pulled out in front of him and he had to brake suddenly. The mare in the horsebox behind the car slipped and fell on her side. Thankfully, she emerged unscathed. The Moscow Flyer story could easily have ended before it had even begun.

As it was, on 10 May 1994, Meelick Lady gave birth to a little bay colt. Within two hours the foal managed to get his spindly legs under his body and push himself up. This achievement ranks up there with all the feats this little foal would go and accomplish in later life. But you have to start somewhere. And you have to get up there if you are going to reach your mother's milk. Needs must.

It is easy to be wise in hindsight, when you know that this foal who sprawled shakily around the field, never allowing his mother to get too far away, has won 26 races and over a million pounds in prize money, but even then Eddie thought he was a smasher. To the untrained eye his lanky legs may have looked too long for his body, and his tail may have looked like it belonged on the end of a rabbit instead of a horse, but Eddie knew that everything was where it should be. A leg in each corner, as Jim Mernagh would say later.

Everybody loved the little foal. He wasn't over big, but he was well proportioned. Dr Ryan loved him. Eddie's friend James McMahon loved him. James bred Merry People, Merry Masquerade and Over the Bar, and lived just down the road. At the 1998 Derby Sale, James walked around telling anyone who would listen that they should go and see this fine-looking horse over in Barn A.

Eddie looked after Meelick Lady, and she looked after her young son. The little foal drank three gallons of his mother's milk every day and grew stronger. After ten weeks Eddie began to give the foal some feed to supplement his diet. Four months later, the bay colt – not so little any more – was completely independent.

When he was a foal, Dr Ryan asked Eddie if he could keep him and rear him at Ballymorris, just down the road. Ballymorris is the most scenic of stud farms, situated, as it is, in the parish of Cratloe on the banks of the Shannon's estuary. It is a farm of fertile limestone land where the grass is luscious and sweet. Horses love it. Eddie thought that Ballymorris would be a good home for Meelick Lady's yearling. He could sacrifice being able to see him from his kitchen window once he was happy in the knowledge that he was getting the best possible upbringing.

And he was. During the summers the young horse grazed on the limestone-enriched land and drank the fresh spring water that came from a stream in the limestone hills of Cratloe. He spent the winter nights in stables on the upland hills and was fed the best of oats, minerals, vitamins and home-grown hay. He was let out during the day. By the time he was two, he had doubled his body weight from the day he was weaned. He was always a very healthy horse who never needed veterinary attention. He was also a friendly horse, according to Dr Ryan. He would come up to him in the field just for a chat and a pat on the neck. He had a first cousin for company during those days – Myelife's two foals who would later be called Life of a River.

When he was four, Eddie offered him as a gift to his father-in-law, but Dr Ryan wouldn't take him. He said that he was too valuable. He told Eddie to enter him in the Derby Sale and that he would make at least 20,000 guineas.

Two months before the 1998 Derby Sale, Eddie met Tom Costello at a point-to-point in Athenry. Tom had stopped training at the time and was just concentrating on buying and selling.

'What about that oul Moscow Society horse you have down there?' Tom asked Eddie. He had obviously heard about him. Moscow Society was not a very fashionable stallion at the time. 'I'll give you three grand for him.'

'Ah no, Tom,' said Eddie. 'Sure he's going to the sale.'

'I'll tell you what, then,' said Tom. 'I'll meet you down at Ballymorris tunnel tomorrow morning at nine thirty. Sure we can have a look at the horse then.'

Eddie met Tom at the tunnel the following morning. The four-year-old gelding out of Meelick Lady was just up the road in a field belonging to Ballymorris Stud. Tom arrived with his son John, and he followed Eddie up from the tunnel to the field. The two men got out of their cars, climbed the stile into the field and beckoned the horse over.

'Jesus, he's a grand horse,' said Eddie.

'He is,' agreed Tom. 'You could stand him up in the field there and he'd talk to you. I'll give you what I was giving you for him.'

It was a good opening negotiating position, but both men knew it was only a negotiating position. Tom had to have known that if Eddie wasn't going to agree to sell him for three grand at the point-to-point in Athenry, he wasn't going to sell him for three grand the following day.

'Ah, I'll leave it alone now, Tom,' said Eddie. 'You're fine.'

In fairness to Tom Costello, he did like the horse and he was there to buy him.

'I'll tell you what I'll do, Eddie,' said Tom. 'I'll give you ten grand for him. Here and now. And I'll have him away with me before lunch.'

Eddie thought for a moment. Tom Costello was not a man you refused easily. And ten grand was a decent price. It was a fair step up on the three that Tom had offered initially. Ten grand in the hand, or take your chances at the sale. But he could do very well at the sale. The fact that Tom Costello was offering ten grand meant that he thought he was value at that. There would probably be others who thought the same. And his father-in-law had said that he would make twenty. Then again, although Eddie had bought at the sales befor, he never sold one~. It can fray your nerves, he had heard. You could have a very nice horse there who could fall through the cracks. Two buyers want your horse and you can do very well. But the sales ring at Fairyhouse can be a lonely place when you are looking down at your horse being led around as the auctioneer pleads for an opening bid.

All of this flashed through Eddie's mind in the space of a couple of seconds as Tom stood patiently awaiting his response. Tom would have the horse away now in his box and Eddie would be ten grand richer. If he didn't sell to Tom now, it was possible that he could bring him up to Fairyhouse on 26 June and have him home with him on 27 June. Eddie looked at his horse, then turned slowly to Tom.

'I won't, Tom, I'll tell you,' he said. 'I'll bring him to the sale.'

Tom's face remained expressionless. If he was disappointed, you wouldn't have known it. He nodded slowly and walked back towards his car. He could have said fourteen, but he didn't. As he got to his car, he stopped and turned round.

'Eddie,' he said, 'you used me for a fecking mark.'

He got into his car, closed the door and drove off.

That was the last conversation that Tom Costello and Eddie Joyce had. Tom had a look at the gelding at the Derby Sale all right, but he was never in the running to buy him. Every horse has a value in the Costello book. This one was value at ten grand, not at seventeen.

A few weeks later, Eddie met Jim Mernagh at Punchestown. It was Jim's mother who had bred Quiet Life, Meelick Lady's dam, whom Tommy Wade had bought at Ballsbridge for Eddie's uncle Dermot. By now, Jim had taken over Coolamurry Stud and ran a fine operation there. Eddie was a novice when it came to selling at a sale. Eddie didn't have the time to prepare a horse for sale. He had a young family – three girls and a boy – and he had a meat business to run. With the family connection to the horse, it made complete sense to Eddie that Jim should prepare his four-year-old gelding.

Jim loved him from the moment he saw him. He was a bit big, and he only had about eight weeks to get him toned for the sale, but he loved everything about him. A leg in each corner. 'You couldn't knock that horse off balance,' Jim said to me when I first went to have a look at the horse at the sale.

Jim had seven horses in total to consign at the 1998 Derby Sale. Every morning in the lead-up to the sale he would take each one out for lungeing. And every morning he would take Moscow out first, because he was such a lovely mover. You could watch him all day. He was just such a beautifully balanced horse. But he did need more work than most of the others. Eight weeks is not a lot of time, and Coolamurry Stud are not known for sending their horses into the sales ring looking big and stuffy. Sharpness and athleticism are Coolamurry's hallmarks. Fortunately, Moscow Flyer loved his work. He would bound out of his box every morning, dying to start. You'd just put him in the lungeing ring and he'd canter around on his own. The only struggle was to get him to stop.

I don't know if Jim Mernagh was tempted to keep him. Jim is a horse trader. He makes his living from buying and breeding horses and, essentially, selling them on. He would have had enough horses around the place left unsold for himself without going out and buying another one. However, he did say to me a number of years ago that he had made a mistake in not keeping that horse. I'm not sure if he was serious or not. I'm not sure if he really did consider keeping him himself.

Of course, if he had, we would not have been able to buy him for Brian Kearney. We would not have gone through the life-changing experience that he has effected on us. Brian might not have fallen as deeply in love with the game as he has. He certainly could not have scaled the pinnacles of the sport on his debut as a racehorse owner without him.

CHAPTER FOUR

BRIAN KEARNEY

The name Kearney comes from two old Irish names: Ó Catharnaigh, 'son of Catharnach', a byname which means 'soldier'; and Ó Cearnaigh, a derivative of 'cearnach', meaning 'victorious'. It is quite an appropriate name for the man who would come to own Moscow Flyer.

Brian Kearney's parents hailed from West Cork, just outside Dunmanway, which is about equidistant from Macroom, Clonakilty and Skibereen. Brian's father, Pete, was from a farming background. Both of his parents died of TB when Pete was very young. In fact, several of Pete's brothers and his sister died of TB when he was just a child. Only Pete and his elder brother survived. By the time Pete Kearney was thirteen years old, he and his brother were orphans.

Their uncle looked after them, and the intention was that the proceeds of the farm would put the two boys through school and university. While Pete's brother followed the script, Pete himself got no further than one year into his studies at University College Cork. He thought that his time would be better spent out fighting for Ireland than studying for a degree in medicine. He was an officer in the Irish Republican Army during the War of Independence, which ran from January 1919 to July 1921. Some of the major battles of the war were fought in West Cork. There was an account of one particular battle in a recent book commemorating the 75th anniversary of the war in which 110 Irish faced up to 1,200 British soldiers. Pete Kearney was a member of one of the units that came very close to getting cut off from the rest of the Irish force. If that had happened, it is highly unlikely that Brian Kearney would be here today.

Shortly after the Irish Free State came into existence in 1921, trouble broke out between the republicans and the Free State government. Dáil deputies were shot and IRA prisoners were executed. The IRA instigated a burning campaign against the houses of people who were seen to have British allegiances. There is a chance that Pete Kearney plotted to torch my father's house at Rahinston. After all, my family home was representative of a lot of the things that would have irritated a republican. But actually, it appears that all large estates owned by Protestants were not targeted; rather, it was only those belonging to people who were thought to have been providing information to the British, or helping them out in some way. If such was the case, Rahinston was probably not on the list. Although the house was damaged by a bad fire a while later, it was a negligent painter and not a rebel who caused it.

Brian's family didn't talk much about that period in his father's life. This was not unique to the Kearney family. Not many Irish families spoke about those times when Brian was growing up in the 1940s and 1950s. They were in the past, and that's where most people were happy to leave them. Brian's father died at the age of 68, when Brian was only 28. Brian reckons that if his father had stuck around for another decade or so he might have got a few more stories out of him.

But Brian did meet people who had been involved with his father in the struggle. Tom Barry was one. One story Pete Kearney did tell was of the time when he and Tom were coming into one of the towns in West Cork. They were part of the Flying Column, which was an elite group within the IRA at the time, and they were moving all over the country. Before they entered the town, they met up with one of the local volunteers and asked him to go in front of them to make sure that the coast was clear. Once he was satisfied that it was, Pete and Tom could proceed. Some twenty years later, Pete bumped into the man, the local volunteer, who was by then a Benedictine monk. They got to talking about that time. After a little while, the monk came clean. Instead of going into the town that day, he had gone down the road, around the corner, and jumped into a hedge. There was no way he was going to risk being shot just so that Tom Barry and Pete Kearney could have a free run into town!

Pete Kearney believed that Ireland should be free, and he was willing to fight for that. He was known for his bravery, and for the care he showed towards those serving under him. He probably had to leave Ireland when the war ended, like most people who were on the republican side. He had a little bit of TB in his left knee at the time, but he managed to doctor his medical certificate, so to speak, and gained entry to America, where he worked for the Metropolitan Life Assurance Company in New York. Brian's mother had trained as a nurse at Baton Rouge in Louisiana and had moved to Bellevue Hospital in New York as a teaching sister. His parents had lived about eight miles away from each other in West Cork, but they had to go to New York to meet. They came back to Ireland in 1933, got married in Ballybrack in Dublin the following year, and settled in Clontarf, just on the north side of the River Liffey.

Brian and his elder brother Brendan went to Belvedere College. The Irish Hospital Sweepstake was started in the 1930s with the objective of raising funds for the building of Irish hospitals. A lot of the money came from America, where it was illegal. Connie Neelan, who was head of the American operation of the Sweep, was a good friend of Brian's parents, and the Kearneys acted as Sweep agents, filling out forms and shipping tickets back and forth. Brian reckons that he has the agent's commission of the Sweep to thank for putting him through college.

Connie was a good friend of the McGrath family at the time, and it was through Connie and the McGrath family that Brian caught his first glimpse of racing. Brian used to go racing as a youngster and follow the McGrath horses. Later on he had a college friend, Frank Glavin, who was friendly with the bookmaker Eddie Hannigan. Eddie's father used to do a lot of betting for Vincent O'Brien and a few others, with the result that, before they went to the races, Eddie, Brian and Frank used to know what horses were going to be backed. They didn't know if they would win or not, but they were sure to be on the hot ones with their five or ten shillings before the real money went down.

Brian graduated from UCD with a masters' degree in engineering in 1961, and joined Irish Cement. He worked in Limerick for a year and was a regular at the racecourse and the dog track there. The company used to source all of its equipment from Denmark, and it had a lot of Danish shareholders, so Brian was sent off to Copenhagen in 1962 for three years. He tells the story of the day he went to the races in Copenhagen with a colleague, Pat McGrane. They couldn't read the form, they couldn't understand the odds, and they didn't know too much about Danish racing. So Brian decided that they would back the best-looking horse in the race. Forty kroner win. They watched as the horse they had backed won with his head in his chest. The whoops of delight and celebrations ended when they went to collect, however. Forty-two kroner.

Brian went up the ladder quite quickly at Irish Cement. But in 1970 the company merged with a smaller company called Roadstone. Well, it was billed as a merger, but in practice it was a takeover by Roadstone. And so Cement Roadstone Holdings (CRH), one of Ireland's largest industrial companies today, was born. All the top jobs were filled by Roadstone people. Brian was a senior member of the project team at the plant in Platin just outside Drogheda, but he could see no path of progression. He was ambitious, and decided that it was time to move on. His boss, Jim Walsh, was suffering similar frustrations and gradually came to the same conclusion for himself. The two left together in 1974 and set up Project Management.

Brian and Jim rented a small office in Ranelagh in Dublin and took no salary for six months. They kept their overheads down and worked on building up the business. They had the archetypal small-business dilemma: how do you have enough time to get the work done in order to keep money coming in, while at the same time succeed in attracting new business? They managed. They turned Project Management from a three-person start-up company into Ireland's largest professional engineering services firms, which employs over 1,200 people today. They have worked for some of the largest multinational organisations in the world, including IBM, Merck, Pfizer, GlaxoSmithKline and Schering-Plough, and had the capability to build five factories simultaneously for the Xerox corporation in fifteen months.

Amazingly, when they set up Project Management they set up a very strong pension scheme that would allow them to retire at the age of 60. It probably isn't the first thing most start-up businesses put in place. But Project Management wasn't like most start-up businesses. The agreement was that you retire at 60 and remain on the board as a non-executive director for three years. That was just about long enough, they figured. After that you would begin to lose touch with what was going on in the industry and your contribution to the board would begin to get weaker.

During the last six months before he retired, Brian decided that it didn't make sense for him to get involved in new projects as he wouldn't be there to see them through. He had had it in the back of his mind to write a book about his business, and he decided that his last six months in the company would be the ideal time to do it. Together with his late colleague Joe McClean, he wrote the book

The Celtic Tiger at Your Service. It is a must-read for anybody thinking of setting up a business.

Brian met Patricia, a fellow native of Clontarf, when he was about eighteen, and they were married when they were 23. They have four children: Peter, Conor, Emer and Lise. Conor is the racing enthusiast, and it was through him that Brian and Patricia first met Arthur Craigie.

Brian would have been no more than a casual racegoer at the time. He would have gone to Baldoyle as a youngster, and he'd go to Phoenix Park and Leopardstown. In 1980 he backed Tyrnavos at 25–1 to win the Irish Derby because he had just come back from holiday in Greece. He enjoyed his racing, but would never have claimed to be an expert. Still, he had entertained a vague notion over the three or four years before he retired about owning a racehorse. He thought it might be something good to concentrate on in his retirement years, when he would have the time to go and watch his horse race. But his idea was that some of his and Patricia's friends would come into a syndicate with him. He raised the idea a couple of times over a few drinks. While the idea was generally greeted with unfailing enthusiasm late at night, it would rarely get a mention over breakfast.

On Hennessy Gold Cup day in 1998, Brian and Patricia went to the races at Leopardstown. Their son Conor was there with his friend Arthur Craigie. Dorans Pride was taking on Imperial Call in the Hennessy itself, and Arthur owned a horse who was going in the bumper. Shean Town had finished third in a bumper at Leopardstown over Christmas on his only previous outing, and they were hoping for a good run. Brian and Patricia had a small bet on the horse and joined Conor and Arthur in the bar to watch the race. As it happened, the horse won. He just held on by a head. The excitement that this race engendered in Arthur and Conor and all their mates, and the celebrations that victory inspired, greatly surprised Brian and Patricia. They had never been so close to a winning owner before. The champagne popped and the cigars sparked. Whatever it was that instigated these scenes of joy, Brian decided that he wanted some of it.

He had listened to owners telling him that whatever you invest in a horse, you have to be prepared not to get any of it back. If you are lucky you will get some back, but only if you are lucky. Write it off, consider it gone, and if you get some kind of a return it's a bonus. All Brian and Patricia's children had had their schooling by the late 1990s. They had gone through college and were basically self-sufficient by the time Shean Town won his bumper. If they were ever going to buy a horse, now was the time. Brian decided that he would do it. He asked his son Conor to ask Arthur to get Shean Town's trainer to buy him a horse. It wasn't a very methodical approach. In fact, it was wholly out of character for Brian, who is normally so meticulous at the planning stage.

As it happened, Shean Town's trainer was me. So I got this message from Arthur that his mate's father would like me to buy him a horse. It couldn't cost any more than twenty grand. We didn't have anything suitable at home at the time, but the Derby Sale was coming up at Fairyhouse in June. That would be time enough.

Brian hardly knew anything about me. He knew that I had had some involvement with eventing and he had heard of Space Trucker, although he didn't know that I had trained him until Arthur told him. The only thing that I had had going for me was that I was Shean Town's trainer.

I contacted Brian before the Derby Sale and asked him if he would like to go to the sale with Johnny and me. Unfortunately, he was tied up with some project at the time and he couldn't make it. So I had this fairly unusual situation where I was setting off to buy a horse for someone I had never met and about whom I knew nothing, except that he was the father of a friend of one of my owners. But I never really worried that Brian would renege on the deal. I suppose, in hindsight, I should have. It happens. It wasn't the most secure footing on which to be going out to spend twenty grand. But I got a good feeling from Brian, and the fact that he came through Arthur was no hindrance.

Brian came down to see his horse during the summer. He seemed to be quite proud of the fact that this was his horse. His first horse. I'm not sure if he had ever been in a trainer's yard before, and he seemed to be quite bemused by everything that was going on. Commonstown is a hive of activity even at the quietest of times. Dick McElligott, Brian's friend with whom he shares a box at Cheltenham, had told him that the gallops went through the kitchen, so I'm not sure what he expected.

The name and the colours were all Brian's. That's the great thing for an owner when they buy an unraced horse: you get to choose everything. The colours had to be black and white for Belvedere; also, Brian felt that they would be quite easy to spot in a big field. The black and white hoops had already been taken by Sir Anthony O'Reilly – the quintessential Belvederian – so Brian had to settle for chevrons. Another of Moscow Society's sons, Moscow Express, was doing very well at the time, so Brian thought that he would keep the Moscow name. You send three names off to the Turf Club in order of preference, and they come back and tell you which ones you can have. Moscow Max was one name Brian chose, after his grandson Max, but for some reason the Turf Club wouldn't accept it. Moscow Flyer was another, and Moscow Flyer it was.

It must have been a strange experience for Brian. He is an extremely successful businessman who was used to planning every detail so that his company, Project Management, could flourish and grow. With his business, he made sure that timesheets, expense sheets, purchase orders and written agreements were used from the very beginning. Even when it was only a three-man operation. Yet here he was having spent 17,000 guineas on something about which he knew next to nothing. The investment had been selected by someone about whom he knew next to nothing. He didn't even see the horse before it was bought. Even when he came down to Commonstown to see his purchase for the first time, he couldn't have known if his money had been well spent. Four legs, a head and a tail. Definitely a horse. That was as far as it went.

But in order to be successful, you don't have to be an expert in everything. You just have to know someone who is skilled in each of the areas in which you are involved. Brian was utilising his skills of delegation in this latest escapade. I thought that we had spent Brian's money well, though I didn't know just how well. None of us did. Over the following months and years, we would learn that Brian Kearney had bought a priceless commodity for next to nothing.

CHAPTER FIVE

GROWING UP

My family's association with Ireland goes back to the eighteenth century. The first Fowler to cross the water from England was the private confessor and personal chaplain to King George II. When the king died, his chaplain was out of a job. In reality, however, a chaplain was never really out of a job in those days. Especially not when he had been personal chaplain to the king. It was a bit like the way you are never out of a job in politics these days. You are just moved to the House of Lords, or to the Seanad. Or to Brussels.

He was sent to Ireland as the Protestant Bishop of Killaloo in 1763, and he progressed from there to become Archbishop of Dublin. His son got his Doctorate of Divinity from Trinity College, and was given the parish of St Anne's. St Anne's church is still on Dawson Street in the middle of Dublin city today, just on the corner with Molesworth Street. Amazingly, it is the church in which I was married. Soon after being granted the parish, however, the archbishop's son decided that he was unwell, and that he needed to go to Switzerland to take the fresh air. He stayed for all of five or six years. He was drawing his stipend from the parish and drawing an annual allowance from his father, and had enough income to live like a lord. There were a lot of young ladies in Switzerland at the time who were refugees from Paris. They may have been more of a lure than the fresh air. Eventually his father told him that he would have to come back or he would lose his parish. So he returned to St Anne's and, after a few years, was made Bishop of Ossary and Ferns, a diocese that runs from Borris-in-Ossary in the north of County Kilkenny to Ferns in County Wexford.

Being a bishop in those days wasn't terribly demanding. This particular bishop found himself a rich wife whose brother was the last Earl of Blessington. The Earl died without any children, so the bishop and his wife inherited his estate. This included a lot of the land in Dublin city centre, all around Mountjoy Square and Gardiner Street. Actually, their family name was Gardiner.

This enabled the Fowlers to move out of Dublin. They sold bits and pieces of the land in Dublin city and moved out to County Meath. By 1860, a couple of generations later, the Fowlers had acquired about 6,000 acres in County Meath. All of it was tenanted except for the Rahinston estate, just outside Summerhill, where we grew up and where my brother John now lives.

In the 1880s, when William Gladstone was trying to curry favour with the Irish, he started passing various acts that returned the land to the tenants. The Land Commission continued in this vein during the 1930s, mainly targeting absentee landlords. The net result for the Fowlers was that by the 1950s, when my parents moved back to Ireland with John and me, all the tenanted land was gone except for a few little isolated pockets of woodland. We were left with the Rahinston estate. I suppose we couldn't grumble about 850 acres.

My father's uncle, Captain Harry Fowler, was born in 1856. He spent a lot of his youth in foreign countries with the army, most of the time in what is now called Afghanistan. He came back around 1890. He had a bad fall out hunting one day and smashed his ankle to bits. In those days they weren't very good at repairing things, so they just cut his foot off and welded a lump of wood to the bottom of his leg. It didn't stop him hunting, however. We have a photo of him out hunting as master of the Meath Hounds – him and his wooden foot. He had a stud farm, which he gradually ground to a halt. He also had a lot of female admirers, he had his hounds and he had a few racehorses. He retired from hunting in 1935. He figured he was just getting a little too old for it.

My father's father was the youngest of three brothers. Captain Harry was the eldest, and General John Fowler was in the middle. General John had two daughters, neither of whom ever married. Captain Harry had two sons. His youngest was killed in the First World War in 1915, and the other died of leukaemia in 1929 at the age of 35. Then his wife died. They are all remembered on the tablets in Rathmolyon Protestant Church. I used to read them all when I was at church as a kid. Sitting there, really bored. You'd nearly know them all off by heart. Actually, Captain Harry's eldest son, after surviving the war, became a very high-class cricket player. He used to take English teams to America and Canada and try to show the North Americans that there was a viable alternative to baseball. He would arrange cricket games in the Chicago White Sox baseball ground, and in Los Angeles. There were a lot of English people in Hollywood during the late 1920s and there were several cricket teams there.

I was born Jessica Jane Fowler in London on 25 February 1947, and I spent the first two years of my life in a place called Ravensthorpe in Northamptonshire, England. I know this because I was told. I don't remember too much about the first two years of my life. I don't suppose many people do.

In 1949, when I was two and my brother John was three, we moved back to Ireland.

My father had an elder brother, Uncle Frank, but he didn't want Rahinston. He didn't want the hassle. Frank never married, he lived in the north, and he loved sailing. None of that fitted in too well with owning and managing an 850-acre estate, so my father was next in line. Initially we rented Culmullen House, which wasn't far from Rahinston. Culmullen House was owned by a big Dunshaughlin family, the Leonards, at the time. It was later sold to Sam and Ada McCormick, who later owned the top-class mare Maid of Money whom my brother John trained to win the Irish Grand National in 1989. I remember having chicken pox while we lived in Culmullen House, but I don't remember much else about it.

In 1951 we moved to Rathmolyon House. It was another old house that was owned by Captain Harry and hadn't been lived in for the best part of 50 years. We lived there until Captain Harry died, and then we moved to Rahinston. Captain Harry was just six weeks off his 100th birthday when he passed away. He was in the full of his faculties right up until his very last breath. Actually, he didn't stop driving until he was 97, after his last car crash, when he drove off the back avenue going down to the farmyard one morning. After that he decided to hang up his keys.

To be honest, I found him to be a rather fearsome man. We used to go to Rahinston for Christmas and such like, and we'd be taken to see him regularly as he lived only three miles down the road. I was fascinated by his wooden foot, but I'm not too sure that he liked small children. Especially not small girls. I would always be afraid to ask him if we could gallop our ponies around the farm. We had twenty acres down in Rathmolyon, but there were 850 acres at Rahinston. There was no comparison. After a while you'd get bored with twenty acres when you knew there were 850 acres just up the road. My brother John and I would come up to Rahinston about three times a week during the summer. We'd put our ponies in the stables and come into the house. We'd chat him up for a little while before asking him if we could go for a gallop. I'm sure he knew what we were up to. John was great at that. I'd be petrified, but it would be worth it once we were out on the ponies.

Interestingly, I don't remember learning to ride. I suppose I have just always ridden. There are photos of me sitting on a little white pony in Rathmolyon when I was very small, but I don't remember any of that. When my father thought that I was at a stage where I needed to learn how to ride properly, he gave me some tuition. Show-jumping, dressage, everything.

My father was born in Kells, County Meath, and joined the Gunners' Royal Artillery during the First World War. Brigadier Fowler. By Easter 1916 he had just graduated from the Royal Military College. He was at the races in Fairyhouse that Easter Monday when he was ordered to go to Drogheda to help defend the town against the revolutionary mob. By the time he got there, however, thankfully the thing was over. In 1917 he was sent to Passchendaele in Belgium to fight. There was frightful carnage there. Some 250,000 soldiers were killed as they fought one another to a standstill in the mud. Fortunately my father survived. He returned to England after the war to become an instructor at the Army Equitation School at Weedon.

He lived the life of Reilly between 1920 and 1940. I suppose he had earned it. He was sent all over the world with the army, posted at various times to Egypt, India, Iraq and Iran, or Persia as it was then. He had some army duties to do of course, but they weren't very strenuous. If he was in England during the winter, he used to come back to Ireland to hunt. He would get the Irish mail train from Euston at 8.45 on a Friday evening and he'd be in Dun Laoghaire on Saturday morning at seven o'clock. He'd hunt on the Saturday, shoot on the Sunday, hunt again on the Monday, and be back at the barracks at six o'clock on Tuesday morning.

There were a lot of great riders at Weedon at the time. People like Brigadier Bolton and Colonel Nicholl, who rode for Great Britain in the 1948 Olympics. My father was on the British polo team that went to the 1936 Olympics in Berlin and won a silver medal. Actually, the British team was full of Irish people. Every one of them was born in Ireland before the turn of the century, so they were part of the British Empire at the time. It must have been a huge deal, to win a silver medal at the Olympics, although it is difficult to judge because that was the last time polo was played as an Olympic sport. They were beaten 13–2 by Argentina in the final, but it must have been great for him and for the team to get that far.

I don't think many people felt that the peace that reigned after the First World War was going to last indefinitely. Still, they probably underestimated the extent to which Germany was on its hands and knees in the 1920s. When Hitler got into the Reichstag, people began to get worried again. If the Berlin Olympics had been held two years later, I don't think Britain would have sent a team.

My father was very reluctant to talk about his wartime experiences. Occasionally he and a couple of his old army buddies would get together in the dining room, and they'd sit there half the night talking about it over port. But he was very disinclined to talk openly about it. If you asked about it a couple of times and weren't encouraged to ask again, you sort of didn't pursue it. I think they were happy that it was over, happy to forget about it. They had lost a lot of friends. My father stayed on in the army until 1949. John remembers him going to meet him at Rugby train station with me and our mother after he had left the army. He wasn't cut out to be a staff general. He didn't want to just sit behind an office desk until he retired. Anyway, it was fairly obvious that, barring the occurrence of something untoward, he was going to have to go back to Ireland to look after Rahinston.

My mother was born in England, but she had a lot of Irish relations and she used to come to Ireland as a child. She drove ambulances and trucks during the war. I suppose if you were able-bodied you got a job during the war. She had a heavy-goods vehicle licence, so she was recruited as a driver. My mother's first husband was killed in a plane crash at the start of the war, in 1941. She was left as a young widow with two children. My father knew my mother's first husband very well – they used to play polo together – so my mother and father had known each other for some time. In May 1944 they decided to get married.

My father was 49 when I was born. In those days you were considered old at that age, but he was an amazing man. He rode right up until he was in his eighties. He used to exercise my great eventing mare Amoy for me, right up until she retired. He was tough, in that he liked things to be done correctly, but he was fair. He had a great sense of what was right. I remember one Christmas all my school friends were going skiing, so I asked if it was OK if I went with them. My father said, 'Fine, but you won't have a pony to hunt when you come back.' The way he looked at it, there was no point in him getting my pony fit for the holidays if I wasn't going to be around to ride it. If you want to hunt, your pony is there, but if you want to go skiing, there'll be no pony – that was his way. I probably didn't see it at the time, but he was right. It put things into perspective for me. I went skiing for the first time when I was 40.

I have probably inherited a lot of my father's characteristics. I think I have his determination. If he was intent on doing something, he didn't rest until he had accomplished it. Also, he was a horseman in every sense of the word. From riding, breaking and jumping to welfare and diet. A lot of what I know about horses I learnt from my father.

My mother was a beautiful rider too. At the age of sixteen, she was about to give up riding until someone suggested that she ride side-saddle. She hunted side-saddle all her life, all across Meath. She also ran our home and picked up the pieces after us. She was brilliant. If you wanted something done, you just had to ask my mother. I didn't see that much of her children by her first marriage, my half-brother and -sister. Simon was fourteen years older than me and Sarah was twelve years older, and they were away at school most of the time. But when they'd be coming home, we'd get awfully excited. As we got older we got closer. Sarah married the late David Ainsworth, who used to train on The Curragh.

It was great growing up in Rahinston. It was great to have all this land on which we could gallop around on our ponies. You didn't have to hack up the road for miles to get to where you wanted to go, or ask the old man's permission. It was just all there for you in your back garden. Almost all of our friends were friends through pony club. That was the common thread. And Rahinston was very much a part of that community. We used to have competitions in Rahinston which were great fun.

Ireland in the late 1950s and early 1960s was not a very prosperous place. We were probably insulated from a lot of it on our 850-acre estate, and you don't really think about these things as a child, but there was very little money about. The kids in Rathmolyon used to walk barefoot for three or four miles to school, carrying their shoes because they were too expensive to get wet. That's what it was like back then. We only got electricity into the house in Rathmolyon in about 1953. I can remember our late lamented head man, Billy Burns, coming up to the house when we were still in the village with his brand-new pair of wellington boots. He was about fourteen at the time, and he asked my father if he could have a job looking after the ponies. And I can recall seeing cattle being driven to the market in Dublin on foot. These cows coming through Rathmolyon on their way to Dublin, about twenty miles away.

There were always horses around when I was growing up. My father and mother both hunted and my father played polo. We had an old cattle truck and my father used it to take the horses to Phoenix Park to play polo. I used to go with him. I remember sitting in the back, looking out through the little slits and wondering if we would ever get there. It was only about twenty miles, but it seemed to take for ever. We kept a few point-to-pointers too, which my father used to ride. He rode Mr Romford to win a bumper in Mullingar, and he rode Prudent King. He must have really fancied Prudent King to win his bumper – a four-year-old bumper on New Year's Day – because he sent my mother along to back him. He was a huge price, and my father was having £100 or something substantial on him. After he had won, my mother went to collect at the Tote window. 'Madam,' the Tote man said, 'would you mind coming round the back?' My mother was petrified as she thought something was wrong. My father had ridden the horse, and jockeys weren't allowed to bet. She met the man at the back of the building. The man looked at her sternly and enquired, 'Will a cheque be OK?'

My father had bought Prudent King for my mother at Ballsbridge in the Horse Show Sale as a three-year-old. After he won his bumper, Vincent O'Brien offered £1,500 for him. After much consternation, they decided to sell. Or rather, my mother decided to sell. It was a lot of money in those days. So much money, in fact, that they bought a house in Cahirdaniel in Kerry with it (we still have that house). My mother said that she wasn't going to allow my father to buy another horse with it. Vincent later won one of the divisions of the Gloucestershire Hurdle with Prudent King at Cheltenham.

My brother John went off to prep school when he was eight but I stayed at home to be taught by a governess. Judy Preston and I used to have lessons together. Judy later married the top event rider Ronnie McMahon. Twice a week during the winter we would go hunting with the Tara Harriers. We'd do lessons until eleven o'clock and then we'd set off on the ponies to ride to wherever they were meeting, Rathmolyon or Rathcore or Longwood. If we got back from hunting before half past three, we had to do another hour of lessons. Strangely, we rarely made it back on time.

When I was eleven, my pony Whiskey and I were on the team that won the pony club team event in Mount Juliet. Three years later we went over to the UK to the pony club championships, which were held that year in Highgrove, where Prince Charles now lives. We had a great team that year. Patricia McDowell, one of the McDowells from the House of Rings, was on it. The whole McDowell family were great show-jumpers. And there was Judy Preston, and my brother John. I rode Tache that year, and I won the individual class. The team finished third.

I had a few good ponies when I was younger. After Whiskey, when I was in my early teens, I had Tache; a few years later I had Simple Simon. My father was very good with ponies and he always had good ones for me to ride. I show-jumped and hunted and did everything on them. And we did hunter trials once a year. There weren't that many events at the time, but I was lucky enough to win my fair share.

I never really thought about the fact that I was at home being taught by a governess while a lot of my friends were at school. I did think that it was great that I didn't have to go to school, but that was as far as it went. I suppose when you are a child you don't delve into these things too deeply. That was just what we did. We thought it was normal. John went to school, I didn't. That was just the way it was. In those days it didn't really matter if a girl got an education or not. We'll keep you for so long, and then you'll go and get married. That'll do you. That was the thinking back then. There was no such thing as a career or going to university or anything like that.

But when I was twelve I was sent off to boarding school in England, Hatherop School in Gloucestershire. They thought it was about time that I went to England to learn how to behave like a young lady instead of being a tomboy, which I think I was. That was a bit of a shock to the system initially, but I loved it after a little while. I loved being around lots of people my own age. I probably didn't do too much work, but I had a great time.

The school was run by an eccentric woman called Mrs Fyfe. She was about 80 and stone deaf, which was probably just as well given the antics we used to get up to. We lived in a castle that was crumbling around us. We had a bath rota. You got a bath three times a week. I guess it was cold and pretty basic, but we didn't know any better so it was grand. It was a bit like Harry Potter without the magic but with all the adventure. There was an opportunity to ride once a week at Hatherop, but my mother wouldn't let me. She said I spent enough time riding during the holidays and that I'd be better off learning to be a lady at school. Or something like that.

I was lucky to last there until I was sixteen. I didn't do very much work, especially during my final term. I guess I wasn't a model pupil. During my last three weeks I didn't go to breakfast once. There was no badness in it. I guess I just enjoyed the thrill of doing something and getting away with it. Some mornings it would be eleven o'clock before I'd get up. We used to raid the gardens at night time and eat the raspberries. I was good at getting out at night, and I made sure to obey the eleventh commandment: thou shalt not get caught.

I'd fly to England during the summer but get the boat during the winter; my parents thought it was too dangerous to fly during the winter. It might have been fairly scary all right. The planes that flew to Bristol in those days were these big things that used to waggle their wings to get off the ground. During half-term I used to stay in England with aunts and uncles, or sometimes I'd be asked to stay with my school friends. My parents would come over during the summer and take me out for a night. We'd see John at Eton and stay with friends of theirs. That was the only time they'd come over, and apart from the holidays that was the only time I saw them. My mother used to say that I must have had a terrible time at home because I was never homesick. I didn't really think about it too much. I suppose I was having too good a time at school.

But the holidays were great. I'd do hunter trials in the spring and go eventing in the summer. And we'd always go to our house in Kerry for two weeks during the summer. We never went abroad. Sometimes we'd go to Kerry for the Christmas holiday too. We didn't have electricity in the house then, so we'd have lamps and candles and things. It was almost magical.

When I finished school I went to Paris for a year. I wanted to learn French, and my parents thought it would be a good idea. So they enrolled me in this school that was kind of like a finishing school, and looked for a family to put me up. They found this French lady, Madame Murray, who was a formidable lady. She always wore black. I never saw her in anything other than black. She was married to an American soldier who had stayed in Paris after the war. That wasn't so bad as it meant that if you were really stuck you had someone with whom you could converse in English.

I headed off to France with another Irish girl, Kerry Page, who was from just down the road in Grangecon. Kerry stayed for six months, I stayed for nine. It was really great being there for the summer, though the first three months were tough as you were getting to grips with the language and all the different aspects of Parisian living. I'd say after about three months the penny dropped, and after that it was great. You could go to the theatre or the cinema and understand everything. We lived right in the middle of Paris, opposite the metro station Chambre des Députés at the beginning of the Boulevard St-Germain. My digs were paid and I had an allowance of £2 per week; it was about thirteen francs to the pound at the time. With that I could buy my school books and my metro ticket and still have plenty left over to go to the theatre.

When I finished my year there I wanted to go back to the Sorbonne and read art for two years. But this was the mid-1960s, and there was already a fair degree of tension around the city ahead of the student riots of 1968. After spending nine months in Paris my head was full of ideas. I loved it there and I loved the idea of studying art at the Sorbonne, but my parents wouldn't hear of it. I was a girl, and as I said, in those days girls didn't really go to university. Regardless of the tension in the city and the potential danger to me as a result, I'm not sure my parents were very comfortable with the idea of me spending another two years in Paris anyway. It was absolutely out of the question. It didn't bother me too much. It would have been a nice thing to do, but I wasn't that despondent when it was ruled out. When you're seventeen you just move on to the next thing.

At that point I had no idea what I wanted to do with my life. I didn't really even think about it too much. I suppose I just meandered along from day to day, having a good time, riding lots and enjoying myself. Things just happened, and I suppose I just went along with them. You got a job, you worked for a couple of years, you travelled a bit and then went back home. That was what you did. You'd always be doing something, but you wouldn't be thinking where you'd want to be in five years' time or anything like that. I suppose if I had thought about it I would have wanted to be doing something with horses. But even that wasn't clear in my mind. I just went along with whatever was happening.

I went to London for a few months and then came home and did a secretarial course in Trim. My father was master of the Meath Hounds at the time. For the next three years my job was to drive a car and trailer with my horse and a hunt servant's horse to the meet three times a week, stay out all day and bring it back in the evening. That was great. I also had a job as a secretary two or three days a week for Johnny Alexander at Loughtown Stud. I don't think I was very good at that. I was very organised, but I couldn't spell. Still can't. There were no spellchecks in those days, so that probably equates to being not a very good secretary.

But I loved riding. My father always had a good touch with horses and ponies, and I always seemed to have good ones to ride. I probably wasn't that competitive in those days, though. The horses and ponies were there, so I just got on and rode them. Gold Buck was the first serious competition horse I had. I won a couple of events on him and went to Burghley in 1965 when I was eighteen. Burghley is second only to Badminton in the eventing world in terms of prestige. In fact, I was going to Badminton with Gold Buck the following spring, but it got rained off that year. That was gutting. It would have been my first time competing at Badminton. Gold Buck did a bit of eventing, but he was a bit cowardly and he went point-to-pointing and racing. He found that less daunting. I finished second on him in a point-to-point in Waterford, and my brother John rode him to win one. That was the only point-to-point in which I ever rode in Ireland, although I did ride in a couple in England when I lived there later. I preferred eventing. My father didn't really approve of women riding in races, so it was easy to go down the eventing route.

But the rest of my life began to get in the way of my riding. In the summer of 1966 I went to America with a pal, Roseanne Foster. Her parents and my parents were great friends and we had been at school together. We headed off to the States and travelled around by bus for three or four months – $99 for 99 days on a Greyhound bus was a deal not to be passed up. We stayed with various friends of our parents. We started off in Unionville, Pennsylvania with

Charlie Bird. He was master of the Meath Hounds when I was growing up and he had a farm in Ireland. From there we went all over the place: Washington, Georgia, down to New Orleans, across to the Grand Canyon, Los Angeles and San Francisco. John was in McGill University in Canada at the time so we also went up there to see him. We ended up in Wyoming, staying on a ranch with the Tate family. There we met the Schiffer family – people with whom I am still great friends. They were bringing their cattle down from the mountain at the time, so we rode up and for three days we moved cattle. It started to snow on the first night, so we stayed in a hut up on the mountain. It was unbelievable. We started off in the snow and ended up in a dust bowl. Just gorgeous. But, God, those cows make a lot of noise! It would have been just about perfect had it not been for the noise. It got to you after a while, and unfortunately that is the thing I remember most about the whole escapade.

We tended to travel by night in America. That way you could sleep on the bus and you didn't have to pay for cheap hotels or YMCAs. One morning we arrived at Atlanta bus station at around five o'clock. We were in Georgia to stay with some friends of my parents who used to come over to hunt. Our connection wasn't till nine, so we had four hours to kill. We decided that we'd get the cheapest thing possible to eat. So I was wandering up to this place, half asleep, and I saw this guy standing there eating a sandwich. It was David Reed-Scott, from Grangecon. A friend from childhood. It turned out that he was going to stay with the same people.

Life is a lot about chance. If you hadn't gone there or hadn't done this, that might not have happened or you might not have met this person and your life would have been totally different. That's the way life is. You can't dwell on what might have been; you have to go with what is. If the first two horses we bid on for Brian Kearney at the Derby Sale in 1998 had not been so expensive, we would not have bought Moscow Flyer. He might still have turned out to be as good as he was had he been trained by someone else. But he might not have.

I was in New York just before I returned home. I was on my way down to see Times Square, just to see what all the fuss was about, when suddenly a taxi pulled up in front of me and Johnny Harrington jumped out. I knew him too from home, and I actually knew that he was in New York at the time. Still, what are the chances? In the middle of New York City in 1966? I was nineteen. It was remarkable. But not as remarkable as the fact that less than ten years later, Johnny and I would end up getting married.

CHAPTER SIX

JOHNNY HARRINGTON

Johnny Harrington's family put the H in HGW Paints. Harrington Goodlass Wall. When Johnny was growing up in the 1940s and 1950s, HGW supplied practically all the paint that was used in Ireland at the time, and could boast probably the biggest factory in the country.

Born and raised in Cork, young Johnny was sent off to Ampleforth College in Yorkshire for his secondary schooling. That was the thing to do in those days. If you were Irish, Catholic, had a son and could afford it, you sent him to Ampleforth. It might not have been the right thing to do, but it was definitely the thing to do. About a hundred Irish boys were on the Ampleforth books at the time.

Johnny wasn't exceptionally gifted at school – no more than myself – but he muddled through. When he came out the other side in 1955 he was all set to go on his two-year National Service. But when he went for his medical, which should have been a mere formality for a boy of his age, they discovered that he had a collapsed lung. He had had pneumonia during his final term, but they'd thought he was over it. He wasn't. He was rushed to Middlesex Hospital, where he remained for six weeks. After that he went back to Ireland and played golf. He says that he had to be out in the fresh air because of his collapsed lung, but I have my suspicions about the validity of that claim. It might have had more to do with his golf handicap than with his collapsed lung. After a year of sauntering around the golf courses of Ireland, he was hauled back to learn about the family business.

But paint factories and collapsed lungs don't go together. Not even nearly. Johnny hated the paint factory. He hated being in the office, he hated the smell of paint, he hated everything about it. He lasted three years, which was just about three years longer than he thought he would last. He was then offered a £750 pay-off to get out, which he gladly accepted.

He thought he wanted to get into racing, but he didn't know very much about it. However, his godfather, Arthur Dynan, had horses with Vincent O'Brien, and Johnny had been well acquainted with the social side of racing as a result. They used to go on family holidays with Vincent and Jacqueline. Johnny went to Merano with them in 1953, when Vincent ran Knock Hard in the Grand Prix de Merano the year he won the Gold Cup. He shared a room with jockey Martin Molony, who used to make Johnny get up early every morning to go to mass. After a few days of this, Johnny figured he'd get up half an hour earlier and go down to the racetrack to watch morning work. That was far more interesting.

In 1956 he went to the sales at Ballsbridge with his great friend Thady Dunraven. Now Lord Dunraven, he is paralysed and in a wheelchair, but he is still in great order. A wonderful man. At those sales there was a horse that they both liked and both wanted to buy. There was also a young lady there whom they were both trying to impress. In a joint display of macho bravado, and with this girl looking on, they bid against each other. Inevitably, they ended up paying more than twice what they should have paid for the horse. Thady kept the horse and called him Moment of Madness.

At the same sale, Johnny bought an unbroken four-year-old gelding by King Hal out of Culleen Coup. King Hal was the dominant National Hunt sire at the time and the mare was from a famous breed, owned by Mr Dargle from Mullingar. Johnny paid £150 for the horse, which appeared to be a serious bargain. Johnny kept his horse with Glen Brown in Cork, who was later responsible for buying Arkle for the Duchess of Westminster. The duchess came to stay with Glen one weekend to go hunting, saw Johnny's horse, loved him, and offered £1,000 for him. Johnny was beside himself. Judgement vindicated, and £850 profit to boot. Maxi Cosgrave came down to check out the horse for the duchess before she bought him. He couldn't understand how Johnny had picked up such a good-looking, well-bred horse for £150. When he examined him, however, the realisation dawned. His prognosis was that the horse's heart was so bad that he was dangerous to ride. He could have dropped dead at any second. Deal off. Still Johnny's horse.

Peg Watt was master of the United Hunt at the time. She took a half-share in the horse from Johnny and agreed to pay the training bills as long as he was kept in training with Willie O'Grady, Edward's father. It was a great deal for Johnny. No training bills and the opportunity to have a horse with Willie. He was still in the paint factory at the time, but he used to come up from Cork to Ballynonty, where Edward now trains, every Friday night so that he could ride out his horse, named Hal Culleen, on Saturday mornings. He'd arrive at about six o'clock on Friday evening. Usually Willie would be waiting for him, and he wouldn't even let him get out of the car. Johnny would have to drive Willie to Cahir, where he would go drinking with his mates. Johnny was their chauffeur for the night. They might not get back until four or five in the morning, and Willie's head lad, Tim Finn, who is still down there with Edward, used to call Johnny at seven to go to ride out. One morning, after a particularly late night, Johnny's legs almost went from under him upon dismounting. Willie noticed this and decided to have a bit of fun.

'Do you want to ride another?' he asked Johnny.

'Love to.' Honestly.

After 500 yards Johnny was out of control. His horse left the ploughed gallop, went straight up to where the other horses were walking around and stopped dead. Johnny went right over his head and was knocked out cold. All he remembers is waking up with Willie's dogs licking his face and all the lads laughing. Edward O'Grady was about twelve at the time. He was laughing so hard at Johnny's misfortune that he himself got bucked off. This was a source of even more amusement for the lads. He was, after all, the boss's son. Johnny still talks about the breakfast that morning: the sausages and eggs that Mary served up, how he just about made it to the loo before throwing up, and how Edward's nose was out of joint all through the meal.

It might be an automatic fourteen days for concussion these days, but not then. Willie had him up again after breakfast. As a small concession, he put him up on a nice quiet one that Johnny could only just about persuade to do two rounds of the plough. That horse turned out to be Solfen, who ran in two races at the Cheltenham Festival the following March and won both.

Johnny had a couple of rides for Willie in bumpers that winter without troubling the judge. He rode Hal Culleen in his first race in Tralee, where he finished third of four. His next race was at Limerick. Johnny went up to Willie in the parade ring before the race.

'What are my instructions?' he asked the trainer.

'Instructions?' replied Willie with a laugh. 'You couldn't carry out instructions!'

The lad who led him up, Bunty, told him not to hit the front too early and he would win by a minute. Hal Culleen had other ideas. He went clear at the bottom of the hill. By the time he got to the top of the hill, Johnny had let the whole field – six horses – up his inside and he came round the home turn last. It was a short home straight at the old Limerick course, but it was long enough for Hal Culleen.

Johnny didn't know where the winning post was, but when he reached it he was a neck in front. The entrance to the course was just past the winning line. The horse saw Bunty at it, went straight for him, nearly knocked him down and galloped through the parade ring to the weigh room with Johnny just about clinging on. He was possibly the first jockey ever to get run away with into the parade ring, and probably the only one to present himself at the weigh-in before the clerk of the scales.

Hal Culleen won his maiden hurdle easily and was winter favourite for the Gloucestershire Hurdle – the current Supreme Novices' – at Cheltenham. Unfortunately, the inevitable happened: his dodgy ticker caught up with him and he never made it to Cheltenham. If he had had a heart, Johnny says he could have been anything. The Tin Man wouldn't have had a look-in.

Within a week of Johnny getting his £750 pay-off from the family business, Vincent O'Brien rang him to ask him if he would be interested in a game of cards. Of course he would be. This was a regular game that Johnny was asked to join. There was Vincent and his brother Phonsie, Lord Harrington, Ted Stokes and a few others. It is reasonable to assume that Vincent knew about Johnny's new-found wealth. Arrive early, play before dinner, play after dinner, stop at midnight and stay the night – that was the plan. Johnny didn't win a hand before dinner. He didn't win a hand after dinner. He lost £250 – one third of his fortune. And this was 1957. Back in the days when £250 was a lot of money.

He was sharing a room with a fellow called Don O'Neil Flanagan, an architect from Waterford who basked under the title 'The Social Architect'. He knew everybody, and got a lot of his business through social contacts. Like Johnny, this was Don's first time playing in the game. Also like Johnny, he had done his dough – £1,000 of it. When they were going to bed, Don turned to Johnny.

'That was a wonderful experience,' he said. 'Meeting all those people.'

Johnny looked at him incredulously. 'I've only done £250, and I'd prefer never to have met them!'

But Vincent was Johnny's hero all through his school days and beyond. Ampleforth was a racing-oriented school. There was a priest there called Father Hubert Stevenson who was related to some racing people and was a terrible social climber. One evening Johnny met him after vespers. Vincent had just been warned off, albeit in somewhat questionable circumstances, when a prohibited substance was found in Chamour after he had won the Ballysax Maiden at The Curragh in 1960. 'I had dinner with Noel Murless last night,' said the priest, 'and he tells me that your friend O'Brien is going to hang.' It was all Johnny could do to stop himself from hitting him. But it is a long road that doesn't turn. Some 25 years later, when Vincent's son David began going to Ampleforth, it didn't take long for the priest to befriend the trainer. Johnny used to meet Fr Stevenson regularly down in Ballydoyle. They'd have a laugh about their conversation that evening after vespers, but Johnny never let him forget it.

Johnny's father was great friends with Charlie Rogers, who was Dorothy Paget's racing manager. Daughter of Lord Queensborough, Dorothy Paget was an eccentric lady who owned five-time Gold Cup winner Golden Miller. She was a fierce punter but prided herself on the strength of her bloodstock empire. In 1946 she bought Ballymacoll Stud – later to be owned by Sir Michael Sobell and Lord Weinstock, and birthplace of horses like Dart Board, Troy, Sun Princess, Helen Street, Pilsudski, Golan, Islington, North Light and, of course, Arkle – but, famously, never visited the place. Sir Gordon Richards was her principal jockey when he was riding, and he'd already begun to train by the time Johnny decided that he wanted to work in racing. So Charlie Rogers got him a job with Sir Gordon, who had just moved to Whitsbury. William Hill owned the yard, and Gordon leased it from him. That's the place where David Elsworth is now.

Johnny lived in a hostel and just mucked out and rode out. He used to go racing a lot then, and although he was only with Sir Gordon for two seasons, he got to know a lot of racing people in England. People like Peter Walwyn and John Dunlop. He loved going down to Lambourn. He became good friends with the Duchess of Norfolk, who was effectively training her husband's horses at the time, although Gordon Smyth was down as the official trainer. She was always quizzing him about Sir Gordon's horses. John Dunlop was a pupil at Smyth's at the time, but it wasn't long before the duchess appointed him as trainer. Johnny used to spend a lot of time down there, and he and John became great friends. John asked Johnny to be godfather to his son, Ed, and John is our daughter Kate's godfather.

Johnny got on well with Sir Gordon, who treated him very well. It wasn't until later that Johnny found out that Sir Gordon thought he was Lord Harrington. Things might have been a little different had he realised he was just plain old Johnny Harrington, paint maker, from Cork.

The experience with Sir Gordon made Johnny's mind up for him that he wasn't going to be a trainer. There was no aspiring Noel Murless or Vincent O'Brien lurking inside him. He thought it was too difficult, too much hassle. And there wasn't any money in it. He was supposed to join Peter Walwyn as assistant trainer the following year, but while he was at home for Christmas he was offered a job as a bloodstock agent with the Curragh Bloodstock Agency (CBA). He thought that that would be a safer bet.

Johnny admits that he didn't know much about pedigrees then, and even less about conformation, but in those days it really was a case of who rather than what you knew, and Johnny was very good at getting on with people. Paddy Sleator took him under his wing. He used to pick him up in the afternoon and go down to the middle of Wexford or Cork looking at store horses in fields. Johnny asked questions, and Paddy answered them. He didn't mind. What was back of the knee? What was a curb? And what do they all mean for a horse's prospective racing career? Johnny reckons there are many bloodstock agents now buying horses who chanced their way through it and got away with it. How many of them would pass a bloodstock agent's exam?

One of Johnny's first clients was Fred Winter, who was just

starting to train when Johnny joined the CBA. He knew nothing about conformation. In fairness to Johnny, he told Fred that he should probably get a different agent as he didn't know much about it himself. But Fred wanted Johnny, and they pressed on together. The first call they made was to Dan Moore's yard one morning. Johnny used to ride out there so Dan knew about Johnny's limited knowledge of conformation. They went through the motions nevertheless, looking at horses and feeling their legs, Johnny and Fred competing with each other in their ignorance. After a while Dan could stand it no longer. He virtually kicked the two of them out of the yard. They went back in the afternoon and bought two horses. Both for ten grand. Both by Vulgan. Both absolutely useless.

But Johnny got better. He listened, he asked questions and he learnt. He formed a good friendship with Jonathan Sheppard, who was leading jumps trainer in the States for a number of years. Johnny helped him buy most of the horses he had for George Strawbridge that were so successful out there. I suppose he knew what type of horse was required to be successful over jumps in the States. He also bought a lot of horses for Fred and Mercy Rimell, and for Jenny Pitman. He bought Toby Tobias from Con Power for Jenny. The day we bought that four-year-old bay gelding, untried, unbroken, by Moscow Society out of Meelick Lady, I remember Johnny telling me that he was a real Mercy Rimell horse. A Mercy Rimell or a Paddy Sleator horse. Not too big, but beautifully put together. Very correct. Always standing correctly. Everything in proportion.

Johnny rented Ballylea Stud in Dunlavin on a five-year lease after he joined the CBA. David and Diane Nagle own it now. One hundred acres and a fully furnished house for £2,000 a year. After three years, the owner, Mrs Nicholson, asked Johnny if she could break the lease. She had had an offer of £100,000 for the house and land. A grand an acre was unheard of then. Johnny asked her for £20,000 as compensation. She gave him £12,000. Everybody happy.

Commonstown Stud in Moone came on the market at the same

time. The house was in a desperate state. Another great friend of Johnny's, Jock Wilson, father of Jim Wilson, the last amateur rider to win the Gold Cup (Little Owl, 1981), used to call it Shit Hall. But it had 134 acres and Johnny could see its potential. Two sisters had been living there, the Leonards, with about a hundred cats. Johnny still talks about the smell of the cats.

Johnny bought the place for £80,000. He had his £12,000 from Mrs Nicholson and a few other bits and pieces, but he needed about another £50,000. You would have thought he would have been OK, as his family had founded the old Munster Bank in Cork which later became the Munster Leinster Bank and then Allied Irish Banks. There was always a Harrington on the AIB board up until about twenty years ago. Unfortunately, as Johnny was the black sheep of the family, they wouldn't have loaned him £50, not to mention £50,000. He had bought a few stallion shares, and he had acquired a 25 per cent stake in the CBA for very little money, but he didn't have anything that was readily liquefiable. But ACC Bank had just opened its Naas branch, and Johnny went to see them. They welcomed him with open arms, and they had money to lend. Johnny was one of their first clients, and we still have an account with them today.

Obviously Johnny didn't know it at the time, but this was to be the place where he would settle down with me. It was to Commonstown that we would return after our marriage. We would raise our two children, Emma and Kate, there. It was from there that we would send out our racehorses to compete on racecourses all over Ireland and the UK. More significantly, however, it was in Commonstown that one of the most famous National Hunt racehorses of our time would be broken, schooled and trained, and it was from there that he would be sent forth to capture the racing hearts of an entire generation.

CHAPTER SEVEN

EVENTING AND MARRIAGE

I first met Johnny in 1965 at a big New Year's Eve party in Luttrelstown Castle. I had heard a lot about him before that, so I was glad to finally meet him. People would talk about him quite a bit. 'Johnny Harrington's here. Do you know Johnny Harrington?' There weren't many social gatherings that went ahead without Johnny. He was very popular. He was ten years older than me and he spent a lot of time in the UK in those days, so we didn't begin to hang around in the same circles until I got a bit older. On New Year's Eve 1965, I was eighteen.

That was actually quite a funny night. Ben Hanbury, who was working for Dan Moore at the time, was driving me home to Rahinston when we crashed into Jenkinstown Bridge. I'm not sure if Ben had had a glass of champagne or two, but there probably wouldn't have been too many gardaí on the road around Jenkinstown Bridge on New Year's Eve in those days. We were both OK, so we dusted ourselves down and hailed the first vehicle that came along. Interestingly, that was a cattle truck. God knows what someone was doing driving a cattle truck over Jenkinstown Bridge at two a.m. on New Year's Day, but we didn't ask. We were just glad to get a lift. We abandoned the car there – it was OK to do things like that in those days – and I remember getting dumped off in all my finery at Paddy Gill's house at about three a.m. Paddy – the father of former jockey Padge Gill – was working for my father at the time and he didn't mind getting up out of his bed to drive me home. At least he said he didn't.

I wouldn't say it was love at first sight with Johnny, but I did like him from the first time I met him. He was good craic, and there was a constant twinkle in his eye. I suppose he had the same kind of mischievous demeanour about him as I had, and I liked that. I went out with him a bit then, but I was also going out with David Lloyd at the time. My brother John had gone to school with David. I had met him at a dance that I co-hosted in Rahinston along with my friend Sarah Macgillicuddy. Our parents threw a 'coming out' dance for the two of us together as, in theory anyway, we were coming of age. Sarah is now godmother to my daughter Emma, and we're still the best of friends.

It may have been down to the fact that Johnny was ten years older than me, or it may have been because we were so alike, but we used to fight a lot. Over nothing really. I have to admit that most of it was my fault as I was very headstrong. Then again, I suppose we were both headstrong, and that's why we fought. We liked each other and everything, but we were just two people who couldn't get along. If I had married Johnny then, it wouldn't have worked. No way. We would have killed each other. It was one row after another. Johnny says that the second time around I had more manners on me.

Also, I was from an old Protestant family and Johnny's family was devout Roman Catholic. At that time, my father had slight inhibitions about mixed marriages. Instructions in Ireland were very specific in that children of mixed marriages had to be brought up as Catholics. My father didn't agree with that. He didn't prevent me from marrying Johnny, or ever say that I shouldn't marry him, but I suppose he let it be known that somebody else might be better. Johnny points to the fact that never before had a Fowler married a Catholic. He says that, worse still, he was a Catholic with apparently limited prospects, so he reckons he was long odds against from the start. To be honest, I didn't think about that aspect too much. I was governed exclusively by my head and my heart at the time.

David had been on at me to marry him for a while. I was flattered, but I didn't think about it too much. I was riding, hunting, having a great social life and just generally enjoying life. Then one day I had a particularly bad bust-up with Johnny. I can't even remember what it was over – probably nothing at all, like all our little squabbles. I don't think that the two were interconnected, but after that I decided to accept David's proposal. It was the winter of the foot and mouth outbreak in 1967. I was in Ireland and David was in England, so it was quite difficult for us, but we finally got engaged in April 1968 and got married that August.

Johnny was disappointed. Of course he was (at least I hope he was). But that was just the way it went. He dealt with it and moved on. I'm a firm believer in things happening for a reason. I wasn't meant to marry Johnny then. We weren't ready for each other. It's amazing how time and circumstances brought us back together again.

After I got married to David, I moved over to England with him. That was a bit of a change for me, but it made sense as David was farming over there, his family was there, and we were able to take on one of the farms. It was no big deal for me. It was just accepted that that would be the way. Again, I didn't really think about it too much. My parents were OK with it too. I suppose my father missed me being around the place, but they accepted that it was my decision. My life. That was the way with my parents. They allowed you to do whatever you wanted to do, within reason. Make your own mistakes if you need to, and learn from them.

So I headed off happy to the Cotswolds. It was the start of something different. Something new. I was 21 and full of youthful optimism. I was carefree, and I went with the flow in many ways without thinking too deeply about things. I didn't dwell on decisions or their potential consequences. I was happy to live life for the now and get on with it.

Initially we lived in Oddington before we bought a farm in Adlestrop, about three miles down the road. We lived in a place called Hillside, just around the corner from where Richard Phillips now trains. I helped on the farm. I did the wages. Whatever needed to be done. And I hunted a bit. We both hunted. I hunted with the Heythrop Hounds, and I evented when I had horses. I took a couple of my father's horses over with me and I had a mare who had been bred over there. But before long I had children to look after. James was born in 1970, and Tara was born three years later. I still hunted and pottered around with horses, but I wasn't as deeply involved as I had been before I got married.

I had made my debut at Badminton on Ginger Nut in 1967 between coming home from America and getting married. That was an absolutely unbelievable experience as all my childhood heroes were riding that year. People at whom I used to look in complete awe: Harry Freeman Jackson, Eddie Boyland, Ginny Petersham. To be in there competing against them was just incredible. I really did have to stand back and rub my eyes a couple of times during the week.

And the course was phenomenal. The fences were so much bigger than I had expected. I had been there before a few years earlier when my half-brother Simon Walford had been competing, and I had seen the course, but I suppose it's different when you go there to compete yourself. I must have walked the course at least five times that first year, figuring out my route and how the hell I was going to negotiate those massive fences.

I remember being bowled over by the crowds too. It would probably only have been about half the size then that it is now, but I remember thinking that there were an awful lot of people and that they were all going to be watching me compete. It was a lot for a twenty-year-old to take in.

The dressage was more or less the same then as it is now. But in the cross-country, instead of having penalty points if you were above a certain time, you got bonus points if you were below a certain time. So you went in with a 'plus' score instead of a 'minus'. Also, if you have a fence down now in the show-jumping you get four penalty points. Back then you got ten. I had three fences down in the show-jumping on Ginger Nut in 1967. That was very expensive, but we still managed to finish fifteenth. The scoring system was completely against her because show-jumping was her weakest discipline of the three.

We went on to the European Championship later that year at Punchestown. My brother John had ridden Ginger Nut to win the first ever Punchestown novice event the previous year, but he had gone more into racing in 1967, riding as an amateur mainly in bumpers and point-to-points, although he did come back that year to ride a horse called Dooney Rock for the Phillipses – the people who started the Ballyfree chickens business – on the Irish team in the European Championship. I didn't make the Irish team for Punchestown in 1967, so I was just riding as an individual.

Jock Ferry used to come down to Rahinston to give John and me lessons every morning. Unfortunately, that was during horse show week in Dublin when it was difficult not to socialise. Our quandary every night was whether we would go home to bed and try to catch a few hours' sleep, or go straight to meet up with Jock for our training. Invariably we went straight there. By the time we finished training, our friends would have been home to bed and would be all set for lunch, so we'd have to go straight out again. That year at Punchestown, all the teams stayed at the Blessington Hotel. But there wasn't enough room for everyone, so the younger members of the Irish team – that was me and a few others – were put up in caravans at the back of the hotel.

Ginger Nut and I were quite late in that competition. We were twelfth after the dressage. An Argentinian technical delegate had passed the course and he had put these rather flat aprons on the steeplechase fences, which made them look a little like a bank. A good few people had falls at them because their horses tried to bank them. We did OK there, though, and in the cross-country. Going into the last day, I was lying in fourth position in the individual competition and John was in fifth. Either we had had a good party the night before after the cross-country or we were just not much good at show-jumping. I should have done better, but show-jumping was Ginger Nut's worst discipline. She used to scatter the poles for fun. I dropped down to sixth place, and John dropped down to twelfth.

John went to the Mexico Olympics with the Irish team in 1968. I didn't. I got married instead. I didn't think that I'd be selected for the Irish team anyway. Ginger Nut hadn't gone so well that spring, and we were probably too far down the pecking order.

Those early years of married life in England were good. We didn't have a huge amount of money, but we were able to get by. I hunted, had children, and worked on the farm. That was what I did. And I used to go racing a bit then as we were right beside Cheltenham racecourse. We were very popular around Festival time. We used to have a lunch party in the house at twelve o'clock and everyone would drive down to the racecourse to be there before the first race. Different times. You would hardly be able to make it these days in a helicopter. I went to the Festival every year when I lived in Gloucester, from 1968 to 1973. I was at Cheltenham when L'Escargot won his two Gold Cups in 1970 and 1971 for Dan Moore and Tommy Carberry. And I remember Frank Berry winning the Gold Cup the following year on the little mare Glencaraig Lady. It was great to be an Irishwoman in Cheltenham on those occasions.

I had an interest in racing, but I wasn't totally immersed in it then. John was riding a lot and starting to train, so I followed his progress and I knew what was going on, but not a lot more than that. I suppose I was as much into it for the social side as I was for the racing. I remember John falling at the last fence in the Kim Muir on Rag Trade in 1975, and Terry Biddlecombe slagging him on the television, saying that he should have held the horse's head up and not kicked him into the fence. But John had kicked him into every other fence on the course and he had jumped like a buck the whole way round. In fact, his instructions were to kick him into every fence. It was a shame, because Rag Trade belonged to Ian Williams, who was a nephew of Kim Muir. It would have been fantastic if he had been able to win the race named after his uncle. Rag Trade never fell again and won the Grand National the following year.

I continued to ride after James was born. Probably not with the same intensity as I had done when I was at home, but I was happy riding and hunting. I managed to get back to Badminton in 1971 on a mare called Chopsticks. Unfortunately, she reared up, fell backwards and injured herself just before the cross-country. We went in the cross-country, but after two fences I knew she was wrong.

Shortly after Tara was born in 1973, things began to get tough at home. David was doing less and less around the farm and I was having to do more. It wasn't easy with two small children. Things weren't getting done. I was working furiously just to stand still. David also began to spend less time hunting. Communication became difficult. I stopped trying to talk to David about what needed to be done and started just trying to do it myself. It was a gradual disintegration. And you didn't notice. It's a bit like the frog and the boiling water. If you throw a frog into a pot of boiling water, he will jump straight out and save himself. But if you put him into a pot of cool water and gradually raise the temperature to boiling point, he won't jump out. I stayed in the pot. Almost too long.

I was so deeply involved with it that I was the last person to see it. I knew things weren't right, but you make excuses to yourself. You want things to be right so you put up with them and drive on. There'd always be a story. You push it to one side and say it's not happening. That's OK when it's just you. Well, perhaps it's never

OK, but when it's just you, on your own, you make your own bed and you lie in it. You have only yourself to blame if things go wrong and you don't do anything about it. But when your children are involved, it's different. They have no say. Little lovable people who are completely dependent on you. People who will thrive or suffer based on your actions or inactions.

It was a real wake-up call for me. It made me face something that I had buried deep in the back of my mind. If you didn't admit that something was wrong, then maybe nothing was wrong. It's quite ironic really.

I packed the kids into the car and drove to the ferry. I just arrived home and said, 'I'm here.' It was 13 February 1974, my mother's birthday. A birthday to forget. My parents weren't best pleased, but they were great. They put up with me until May, when I went back to England. It would have been much easier to stay at home, but I was determined to stand on my own feet.

In fact, what probably made up my mind for me was a telephone conversation that I had with David. One of those wonderful conversations that you have. He said that he always knew I'd go back to Ireland. That I'd go running back and hide behind my parents. That I'd been leaning on him for the last six years and could never do anything on my own. So I said I'd show him.

I went back to Northamptonshire with James and Tara. I lived in a lodge in Hazelbeach belonging to my uncle and aunt, Peter and Cecily Borwick. Tara used to go to a childminder once the holidays were over, James would go to school, and I would go to work. I worked in a conference centre next door to where I was staying. I would do whatever they wanted me to do. They had a couple of horses that I used to look after. Or I would work behind the bar or in the office.

I had met Johnny a couple of times while I was with David. He had become great friends with my brother John, and I used to see him at a lot of the big social occasions during the year. They got involved in a few horses together and they used to go racing together a lot. In fact, Johnny and John became such good friends that John had asked him to be his best man when he got married in 1971. The day that John asked him, Johnny was in hospital, at 96 Leeson Street, where Vincent's Nursing Home was in those days. Johnny suffered a bit from brucellosis then – a bacterial disease that causes fever in humans – and he had just suffered an attack. At first, Johnny refused to do the best man duties. He couldn't possibly. Sure he wasn't the right religion or anything. But eventually, after some persuasion, and the assistance of Johnny's nurse, he agreed to do it.

Fortunately, Johnny hadn't got married in the six years that I'd been away. Not because he was waiting for me or anything. Absolutely not. He had written me off, which I suppose was quite a reasonable thing for him to have done, given that I was married. He was too busy working with the CBA and off enjoying himself. He reckons that there was hardly a party that went ahead in Ireland without him in those days.

He was in Australia when I returned to Ireland, but we got back in touch around April. We moved in the same social circles, so we were bound to bump into each other. Even though we began to see each other again, I still went back to England. I was determined to do things on my own. Johnny would come over sometimes and I'd get the odd weekend off. The little fights were gone. We were older and more sensible, and I wasn't as fiery. I was probably very immature when we were together first, and I think I had grown up second time around. I suppose a separation will do that to you. I had lost a lot of my energy, which may not necessarily have been an entirely bad thing. Perhaps that comes with growing up anyway, or perhaps it was simply a result of my marriage breaking down. Maybe it was a combination of both. I remember the first time Johnny brought me to stay with Peter and Bonk Walwyn for a weekend. Johnny asked Peter what he thought of me, as gentlemen did, and still do, I believe. 'Lovely girl,' was Peter's verdict, 'but she hardly opens her mouth.' That wasn't me. I had obviously lost a lot of my confidence. Gradually, it began to come back.

I don't see David that often now, though I kept in regular contact with him until the children were eighteen. I felt it was important for them to have him in their lives. Once they turned eighteen, however, it was up to them. He came over to Ireland for both of their weddings. We're still in touch, but not too much.

The divorce came through over a year after I went back to Northamptonshire, and Johnny and I got married soon after that. I did suggest that it might be a good idea if I came over to Ireland for a little while before we got married, but Johnny wouldn't have it. Or rather, his mother wouldn't have it. His poor mother. Whatever misgivings my parents had about me marrying a Catholic, they were negligible compared to what Johnny's mother went through. It was bad enough that her darling Catholic son was marrying a Protestant – her Johnny, whom she thought would never get married – but a divorced Protestant with two children?

We got married in London on the first Monday in August 1976 in what was a very low-key event. We just had a lunch for twelve of our friends afterwards. We didn't ask any of our family to come at all. I suppose we didn't want to create much of a fuss. My parents had already given me a wedding, so I wasn't going to ask them to pay for another. And I didn't think that Johnny's mother would be inclined to see her darling son getting married in a registry office. So we just went ahead and got married, and had lunch in the Berkeley.

That evening we went down to Goodwood to see Peter and Bonk Walwyn, who had taken a house down there during Glorious Goodwood and for the week after. Bonk's mother, who was a wonderful person, put flowers in our room for us. She was always very thoughtful like that. Unfortunately, she didn't realise that Johnny suffered from hay fever.

'How did you sleep?' she asked us the following morning when we came down for breakfast.

'Absolutely terribly,' Johnny retorted without thinking too hard. 'Some fecking idiot put flowers in our room and I was sneezing all night!'

We went down to see Johnny's sister, who lived near Portsmouth, the day after, and we flew back to Ireland later that week to begin our life together. Back to Commonstown Stud. What Johnny didn't tell me, however, was that David Morley was going to be on the plane, along with his vet Tommy Robson, and that they were all going down to Francis Flood's to buy a horse that afternoon. Just as well I wasn't expecting him to whisk me off on a surprise honeymoon. Actually, we had great craic that night, and I suppose you could say that we postponed our honeymoon until the following January, when we went to Australia.

Johnny's housekeeper at the time was Mrs Corcoran. She looked after the house and looked after Johnny. She basically ran his life. I never knew her as anything other than Mrs Corcoran. I don't think I ever knew her Christian name. She was a really great woman, and Johnny would have been lost without her. She was an institution in Commonstown really. She used to arrive on her scooter with her helmet and she'd come straight in and attack the house. She used to get so excited when Johnny had guests staying over that she'd rush in and bring the tea up to their bedrooms often without removing her helmet. It was probably a big change for her when I arrived on the scene – another woman in the house – but we got on great together. Her grandson, John Corcoran, is working for us now.

The CBA were doing well at the time. Peter McKeever had set up a very lucrative shipping business, and the insurance and stallion management end was going well. Paddy Jordan, now one of the biggest estate agents in Kildare, was running their property business. But the ancillary services were propping up the bloodstock business. Johnny maintains that the CBA could never have made money from its bloodstock division. Not on 5 per cent gross commission, sometimes split. The overheads were too high – offices and secretaries and travel expenses. A bloodstock agent can make money on his own with a telephone and a laptop. Not with a huge staff and offices in the middle of Newbridge.

Dick Warden was a co-director of Johnny's in the CBA. He

was the man who introduced the Arabs to racing. He sat in Dubai for three or four weeks awaiting an audience with Sheikh Mohammed. Eventually the Sheik agreed to buy two cheap horses. One of those was Hatta, who won the Molcomb Stakes, and the Arabs were hooked. As the operation expanded, the CBA's shipping business contracted. And as the Coolmore operation got stronger around about the same time, the CBA's stallion management business got weaker. The services that had been maintaining the CBA's profitability were getting squeezed.

Johnny also had a permit to train. Under a permit at the time, you could only train for yourself and your immediate family, and permit holders rarely had large stables of horses. Johnny had four young horses and a couple of mares, but he was so involved with being a bloodstock agent and with being a director of the CBA that he more or less left it to Eamonn Leigh to look after the horses. Of course, Eamonn is a key cog in the wheel today. In fact, I only get to ride Moscow out these days when Eamonn is sick or away – i.e. very rarely.

Johnny used to go to all the yearling sales at the time. In those days he also used to go to Australia from mid-January until Cheltenham. After we were married, I used to go with him. It was fantastic for me as I had never been to Australia before. We'd go around all the main studs, starting at Perth, on to Adelaide, across to Melbourne and down to Tasmania. We usually flew home from Brisbane, via Hong Kong.

I was always going to hunt after I married Johnny, but I had no intention of resuming competitive riding. My father used to give me this black yoke that he had bred in order that I could hunt with the Meath Hounds in 1978. Her name was Amoy. I didn't think too much of her in the beginning. She was a cowardly little thing. We went to jump over a ditch the first time we went hunting, but she changed her mind at the last minute and ended up jumping into it. There was water in the ditch and it was all I could do to stop her from drowning. I was pregnant with Emma in the autumn of that year, so some of the kids my father used to teach at pony club hunted Amoy. Noreen Whelan rode her in the pony club championships that year at Punchestown.

Amoy actually did a lot of hunting and point-to-pointing while I was off. When I was able to ride again, my father asked me if I would event her and another mare that he had called Lucinda. I didn't fancy it at all. I had a small baby and two children – eight and five – to look after. It was a non-runner as far as I was concerned. I had different priorities in my life. But I said, 'Fine. You keep the horses at home, you drive them to the events, and I'll come and ride them. I might come down and ride them maybe one day a week if I can make the time. But only if I can make the time. That's the deal. Take it or leave it.' My father took it. He must have seen a lot of potential in these two mares and he must really have wanted me to get back riding. John rode Amoy in a couple of novice chases the following season – she finished third at Leopardstown – and then I started eventing her.

Amoy turned out to be a wonderful mare, which was quite incredible given how cowardly she was. When she began to win things I got quite nice about her and I would take her down to Commonstown about two or three weeks before an event. But apart from that, my father did all the work on her. All the training and schooling. He was in his eighties at the time. Amazing man.

Coming up to the 1980 Olympics, it looked like I had a good chance of being selected for the Irish team. But the Olympics were in Moscow that year and the Russians had just invaded Afghanistan. There was a lot of talk about a boycott. Johnny was totally against me going. I couldn't understand it. This was my chance to compete at the Olympics. We nearly fell out over it.

'There is no way you can go after what the Russians have done,' he said to me one evening. 'Walking into Afghanistan like that. Absolutely despicable. You've got to write a letter telling them that if they decide to send a team to Moscow, you don't want to be considered for it.'

'But I don't want to,' I retorted. 'Why should I?'

My protests went unheeded. Johnny was not for turning on this one. He is rarely so set against something that he won't even discuss it, but this was one of those things. If I hadn't written the letter I would have been in terrible trouble. It was a difficult letter to write.

As it turned out, we didn't send a team. Ireland did send athletes to the Moscow Olympics, but there was such a groundswell of opinion against it among the horse people that it was decided we should not be represented. Almost every other country in the Western world, led by the Americans, followed suit.

An alternative event was organised at Fontainebleau in France later that year. The substitute Olympics. All the equine teams in the world were there, except Italy, the USSR and the Eastern Bloc countries like Poland, Czechoslovakia, Romania and Hungary. Amoy and I were indeed selected for the Irish team. We finished seventeenth in the individual competition and the team finished fourth. Just outside the medals.

But Amoy was a fantastic little mare. We also went to Badminton that year and finished thirteenth. In 1981 I won Punchestown on her, and I finished fifth on her at Badminton. In 1982 we went to Badminton again, where she flew around but jumped me off. Then, in 1983, we went back to Badminton again.

The dressage went OK. It wasn't Amoy's strongest discipline and we ended up with 58 penalty points. The leader was on 40, so we weren't too far off the pace. The following day I remember coming back in after the steeplechase, down the big, long, grassy avenue in front of the house, and thinking, 'Christ, there are a lot of people here.' I was early to go in the cross-country. Yogi Breisner, the present-day jumping guru to whom a lot of the top trainers in the UK now send horses who are finding it difficult to get the hang of jumping steeplechase fences, went before me. He went clear and was inside the time allowed. That put the pressure on me.

I never used to wear a watch when I was going in the cross-country. I always felt that it was unnecessary, and that, if anything, it could be a distraction. I just used to go as fast as I could. There was a new fence there that year called the Pig Sty which had caused a bit of trouble for the early competitors. I was never going to jump it the quick way because there was a big drop at the back of it that you couldn't see, and Amoy was never good at that type of obstacle. There was an alternative route which was longer but safer, and that was the one we took. And there was another fence called the Foot Bridge with a big ditch. We took the alternative route there as well. We went clear, and finished within the time.

When I finished I was in first place overall. It was a great feeling to be leading the field, but I knew there were a lot of top-class riders and top-class horses to come after me. I remember watching for the rest of the day on CCTV in a caravan. One by one they fell by the wayside. By the end of the day, only Lucinda Green and Mike Tucker were ahead of me.

I spoke to Con Power before the show-jumping on the Sunday. He told me that all I had to do was jump a clear round and I would definitely be in the first three. 'No bother to me,' he said. As it happened, we had one fence down, but we had enough in hand over Yogi Breisner in fourth place for it not to matter. It was a fantastic feeling to finish third at Badminton. I was very proud of Amoy that day. She was brilliant throughout the whole weekend. In those days, the Queen always presented the prizes at Badminton, and that was a real thrill. No Irish person has attained as high a placing at Badminton since.

That little mare took me all over the world. She took me to the European Championship in Denmark in 1981, to Luhmuhlen for the World Championship in 1982, and to Fravenfeld in Switzerland in 1983. But she was better at Badminton than she was anywhere else. For some reason she just loved it there.

As ill luck would have it, she injured her shoulder in the autumn of 1983 and never competed again. It was a real pity because she was still at the peak of her powers and could have gone on for another three or four years at least. She was by some way the best eventer I have ever ridden. And she was bred by my father, by Chou Chin Chow out of a thoroughbred mare called Miss Jennifer, who won a point-to-point. My father and my half-brother Simon hunted Miss Jennifer with the Tara Harriers for years. One day, Simon got off her and said that she wasn't going at all, so my father looked up his book and discovered that she was sixteen years old. He retired her to the breeding shed and she had four or five foals, one of whom was Amoy. Directly after giving birth to her last foal, Miss Jennifer had a heart attack. They just about got the foal out of her before she did. She just keeled over and died, missing the vet Joe Clarke by a whisker. Joe says it was the closest he has ever come to certain death.

In the meantime, I had taken over a lot of the training of Johnny's horses at home. We didn't have many, but Johnny was still busy being a bloodstock agent, so it made sense that I did the training. I was there most of the time. And when I was away at an event or something, Eamonn was well able to look after things.

I went back to Badminton in 1984 with a horse called Delahunty. In 1986 I won Punchestown again on another mare my father bred called Coppit. She was another very good horse. I went to Badminton with her in 1986, but it was rained off that year so we didn't get to compete. Then, that autumn, she broke her leg at Burghley. Just turning. Going between two fences. She just put her foot down the wrong way.

Eventing has been very good to me. People often say to me that I missed out on what were probably my prime riding years because I was off in England, busy being married. But that's the way it happened. You have to play the hand you are dealt. You never know how things are going to pan out. Who knows, if I had been riding then, I might not have been so successful. I might not have had the horses during those years, and I might not have happened upon Amoy or Coppit.

I still keep in close touch with the eventing world. All of my children – James, Tara, Emma and Kate – have evented. Tara, Emma and Kate have represented their country at European level, and Emma and Kate are still eventing. I go to a lot of the shows with them whenever I can, but, unfortunately, with so much racing on these days, especially at weekends, it's quite difficult. I love watching them. I probably get more nervous when I watch them compete than I get when I watch Moscow Flyer race.

I used to keep a few young horses who I would make and sell on. I'd sell about one a year. That was the problem in Ireland at the time: all the good horses would be sold in order to keep the thing moving along. It's a significant contributory factor to the reason why no Irish person has won Punchestown since I did on Coppit in 1986. And why no Irish person has attained as high a placing at Badminton since I finished third on Amoy in 1983. You could make money buying and selling horses for sure, but in order to make a living out of eventing, you needed sponsorship.

Lucinda Green was the first person to get sponsorship. After her, some of the other good riders in the UK started doing it. I never sought sponsorship. If you are sponsored, you have to do what the sponsor wants you to do. I thought I was better off remaining independent. I had so many other things going on in my life at the time. If your sponsor wanted you to go to a show, you couldn't say that you couldn't go because one of your children was sick, or because your husband needed you to do something else.

Johnny was buying a lot of yearlings for Hong Kong at the time. The Hong Kong Jockey Club used to buy 30 horses from England, 30 from Ireland and 30 from Australia. They had to be untried, unraced two-year-olds who had cost less than about £3,500 at public auction. Griffins, they called them. We'd break them here and then send them out in June the following year. Johnny had a lot of success in Hong Kong. He bought Indigenous out of Kevin Prendergast's yard for £80,000 for Stephen Leung. He was bred by Robert Hall, the television presenter, and he went on to win the equivalent of about €2,500,000 out there. We also began to buy store horses – unbroken National Hunt-bred horses – and three-year-olds that we'd sell at the Doncaster sales as four-year-olds mainly. And we started buying foals and yearlings to sell on.

In 1984 we decided that I should take over the permit. Johnny reckoned that he didn't recognise any of the horses any more, and whatever training was going on I was probably doing it anyway. We had a few years then when we bought horses and couldn't sell them on. The usual thing. Horses that were wrong of their wind, or were just wrong at sale time. Quite quickly we had quite a few horses about the place, but we couldn't afford to keep them all in training ourselves, so we thought we had better take out a public licence.

So that was how it began. We had two horses in the beginning for Michael Buckley, two for Thady Dunraven, and a few of our own. I had a horse for Chris Cronin that was supposed to be going to Charlie Brooks, but it had a bad heart and it ended up here. Johnny said that he would take a half-share in it and that we'd train it here. That horse turned out to be Brockley Court. He won ten races including a Grade 3 hurdle, and he beat Klairon Davis in a handicap chase at Punchestown.

But things didn't really get going until Johnny met Peter Queally, through the St Mellion people, who had a golf course and were interested in designing one at Rathsallagh. In fact, it was Johnny who introduced them to the O'Flynns at Rathsallagh. Peter Queally was their main backer. Peter was fascinated by the whole racing and bloodstock business. He decided that he wanted to buy a horse, so he bought a half-share in Boom Time for £3,000. He won his first race after Peter bought him, a handicap chase at Fairyhouse in February 1993, and Peter was hooked.

The horses were going quite well at the time, but the finances weren't. We had a huge overdraft which represented a substantial amount of money twelve years ago. We couldn't see any way out of it. Interest rates were quite high and we had to do very well just to service the debt.

Peter used to call in quite a lot. He had a Q&K store up in Naas and he used to drop in at Commonstown for supper on his way back. One evening, he told us that he wanted to invest in our horses. The BBA came down the following week and valued everything – mares, foals, young horses, racehorses, the lot. Peter was down the next day, didn't look at any of the horses or anything, and wrote us a cheque for half of everything, which was great for us. It paid off our overdraft and gave us cashflow. Of course Peter was on a good deal for training fees, but it meant that there was cash going through the place. Peter always said that we needed cashflow if we were going to be serious about training racehorses. We definitely wouldn't be where we are today without Peter's backing.

We had a lot of success with Peter from the start. Oh So Grumpy won the Galway Hurdle during his first year with us. He also won at Ascot, Kempton and Punchestown. Dance Beat won at Punchestown and Listowel the following year before going on and winning the Ladbroke Hurdle. And Space Trucker won two bumpers that year.

But Peter was more than just an investor in the yard. He was Johnny's financial adviser. A real fatherly figure. He helped Johnny buy Great Connell Stud from the CBA when he was leaving. Helped him liquidate his 25 per cent share. He rarely gave poor advice. In fact, the only major mistake he ever made financially was investing in a science-fiction film featuring Dennis Hopper called *Space Truckers*, which completely bombed. We lost every penny we put into that. Luckily the horse turned out to be marginally more successful, providing me with my first win at the Cheltenham Festival in 1999.

I was new to training racehorses, but I had often ridden work on my father's point-to-pointers, and if you live around something for long enough you actually take a lot in probably without realising it. We used to go and stay with John Dunlop and Peter Walwyn when we were in England. You'd go out with them and see them training. All the while learning. It was great to be able to watch top trainers like John and Peter at work. I didn't really go with the express objective of learning how to train, but when you spend enough time around people like that and their horses, you invariably pick up a lot. John believed that everything should canter every day. We do that in Commonstown now. And he was a firm believer in routine. Horses like routine. We rarely deviate from the morning schedule in Moone. I also rode out quite a bit with different trainers in Newmarket. I remember getting run away with at David Morley's, having agreed to ride out at two a.m. in the morning. It was just that you'd be there for the night and you'd ride out in the morning. That was just what you did. It's amazing the little things you'd pick up.

Of course I knew about horses through my eventing experiences. I knew about getting horses fit and teaching them how to jump, and once I started training I began to ask a lot of questions of other trainers. Jim Bolger was very good to me. He let me use his gallop and he'd help me when I was there. If a horse can get to this point on his gallop in a certain time, then he'll win a maiden; if he can get to there he's a good handicapper; there, and he's a group horse. Before I put in the uphill gallop at Commonstown, I went to see Paul Nicholls' gallop and Martin Pipe's and Paul Webber's. You're probably going to go and do it your own way anyway, but you may as well see what other people have done. Even now, when we go to Cheltenham we stay with Nicky Henderson and we discuss various things about training. You never know everything in this game.

It was difficult enough in the beginning. There were very few women training in Ireland at the time and I felt that other trainers would be looking at me. 'What's she doing here? It's about time she went home and looked after her children.' You just paid no attention. Some of the owners were funny too. A lot of them wouldn't want to speak to me. They'd want to speak to Johnny instead. They'd ring up and ask to speak to him, but he wouldn't know how their horse was and he'd have to ask me. But you got over those things, and gradually it turned around. I knew I had arrived when the owners started asking for me, not for Johnny.

But Johnny was great from the outset. He has always left the training of the horses to me, but he is always around to help when he is needed. He is a great help in buying the horses. He has years of experience in that game. Johnny has always maintained that we are in the entertainment business. I'd say about 70 per cent of our horses are now owned by syndicates. If they want to come down and see their horse, Johnny says let them come. Once they have an appointment. They can see their horse work, have a coffee, a whiskey, whatever they want. He is still great with people. Never lose the personal touch, he tells me. Johnny looks after the people; Eamonn and I look after the horses.

CHAPTER EIGHT

EAMONN LEIGH

It is difficult to think of Moscow Flyer these days without thinking of Eamonn Leigh. Eamonn is probably the best-known groom in the business today, thanks to Moscow. In fact, the only time Eamonn leaves Moscow out of his care is when he sends him out on to the racecourse, entrusting him to Barry Geraghty. Bring him back safely now.

Eamonn's home was just down the road from Ballylea Stud in Dunlavin. His father was a great stocksman. A brilliant judge of a bullock. It is extraordinary how people who are good judges of cattle are also good judges of horses. Eamonn's father worked for the Mullions of Ardenode Stud and Ragusa Stud. Apparently, animals are either in your genes or they are not.

But ponies were Eamonn's thing. He always had a few around his house when he was a youngster. He hunted them and jumped them, but he never rode on the pony racing circuit. He was probably too big anyway, but he never had a burning desire to be a jockey. He just wanted to work with horses, and he loved being around them. Eamonn will tell you that there wasn't much else for a young fellow to do around Dunlavin at the time. He began buying ponies, bringing them on and selling them in order to make some pocket money for the summers while he was at school. School was a necessary evil, just something that got between him and his ponies. In fairness to him, he stuck it out until his Leaving Cert., but he always knew that he would work with horses. He just needed a start.

As resident of Ballylea Stud, just down the road from Eamonn's home, Johnny was a prime target. One Saturday morning in June 1970, Johnny heard a knock on the back door. It wasn't unusual for someone to come to the back door instead of the front door, but those who did always came straight in. A knock on the back door was unusual.

Johnny opened it. There, sitting on the back of a pony, was a scraggly little boy. He looked no more than fourteen or fifteen, but he sat easily on the back of his pony. Any jobs?

As it happened, there were. Johnny needed someone to help him with the horses. He was away a lot and caught up with the CBA, and he didn't really have the time to devote to training horses. Eamonn started on one pound ten shillings a week.

The trouble was that, while Johnny didn't know that much about training racehorses, Eamonn didn't know much more. He was good with his ponies and all, but he had to make the step up to thoroughbred horses quite quickly.

Paddy Sleator was training just down the road in Grangecon. Eamonn knew some of the lads who worked with Paddy, and Johnny obviously knew Paddy well, so Eamonn used to spend a lot of time down there. He just observed and rode out, and learnt as he went. Being a natural horseman was no hindrance. Johnny had only three or four horses riding out at the time, so Eamonn used to bring them down to Sleator's in order that they and he would have company. It was difficult to train a couple of horses on their own, so it made sense to hook up with Paddy and his team. There were no horse-walkers in those days, and everything was very labour intensive. This was back in the early 1970s when there wasn't a lot of work around for people, especially in rural Ireland, so there were always plenty of lads down at Sleator's who could give Eamonn a hand with his horses.

The first race Johnny and Eamonn won was at Wexford in late 1970 with a horse called Take Pride. It was down as trained by Johnny Harrington, permit holder, but actually it was Eamonn who was doing all the training. Paddy Sleator had a hand in this one as well. The horse was sent off at 10–1. Johnny didn't back it; Eamonn had his travelling expenses of £1.50 on. Of course they were delighted that it won, but they didn't really expect it to. In fact, they didn't really know what to expect. Paddy Sleator did. He was on.

They sent the horse to Limerick the following St Patrick's Day and Johnny and Eamonn both backed it. Liam O'Donnell rode it out the back for most of the way. Never near to challenge. Paddy Sleator won the race with another horse. Johnny laughs about it now. In fact he laughed about it then. 'You are all the while learning in this game,' he will tell you. He knew very little, but he knew that he knew very little. He kept his head down and his ears open. Optimum learning conditions. The smartest people in this game will tell you that they are still learning about it.

As well as spending time with Paddy Sleator, Eamonn spent summers with Peter Walwyn and John Dunlop. It was handy for him, as it was for me, that Johnny was good friends with such fantastic trainers. Grundy had just been retired when Eamonn went over to Walwyn's at Seven Barrows, where Nicky Henderson is now. Peter had about 80 horses riding out at the time and Pat Eddery was his stable jockey. Eamonn was bowled over by Peter's attention to detail. Eamonn was from a stud farming background, and evening stables was a concept that was alien to him. Every evening Peter used to walk around with a dictaphone recording everything he noticed about every horse. He would often bring a vet round during evening stables so that he could spot small things and fix them before they became big things. That was crucial. Peter also believed in always looking smart when you were going racing. You never knew when you were going to meet the next prospective owner, and it was important to present yourself well. And he was great to the lads. It was Peter who set up the first housing scheme for stable staff. Eamonn learnt about the hydration of horses, diet, fitness and general well-being. He absorbed a huge amount during his spell with Peter, and he brought as much as he could home with him.

And it was the same at Dunlop's. Although Peter and John were both at the very top of their profession, their respective methodologies were quite different. John was great on the technical side. He was big on routine. His theory was that horses don't like change, so they should do the same thing at home every day. Also, he always believed in giving each lad or lass responsibility for his or her own horse. Eamonn thrived under this responsibility. John doesn't believe in getting jockeys in to ride out. He never did. Each groom rides his or her own horse. That's the way it is at Arundel.

Johnny had a few mares and foals around at the time, and he was buying a lot of horses for clients. Eamonn looked after the mares and foals mainly in the beginning. After Johnny bought Commonstown, Eamonn set about moving the horses from Ballylea. It was a pretty large undertaking as Commonstown had been a cattle farm before Johnny bought it and there were no stables. Just cattle sheds. Gradually they got the stables built and were able to accommodate the horses. Eamonn lived in a house that Johnny built for him on Commonstown when they first moved in. He married a girl from Kilcullen in 1974. Unfortunately that didn't work out in the end, but he has a great partner now, Teresa, and four great kids. Two boys and two girls. We gave him a plot of land on the corner of Commonstown about four years ago and he built a house there. Andrew is working away with us here, doing very well. In June 2005 one of Eamonn's daughters, Bernie, married the amateur rider Peter Fahey, who used to work with us at

Commonstown and who rode Moscow in three of his four bumpers. Eamonn opened his wedding speech by saying that he couldn't believe he had just allowed his daughter to marry a fellow who couldn't win a bumper on Moscow Flyer.

Johnny and Eamonn did well from the start. Take Pride, Copper Cow and Above the Ground were among their early winners. Actually, my brother John rode Above the Ground to win a bumper at Down Royal. Then Johnny bought Gay Future out of John Oxx's yard as a two-year-old. He didn't have great feet, but Johnny had a very good blacksmith at the time, Mick Donoghue, and he managed to win a bumper at Thurles with him. He was placed in a couple of two-mile Flat races after that, and he was sold at the end of the following season.

Of course Gay Future has a place in the heart of every person who likes a good punt, or at least a good punting story. Neither Johnny nor Eamonn heard anything of the horse after they sold him until he turned up at Cartmel racecourse in England in 1974, on August Bank Holiday Monday. A Scotland-based trainer, Tony Collins, down as the trainer of Gay Future, also had two other horses running on the same day at different meetings – Opera Cloak and Ankerwyke. A large number of relatively small-stakes doubles and trebles were placed on the three horses in the morning, but Opera Cloak and Ankerwyke were subsequently withdrawn, which meant that all the money went on as a single bet to Gay Future. The horse won hard held, but the bookmakers cried foul and refused to pay. The Gay Future affair entered racing folklore, to such an extent that there was even a film made about it – *Murphy's Stroke* – which starred Niall Taibin and Pierce Brosnan.

Johnny and Eamonn had a lot of success for a very small operation. I say Johnny and Eamonn, but it was of course Eamonn who did all the training. Johnny was travelling the world going to bloodstock sales and buying and selling horses. They would never really have had more than three or four horses in training at any one time, yet they managed to win more than their fair share. Jeepers Creepers won three on the bounce. Joanna Morgan used to ride him. On Return won a decent sprint at the Phoenix Park and was sold to the late Robert Sangster for big money. After I joined the team we had good success with Moon Ranger and Hav A Heart, who won the 1984 Irish Lincoln and was the last winner Johnny trained under permit.

It must have been difficult for Eamonn when I arrived. He had been training the horses. He had been the boss. Then, suddenly, I landed in the place and he had to answer to somebody else. It can't have been easy for him, but he coped well. For a little while, however, our opinions differed. Eamonn is a super horseman, but if he had a weakness it would be that he is too easy on his horses. I was of the opinion that they needed to be worked harder than he was working them in order for them to get race fit. After a little while we clicked, and we've been clicking along ever since.

As the operation expanded, Eamonn grew into his role. As well as being an excellent horseman, he was also very good with the staff. With more horses comes the need for more staff, and Eamonn was more than able to manage them. Johnny Peter-Hoblyn was the first person I took on. We also had David Wachman, Ed Dunlop and Philip Rothwell all with us for a while, as well as a lot of local lads who just wanted to work with horses.

Eamonn did not go to the Derby Sale in June 1998. There was nothing untoward about that. He didn't usually go, unless there was something in particular that he wanted to see. He would be buying and selling one or two horses himself, but he would usually do that privately rather than at the sales. He much preferred to be at home with the horses. 'There's enough to be done here anyway,' he would say. He would nearly be hoping that we wouldn't arrive back with too many new horses. More horses means more work, and more strain on the resources. It was a fair point.

A good friend of Eamonn's, Liam Burke, the owner of Burke's pub in Dunlavin, had had a horse with us called Jack Chaucer, who unfortunately got killed before the 1998 Derby Sale. Liam had asked Eamonn to keep an eye out for something suitable that might replace Jack Chaucer.

We actually brought three horses home with us from the Derby Sale in June 1998. Lot 11 was a bay gelding by Le Bavard out of a Kambalda mare, Hillcrest Lady, whom we bought for 11,000 guineas. He was later named Captain Foley. The best he could manage in five starts was a sixth placing in a Kilbeggan bumper, though he did finish third in a point-to-point. Lot 292 was a Lord Americo gelding out of an unraced mare who had produced a point-to-point winner. He turned out to be Pauhutzanka, who finished third in his second ever bumper at Roscommon and looked like he might win one. But he didn't. Nor did he win any type of race in twelve runs for us, so we sold him to David Wintle in the UK. Lot 432 was, of course, the Moscow Society gelding out of the unraced Duky mare Meelick Lady.

When we brought the three horses back from the Derby Sale, we put them out in a field just outside the house along with two other young horses we had. Eamonn went to have a look to see if there was one that would suit Liam. One stood out. The good-looking fellow with the strange white streak running down his nose. Eamonn didn't know how he was bred or how much he cost, but this was the one he wanted for Liam. It still amazes me how many good judges this horse had managed to evade at the sales. The fact that he stood out for Eamonn was further confirmation for me that we had bought a proper horse. Eamonn thought he wasn't as big and rangy as the others, and that he would come to hand a little more quickly than they would. He was nice and compact, very pretty, and proud of himself. I had to tell Eamonn that he wasn't for sale. That he had been bought for a new client. Eamonn wasn't too despondent. At least the horse was staying in the yard and he would be able to look after him.

He didn't choose any of the other horses for Liam Burke. He advised him to wait until something suitable came along. Liam decided to renovate his pub shortly after that and got out of the market for a horse, but he followed this horse's progress with intense interest. The horse he had nearly bought.

Liam went along with Eamonn to see Moscow run in his fourth

bumper at Navan. He had been beaten in his first three, but we expected him to run well in this one and we backed him accordingly. As Moscow was struggling home in third place, nine lengths behind the winner, Liam turned to Eamonn with a smile on his face.

'Well, look on the bright side,' he said. 'At least I didn't buy him!'

CHAPTER NINE

BUMPER YEAR

Like many other good judges, Nigel Byrne was bowled over by the Moscow Society gelding. Nigel was head man in our top yard at the time. He had worked for Francis Flood before he came to me at the beginning of 1995. He was a good lad who had a good eye for a horse. I phoned him from the sales and asked him to have three boxes ready in the top yard. That's where the new horses were going.

I told Nigel that he could choose himself which one of the three he wanted to look after. There was no doubt in my mind which he would choose, if he was half the judge I thought he was. Nigel says that he selected his horse before the three of them had even walked down the horsebox ramp – further confirmation about the quality of this Moscow Society gelding. All the good judges loved him. Nigel says that he filled his eye as soon as he saw him. There was just something about him. He wasn't a big, strong steeplechasing type, but he had all the credentials. A real smart-looking horse. A lovely walker, a lovely mover. He wasn't going to let anybody else have this fellow.

It is important that a horse is broken correctly. If he is poorly broken, he can be difficult to handle for the rest of his life. Nigel was a good man to break a horse. He spent as much time with this horse – his responsibility – as he could in the first couple of days. Just talking to him, brushing him down, patting him. Making him feel at ease with himself and with his new surroundings. He put a headpiece on him and a bit in his mouth in order to get his mouth working straight away. He'd put it on for a couple of hours in the morning, just to give the horse a feel for it. Then he'd take it off and give him a break before putting it on again in the afternoon.

When Nigel started lungeing the new arrival, he liked him even more. He liked his nice easy action. The horse moved effortlessly around the ring. The first time he tightened the girth on him, he had a little bit of a plunge, but that is to be expected. And when he got up on him for the first time, he had a little bit of a go at him. Just a little one. After that, however, he was a real gentleman. Nigel says you could have put your mother up on him.

Moscow was broken and riding within two weeks. That is much faster than average. He was just a quick learner. And Nigel didn't rush him at all. Because he was such a star, he just let him go along in his own time. Sometimes when horses are proving difficult you put a good bit of work into them to get them tired so that they won't have the energy to buck you off when you sit up on them. Not this fellow.

For the first couple of days after he was broken, Nigel took him out with a lead horse. He'd bring him to unusual places. We had a forest of evergreen trees in one of the fields up the back, and he used to take him down there and walk him among the trees. Just to get his mind working. There's nothing to fear here. Easy. You have to think the way you think they think. Everything is new to them. You don't want them to spook at the slightest thing, so you try to show them as many different things as you can.

When Nigel started to ride him out, he said that there was a real feeling of quality about him. He didn't do any serious work on him, but he did give him a few easy canters. He liked the way he felt. He liked the tug that he took. You could settle him easily, but you always felt that, if you wanted, you could go up through the gears and leave your work companions standing. He didn't. That would come later.

I was happy with the way Moscow was progressing. He was nicely balanced in his work and he looked like he was fairly strong. But it is hard to tell. The fastest piece of work he did in those early days was just a little bit faster than a canter. He was still a very young horse who was only just learning how to gallop.

We popped him over a few poles and he jumped them nicely. Again, nothing too strenuous. Just enough to get him thinking about jumping and developing the skill. We had bought him to jump. He was bred to jump. He might as well get his eye in sooner rather than later.

One morning Nigel had him out in the outdoor arena, just warming down after doing a little piece of work. Suddenly, in the blink of an eye, Moscow took a plunge and Nigel was on his back in the ditch. Moscow stopped, turned, looked at Nigel and just had a pick of grass. That was the first time he pulled that trick. He did it many times afterwards with other people. Neither Eamonn nor I was exempt. Eamonn broke his wrist off him once. There is nothing malicious in it; I think he just does it for the craic. He just drops you and then looks at you. You weren't paying attention there, were you?

I was considering letting him make his racecourse debut in a bumper at Leopardstown's Christmas festival meeting that year, 1998. He was going along nicely and telling us that he was ready to run. When my horses are ready to run, I believe in letting them run. I definitely don't believe in wrapping them up in cotton wool and preserving them. They are racehorses. I am a racehorse trainer. My job is to race them. But coming up to Christmas he got a bit of a cold. It wasn't too serious – just a bit of a runny nose – but I didn't want to risk running him. You can set a young horse back years by running him when he is sick. Especially on his first ever run. So we left him off and planned to bring him to Fairyhouse at the end of January 1999.

I didn't know what to expect from that first run. I really didn't. As I said, we hadn't really pushed him at home. We don't tend to push young horses that much. All his work at home was primarily educational. He would have been fairly fit from his slow work, but definitely not 100 per cent race fit. We would know a whole lot more after Fairyhouse.

Brian Kearney came to Fairyhouse that day. Of course Brian Kearney came. He had had the date in his diary for some time: 30 January 1999, Moscow Flyer's debut. He wasn't going to miss this. No way. His first outing as a real live racehorse owner. His wife Patricia was there, and their son Conor, and his wife Ciara and their son, Brian's grandson, Max, who was two – three years younger than Moscow. He was wearing a little green pixie hat which later became known as the lucky hat. Though I'm not really sure how it came to be known as the lucky hat, given that we didn't really have that much luck in Moscow's bumper year. They were all in the parade ring beforehand. That was great for them, and Brian got a great thrill out of it. Just having his family there with him to watch his horse run. His first horse. He couldn't stop smiling.

Peter Fahey was my amateur rider at the time. Peter is a very good rider. He still rides a little for me, but he now rides in bumpers mainly for the Wexford trainer Pat Fahy – no relation and no 'e'. He had ridden Moscow out at home and he was the man to ride him on his racecourse debut. And Moscow ran well. He raced in the middle of them in the early stages and moved up to take third on the home turn before fading to finish sixth. The race was won by a horse of Edward O'Grady's called Aonfocaleile, whom J.P. McManus had bought with the intention of winning the Cheltenham bumper the previous season. The horse had developed leg trouble and was just on his way back. He was a good winner, and it looked like a decent race. I was delighted with Moscow. I thought it was a great first run, and I told Brian as much.

At that stage we thought that two miles was too short for Moscow. He had a stamina-laden pedigree and I hoped that he would develop into a decent staying chaser. He had just blown up at Fairyhouse, I suspected. It was his first run ever and there was no way he was going to be as fit as those with experience. There was a two-mile-one-furlong bumper at Gowran Park three weeks later and we decided that we would aim for that. We thought he would be fitter then, that the extra furlong would help him, and that the heavy ground would bring his undoubted stamina into play.

A lot of other people must have been thinking the same. Brian went down to the betting ring to back his horse, thinking that he would be a 4–1 or a 5–1 shot. He had only finished sixth in his first race, went Brian's thinking. There were sixteen horses in this race. He had to be at least 4–1. So he couldn't believe it when he heard the bookmakers calling 7–4. Brian joked that some people in Dunlavin must have backed him. But our yard is not really a gambling yard. The lads wouldn't really have a decent bet, even if they did think that one of their horses was going well at home. If they were having a bet, it would only be a fiver or so. If they lost €20 they'd be gutted. Anyway, it would be enough for them to see their horse win without ever having backed it. I would say his short price was just down to punters fancying him. The winner of his first bumper was a good horse, and it would probably be well known that our bumper horses usually improve for a run. That we don't overwork them at home. Though Brian was disappointed to be trading at such short odds – of course he backed his own horse – he did get a kick out of the fact that his horse was favourite for a race. That the bookmakers who were betting win-or-come-second were betting without his horse!

Again Moscow ran quite well, but he could only finish third. On the way down we were expecting him to run well, but I suppose the fact that other people had made him favourite heightened our expectations. Peter gave him a lovely ride around the inside the whole way, but, as at Fairyhouse, he didn't seem to be able to go with them when they quickened. The leaders ran away from him at the top of the home straight, but he stayed on well to finish third, beaten only three lengths.

This gave further credence to my hypothesis about Moscow needing a test of stamina. He seemed to be hitting a flat spot in his races and then staying on. He didn't seem to be able to change gear when the pace quickened. At the time, I didn't think that this was because he was still a developing young horse, that he was still weak and that he just didn't have the strength to go with them on soft ground under those big weights that National Hunt horses have to carry. That realisation came later.

We gave him a little bit of a break then. He had had two runs in three weeks – quite a lot for a young, inexperienced horse. I didn't want to put too much pressure on him or sour him against the game. So we just took him home and let him out in a field for a few days. Then we brought him back in. We did some light work with him and we schooled him a little over hurdles. All our bumper horses are schooled over hurdles from quite early. I think it's important for them to get the practice in when they are young. It also means that we can start racing them over hurdles quite quickly after their bumper days.

I still felt sure that he could win a bumper, so we entered him at the Fairyhouse Easter meeting at the beginning of April. It looked like a fairly decent bumper – it was as difficult then as it is now to find a weak bumper in Ireland – but we thought we had a good chance of winning it. Peter Fahey was suspended, so I got Anthony Ross to ride him. Anthony was, and still is, another talented rider who could claim five pounds in bumpers at the time.

Moscow took it up with about five furlongs to run. He looked the likely winner for a while. But shortly after he turned into the home straight in front, he was swamped. He eventually faded to finish fourth, beaten just over five lengths. It wasn't a bad run, though. Indeed, it turned out to be a much better run than it looked at the time, as the race was won by subsequent Hennessy winner (later disqualified) Be My Royal. But it was getting a little frustrating. He had now run in three bumpers and he hadn't really got close to winning one.

At this stage I thought he was a good horse, though I have to admit that I didn't think he would be a great horse. I thought he would be better when he stepped up in trip and possibly when he jumped a hurdle or a fence. But even the top stayers manage to win a bumper. If Moscow Flyer couldn't win a bumper, it didn't augur well for the rest of his career.

We decided that we would have one last shot at a bumper before we wrapped it up for the season. There was a two-and-a-quarter-mile bumper at Navan at the end of April. Navan is a stiff track with a good uphill finish. If the ground gets soft there, even two-mile races can turn into real tests of stamina. I thought he would win. We all thought he would win. This was the day when Eamonn's friend, the publican Liam Burke from Dunlavin, on whose behalf Eamonn had asked about buying Moscow before he realised that he had been bought for Brian, came along to see him.

Peter was back on board. He had him handy all the way around and down Navan's long back straight. He moved into second place about a mile out, travelling well. This could be it. This could be our bumper. Then the same thing happened: when the pace quickened, he floundered. Peter began to drive him at the top of the home straight, but he couldn't go forward. He dropped to third and just kept on at the same pace to hold that position at the line, behind Boley Lad and Paircin. Again, it wasn't a bad run. He had finished third of 27 runners. Brian seemed to be quite happy, and I suppose on the face of it he should have been. We all should have been. But I'd expected better. I'd expected him to win a bumper. Perhaps he wasn't going to be so good after all. Perhaps he wasn't going to prove to be as good a racehorse as his looks suggested. Some of them don't, you know.

That was it for the season. As I drove home from Navan that day, I thought we might have another go for a bumper early the following season before sending him over hurdles. Or we might just go straight over hurdles. He schooled well, and Nigel Byrne said that he felt like a better horse with a jump in front of him. He probably won't be a superstar now, but he should win races. At least one or two. Yeah. And we just might have better luck over hurdles.

CHAPTER TEN

HURDLES AHEAD

Summer means different things to different people. For us, the lengthening evenings and the rising temperatures are generally a sign that we should begin to take stock of the season that has just gone and think ahead to the one that is coming. We are kept going during the summer all right, but the real business is done during the winter.

We were disappointed at the start of the summer of 1999. No question. The horse for whom we had had so many hopes and aspirations – the good-looking Moscow Society gelding we had all but stolen at the 1998 Derby Sale – had failed to gain a foothold on the first rung of the ladder. If I had harboured any notions of this horse taking us towards the top echelons of National Hunt racing – and I have no doubt that I had – they had all but dissipated by the summer of 1999. Future champions don't fail to win a bumper. Not in four attempts. This horse might turn out to be decent, but decent was probably as high as we could aim. I was disappointed with the way he seemed to be hitting a flat spot in his races before running on again. I wasn't sure why that was. Maybe, as I had suspected all along, it was because he needed more of a trip and that he couldn't go with them when they speeded up. Maybe it was because he was still a little bit weak and needed to strengthen up. Or maybe, last-gasp option, he just wasn't that good.

Moscow Flyer was de-saddled and de-bridled at the end of April 1999 and put out into a field at Commonstown. It was a good time for him. If he had felt that there was any pressure on him to win a bumper during the winter and spring, the summer was a release. The opening of the valve. Summer for top National Hunt horses is all about the three Rs: rest, relaxation and rejuvenation. They are no different to humans. They need their time off if they are to be able to perform to the best of their ability in the future. Moscow enjoyed his summer off. He bucked and kicked and generally acted the maggot in his field, as is his wont.

As a five-year-old, he was still a young horse. Still growing and developing. Ireland is ideal for young horses. The limestone-enriched Irish soil puts the calcium in the grass that is essential for strengthening their bones during their crucial formative years. Moscow, like his stable companions and compatriots, was a prime beneficiary. He thrived during the early part of that summer. By the time he came back in to get down to work in early August, he looked like a different horse. He was obviously on the plump side, having spent the past three months eating and sleeping, with exercise limited to a few bucks and kicks. But even in that short space of time it was apparent to me that he had strengthened up considerably.

Brian came down to see me and Moscow in the middle of August. That was the agreement. Every August Brian would come down and we'd formulate a plan for Moscow for the season ahead. He would come during the season to see Moscow as well, but in August it would be a big deal. He and Patricia would come down, watch the horse do a little piece of work, and we'd go through the plan for the following season over a cup of coffee.

I thought it was an unusual arrangement at first, but ultimately it made a lot of sense – I suppose because Moscow turned out to be so sound and so good. Such a meeting with owners of most horses could be very short. We'll try to get him into a race or we'll try to get him to a racecourse – that would be the extent of the plan. But with the good ones, at least you can have a plan. Although even with the good ones and the sound ones, it was always a good idea to have a contingency.

Such a meeting was also consistent with Brian's business methodology. You appoint someone to do a job, so let them get on and do it. If they are not able for it, then you take remedial action. But you have to allow them enough leeway to do the job as they see fit. And you have to give them direction. This meeting was all about agreeing the direction. But Brian never tried to get involved in training the horse. He had appointed me to do that, and he let me get on and do it. Thankfully, he hasn't seen the need for remedial action. Not yet anyway.

We kicked around the options at the first Moscow Flyer AGM that August. Another bumper, or straight over hurdles? He had been schooling well over hurdles throughout his bumper year and I was looking forward to seeing how he would go in a maiden hurdle. But he hadn't won a bumper, and I still felt that there was one in him. It would be good to go and win one before sending him over hurdles later in the year. Brian agreed. One more bumper, then hurdles.

From the time that Brian first came down to see Moscow in Commonstown, he had often asked me if I thought he had a good horse. That was his dream, to own a good horse. Not an Arkle winner or a Champion Chase winner or a horse who was almost unbeatable over two miles and twelve or thirteen fences, just a good horse. His directness was unusual, and rather endearing. I always told him that I thought he had one, but that you could never tell in this game how they would turn out. It depended on so many things.

That morning in August 1999, over breakfast, he looked me straight in the eye and asked me again. 'Do you think I have a good horse? This horse who hasn't won a bumper in four attempts? The one that we just saw this morning, looking as big as a house? Is he a good horse?' And I remember feeling completely at ease when I told him that he could still dream that he had a good horse. We didn't know for sure yet that he hadn't. We had barely played out the opening moves. The dream was still very much alive.

Brian was hell-bent on Cheltenham. He had been over to the Cheltenham Festival that year as a guest of Jed Pierse's. Jed owns Pierse Construction and a good few National Hunt horses besides. He also sponsors the Pierse Hurdle – formerly the Sweeps Hurdle – run at Leopardstown in January every year. Brian had been blown away by the parade ring at Cheltenham. He reckoned that that was where he wanted to be. He had no aspirations to win a race or anything. That would just be ridiculous. But he did want to be there. Just to stand there on the turf that looked like it had been cut with a pair of scissors. Just to stand in the ring as an owner. It was like I had told him: he could still dream.

I entered Moscow in a bumper at Cork in October. He was going well at home and I got to thinking that this would be it. This would be his first bumper win. He was fit enough, he was definitely stronger than he had been at the end of the previous season, and he would be racing against horses who were far less experienced than him.

Then another bumper blow. When we pulled him out of his box on the Saturday, the day before the race, he was lame behind. Stone bruise. He must have stood on a stone or something sharp on the gallops the previous day. Nothing serious, thank goodness – it would just be like you or me standing on a stone in our bare feet – but it meant that he couldn't run the following day.

That's the way it goes sometimes. Horses are living, breathing, moving creatures. They are more fragile than the majority of species on this earth. Have a look at their four spindly legs and marvel at the fact that they can even support the half a ton of body, neck and head that rest on them, much less carry them at 35mph across often rough terrain and over black birch obstacles. They pick up injuries, they have falls, they get colds, they cough, they stand on stones. That's what they do. And they all do it. You frequently hear people saying that it only happens to the good ones, that only the talented horses get injured. Nonsense. The truth is that it happens to them all. It's just that you only hear about the good ones.

The toughest thing you will ever do as a trainer is contact an owner to communicate the news that something has happened to his or her horse. Telling John O'Flaherty about Ulaan Baatar's fatal injury on the gallops in April 2005 was probably the most difficult thing I have had to do since I started training. He was a lovely horse who was only just beginning to realise his true potential. He could have been a real superstar. Dance Beat was killed on the racecourse. That is arguably more difficult as it happens in public. The fact that I didn't have to relay the news to Peter Queally was scant consolation. Of course, on a scale of one to fatal injury, a stone bruise doesn't even register. Nevertheless, it was disappointing to have to tell Brian the day before the race that his horse wasn't running. It wasn't a huge deal in the broad scheme of things, but Brian was all set to go racing, and we were expecting to win. Brian was hoping to register his first win as an owner.

There was a schooling hurdle at Punchestown the following Tuesday and I told Brian that we would run him in that, that Moscow should be fully recovered by then. They usually get over a stone bruise in a day or two at most. We'd see how he went and take it from there.

I entered him in the bumper and the maiden hurdle at Punchestown the following Sunday. I'm not entirely sure why I entered him in the maiden hurdle, given that we had decided to give him his first run back in a bumper. I just had it in the back of my mind that it would be good to have the option of running in the hurdle. If he is in it, you can always take him out of it closer to the time. If he isn't in it, you can't put him in it.

I rang Barry Geraghty and asked him if he would come over to Punchestown and ride one in the schooling hurdle for me. Barry was riding for Noel Meade at the time, but he was a tidy rider and I was using him whenever I could. He agreed to come over and ride this horse for me. This horse who was zero for four, as the Americans say.

Schooling hurdles are an excellent option for young, inexperienced horses. They allow them to compete against fellow inexperienced horses in simulated race conditions, but away from the glare of the public. You are not in the same pressurised container as you are in when you go to the races. You don't have to achieve the best finishing position possible, you are away from the *Truman Show* that is *At The Races*, and there is no betting. All in all, there is less pressure on both the horse and the jockey. And the trainer.

The primary objective of a schooling hurdle is that the horse learns. That is why they were invented. And you never know what you will come up against. Trainers bring their young horses to the training ground, they jock them up and let them off. If you really wanted to find out what you were up against, you could probably ask and the majority of trainers would probably tell you. But to be honest, I couldn't be bothered. I generally have enough on my plate worrying about my own horses without worrying about other people's as well.

The old schooling ground at Punchestown was inside the main racecourse. Although they race right-handed on the racecourse, on the schooling track they went left-handed. Moscow and Barry took up their positions at the start as Brian and I took up ours in the stands. Although it is only a school, you still want your horse to be competitive. Moscow was fairly straight, and if he was going to give a good account of himself back at Punchestown the following Sunday, he was going to have to go well in the school.

There were about fourteen horses in the school in total. I watched as they formed a line. You are always a little nervous when you know that they are going to leave the ground, especially when it's a horse with so little experience. Moscow had been fairly extensively schooled at home, but this was different. This was as close to a hurdle race as you will get.

I was glad when Barry was able to set him off in the front rank. That was the plan. It meant that he would get a good clear sight of his hurdles, and they wouldn't be flicking back in his face as other horses hit them. He jumped the first two flights more than adequately. They turned the corner and jumped another flight just beside the crannogs on the far side. The horse seemed happy lobbing along in front, and Barry seemed quite happy. Consequently, I was happy.

But often, just when you are feeling quite content within yourself, disaster is not too far around the corner. Quite literally, in this case. There was a marker down at the bottom bend that they had to go round before swinging up the far side. I watched as Moscow and Barry headed straight for it. I could see it happening before it did. I don't know if Barry wasn't looking where he was going or how it happened, but Moscow tried to duck to the left of it. Barry grabbed him and tried to yank him to the right. Suddenly they were in no-man's land and heading straight for the marker. No escape. Moscow hit it full on with his chest and just sprawled. The horse went one way, the jockey went the other. Fortunately, these markers are just stakes in the ground with plastic poles around them, so there was a good chance there would be no physical damage to the horse or rider. Nevertheless, we hadn't brought him to Punchestown to have him crash into a marker.

I watched through my binoculars in horror as the horse sauntered off in the opposite direction. That was him all right – non-conformist. At least he seemed to be sauntering painlessly. I panned back to the marker and saw Barry picking himself up gingerly. He seemed to be OK too. Just a hairline fracture of his pride perhaps. He appeared to be well up to withstanding the bollocking that was forthcoming.

I dashed down off the stands and got out on to the course. Moscow was loitering around by the two-mile start, evading all efforts at catching him. Eventually we cornered him. He wanted to be caught really. He was just having a bit of fun. Just being Moscow Flyer. He appeared to be sound, both physically and mentally.

There was a schooling bumper on after the schooling hurdle, and I asked Joan Moore, who was managing the schooling at Punchestown at the time, if he could go in that. I was desperate that he should derive some educational benefit from his first visit to Punchestown. Brian was fairly surprised that I wanted him to run again. It had taken us about ten minutes to catch him, but he'd hardly taken anything out of himself. Once I was happy that he was sound physically, there was no reason why he shouldn't go again. He needed a good blow. Brian was happy to trust me on it.

Barry had committed to ride something else for Willie Mullins in the schooling bumper, and there was no swaying him, so I put Peter Fahey up on Moscow. There were no mishaps this time. Peter saw the marker and navigated his way around it. Moscow duly beat the others home hands down.

It was a highly satisfactory conclusion to a day that could have ended in disaster. Like the schooling hurdle, you don't know the quality of the opposition in a schooling bumper, but it is generally safe to assume that it is not too low. Especially towards the end of October when a lot of these horses will be close to a race. The fact that Moscow had beaten the others was highly encouraging, and it gave credence to my belief that he had grown into a much stronger horse over the summer. Brian was thrilled. I was conscious not to make too much of a victory in a schooling bumper, but it was definitely a step in the right direction.

I phoned him later that evening to discuss things. Brian could probably detect the excitement in my voice, as I could in his.

'What do we do now?' I asked innocently. 'I have him in the bumper and the maiden hurdle at Punchestown on Sunday.'

There was silence on the other end of the phone. Going hurdling at this stage would be a deviation from the plan agreed in August. It wasn't Brian's style to deviate from a plan unless there was a clear and valid reason for so doing.

'Brian?'

'Maybe somebody is trying to tell us something,' came the slow response. 'Maybe he isn't meant to run in bumpers. We certainly haven't had much luck in them, with the defeats and the injury and everything. Why don't we just head straight over hurdles?'

Deep down I was pleased with Brian's response. Moscow jumped hurdles well at home and he had jumped the first three flights in the schooling hurdle like an old hand. I suppose I felt that, if he was going to go hurdling that season, he might as well start sooner rather than later. In my view he was ready.

'Great,' I said. 'It might be for luck.'

'Who will you get to ride him?' asked Brian.

Now it was my turn to think for a moment. I thought of the wholly avoidable incident at the marker earlier that morning. I thought of the jockey lying prostrate on the ground, and the horse – my horse – cantering away nonchalantly. Riderless.

'I always use the best available,' I said carefully. 'I'll give Barry a call.'

CHAPTER ELEVEN

BARRY GERAGHTY

I'd first come into contact with Barry Geraghty in November 1997. I was running a mare called Market Lass in a novices' hurdle at Naas. John Shortt had ridden her in her first three maiden hurdles, but he was unavailable at the time. Barry was with Noel Meade, and he looked like a nice young rider. As a bonus, he was able to claim 5lb. I gave Noel a call and asked if Barry could ride Market Lass. Noel didn't have a runner in the race so he was fine. Of course, if Barry rides a winner for me, or for anybody else, it is one less winner that he can have for Noel with his 5lb claim. But Noel is very good like that. He usually gives his young riders enough freedom to go and take opportunities as they arise. He always seems to have a lot of good young riders attached to his yard, so he must be doing something right by them.

Market Lass finished third at Naas. Later that month I ran her in another novice hurdle at Fairyhouse. I got Barry to ride her again, and they won at 16–1. He gave her a lovely ride that day. I remember thinking that for a teenager he was very strong and polished in a finish, and I made a mental note that I would use him again.

Barry had always been a horseman, the son of a horseman and born into a family of horsemen in Drumree in County Meath. It was his grandfather who bred the peerless Golden Miller, five-time Gold Cup winner and still the only horse ever to win the Gold Cup and the Grand National in the same year. The great horse was foaled in the stable just across the yard from the Geraghty house in Drumree in 1927. You can actually see the stable from the kitchen window.

It is no surprise that Barry's first memory is of watching Corbiere beating Greasepaint in the 1983 Grand National. He was three. He also remembers being in the front room in his grandmother's house watching the 1991 Grand National. When Gold Cup winner Garrison Savannah jumped the last clear, it looked like Golden Miller's Gold Cup/Grand National record was going to be equalled. There were fifteen or twenty kids in the room and a few adults as well, all gathered to watch the National. They cheered as one when Seagram got up in the shadow of the post to snatch victory. The record was safe for another year at least.

Barry was riding before he could walk. Quite literally. His dad, Tucker, had him sitting on horses as a baby and he was riding his first pony before he was four years old. Tucker opened a riding school when Barry was about eleven and that gave him and his two brothers, Ross and Norman, great experience of dealing with horses. Other kids would be coming in with ponies they couldn't ride. Barry would be given ponies that kids had spoilt and he would have to straighten them out.

He used to ride in the hunter trials. He rode for Sean Byrne, Susie Macken and my sister-in-law Chich, John's wife. Sean Byrne had a great little pony called Little Tom at the time. Sean used to say that he was a Honda with a Ferrari engine. He was only 11.2 hands so, as the lowest level was 12.2 hands, Little Tom was four inches smaller than the ponies against which he was competing. It didn't matter. He wasn't even four feet high but he'd jump fences that were four and a half feet. Barry used to point him in the right direction and just cling on. The first day Tucker took the boys out hunting, he had a pain in his neck looking behind him to make sure that they were all OK. And he'd count them – one, two, three. All there. The second day he brought them out, he couldn't keep up with them.

Every Tuesday morning at about eleven o'clock, the school principal's voice would come over the intercom asking for Ross, Norman and Barry Geraghty to go to his office with their bags. That would be their mother, Bea, in to collect the three lads to go hunting. They were the envy of the school. The principal didn't mind so much. Bea had started organising equestrian activities for the kids at the school and the principal was hugely enthusiastic about it. The boys had to go and school the horses. That was the story. The fact that they were out hunting for the day was merely by the way. And that was how Barry learnt to ride. He learnt by doing. Tucker didn't believe in wrapping the lads up in cotton wool. He just let them get on with it.

The Geraghtys were always a close-knit family. You can see it in them. They all look out for one another. It is probably their common interest in horses that fosters this. When Barry started riding on the pony racing circuit, if he had a ride in Galway or Ballinasloe or anywhere, even over the far side of the country, his dad would drive him. And when Barry's sister Jill rode her first winner under Rules on All's Rosey at Fairyhouse on New Year's Day 2005, the whole family was there to celebrate the success.

Barry rode for two seasons on the pony circuit. After his first season, when he had just turned sixteen, he was all set to go racing. He couldn't wait. But his father thought it would be better for him to spend another year on the pony circuit, hone his skills and go racing when he turned seventeen. That would be time enough. There is no doubt that that extra season on the pony circuit was a huge help to him, particularly at the beginning of his career.

Noel Meade was a friend of Tucker's. He knew that Barry had

Barry is in full flight after the 2004 Tingle Creek Chase at Sandown as Eamonn takes evasive action.

Same story after the 2005 Champion Chase!

*Moscow Flyer
and 'Galway'.*

*Moscow with me, Brian, Eamonn and Brian's wife Patricia after
he had won the Melling Chase.*

Moscow with all the team outside Commonstown House.
[© Caroline Norris]

On the gallops at The Curragh. Eamonn Leigh is using the new whip he designed himself. From left to right: Moscow Flyer, Riga Lad, Mama Mia and Harpers Pride. [© Caroline Norris]

Eamonn Leigh with Moscow Flyer at Sandown.

Help! Soon they will be off and soon it will be over.

*A young
Barry Geraghty.
[© Peter Mooney]*

*Youlneverwalkalone jumps past Moscow at the final flight in the 2000 Hatton's
Grace Hurdle at Fairyhouse. [© Peter Mooney]*

In full flight on the way to winning the Evening Herald Champion Novice Hurdle at the 2000 Punchestown Festival. [© Peter Mooney]

This steeplechasing game is easy! The 2001 Denny Gold Medal Chase at Leopardstown is in the bag. [© Peter Mooney]

Istabraq and Charlie come down at the last in the Shell Champion Hurdle at Leopardstown in 2001 as Moscow and Barry breathe down their necks. We will never know for certain how this one would have panned out. [© Peter Mooney]

Over the last in a line in the 2000 December Festival Hurdle. From left to right: Stage Affair and Ruby Walsh, Moscow and Barry, Mantles Prince and Norman Williamson and Istabraq and Charlie Swan. We four are about to become three. [© Healys]

Johnny Harrington with Graham Nicholl. [© Peter Mooney]

Almost all the information is in the catalogue. [© Peter Mooney]

been doing well on the pony circuit, so he asked Tucker if he would send young Barry down to him so that he could start riding out. Done deal. Barry's first ride on the racecourse was on In the Evening for Noel in an apprentice maiden at Navan in October 1996. There was to be no fairytale start: they finished seventh of fifteen.

In the Evening's next run was exactly eleven months later, in a maiden hurdle at Clonmel. Barry rode her again. In the interim he had recorded his first win under Rules when Stagalier won his maiden hurdle at Down Royal. In the Evening was in third place with no chance of winning going down to the last. She just stepped at the hurdle and came down, firing Barry into the ground. He had a bit of a pain in his back when he got up, but thought little of it. He dusted himself down and rode Sigma Comms to finish fifth in the next.

In the car on the way home with Noel and Gillian O'Brien, Noel's partner, Barry could hardly sit still for the pain in his lower back. He was in agony the whole way home, and was in pain all that night. The following day, he rode out at Noel's, still in pain. Noel was going schooling horses at Fairyhouse, and Barry told him that he thought he should go and get his back checked out. Noel, apparently, wasn't best pleased. This is a man's sport; you can't be running to the hospital for every little pain you suffer. Barry would be missing almost a whole day's work. 'If you want to go and get it X-rayed, then go and get it X-rayed.' He did. He went to see Dr Shariff in Navan. Crushed vertebrae. He had broken his back. He would be out of action for three months. It wasn't worth it, but there was some hint of consolation for Barry in being able to ring Noel to tell him. Noel was genuinely shocked. 'God, it's just as well you went to get it X-rayed!'

John Shortt was riding a lot for me at the time, but he was starting to wind down just as Barry was getting going. I was running Miss Orchestra in the Grand National Trial at Fairyhouse in February 1998. Barry, of course, had ridden Market Lass to win that valuable novices' hurdle at Fairyhouse a few months earlier, and I thought it would be good if we could claim off Miss Orchestra in the National Trial. There is no doubt that Moscow Flyer was the horse who did most for Barry's career. Barry was a good young jockey – perceived as being similarly talented to a lot of other good young jockeys at the time – before Moscow picked him up and carried him up to the penthouse of his profession. But the horse that got him noticed in the first place was Miss Orchestra.

To be fair to Barry, he gave her a very good ride in the National Trial. He followed instructions, had her handy the whole way, and kicked her on three out. Going to the last, there was nothing to choose between Miss Orchestra and Tell the Nipper, with Richard Dunwoody up. Dunwoody had been Barry's idol when he was growing up. When Barry was playing as a child, he was never Eddie Macken or David Broome, he was always Richard Dunwoody or Charlie Swan. Miss Orchestra met the last a little long. Barry gave her a kick and she just paddled it and sprawled on her head. She gave him no chance of staying on. Barry says that if a horse made a similar mistake under him today, even now with all his experience, he wouldn't be disappointed if he came off. But he would have loved to have fought out a finish with Dunwoody. He probably would have beaten him too as Miss Orchestra was a mare who really found lots under pressure. To say that he was unseated is probably a little unfair, but the mare stayed on her feet, so technically it had to go down as a U and not an F.

Jason Titley rode Miss Orchestra to finish third in a handicap chase at Downpatrick after Fairyhouse, but when I was getting her ready for the Midlands National at Uttoxeter on the Saturday after Cheltenham that year, I was again thinking that I would like to claim off her. She would have a low enough weight anyway, and with Barry's claim she would have a real chance of landing what was a very valuable prize.

Uttoxeter is a tricky enough track to ride, and this was Barry's first ever ride in England. But if I had harboured any concerns about the jockey – and I don't think I had many – they were laid to rest very soon after the race started. Barry rode Miss Orchestra aggressively, as planned. She had never been beyond three and a half miles, but she stayed on so well at the end of her races that I had no doubt about her getting this extreme trip of four and a quarter miles. By the sixth-last fence, Miss Orchestra and Kamikaze, with Norman Williamson up, had drawn clear of the field. Kamikaze made a mistake at the fourth last and Miss Orchestra went on. Barry just kept her going, kept the momentum up, and popped her over the last three fences. It was a good pot to win, and it was a great win for the yard. But most of all it was an invaluable win for Barry. Over and above his 10 per cent of the £40,000 winner's prize, it got him noticed on both sides of the Irish Sea.

By the time of the Galway Festival that year, 1998, Barry was being noticed and used by other trainers. So much so that he had reduced his claim from 5lb to 3lb. He was selected as one of four young riders to represent Ireland in the annual Australia v. Ireland Jockeys' Challenge in Australia immediately after Galway. Things could hardly have been going better for him.

At that Galway Festival, however, he met a full stop. Well, if not a full stop, then definitely a semi-colon. It frequently happens in this game. Just when you think things are going well, something comes to smack you in the face and stop you in your tracks. And you always have to be aware of it. You don't have to go around with a long face every day, thinking that disaster is just around the corner, but you do have to learn not to take anything for granted. Appreciate the good times, because, as sure as the Irish Grand National is run on Easter Monday, there are bad times lurking somewhere in the long grass.

Barry was riding a horse for Paddy Graffin called Verywell in a beginners' chase. Barry's father actually used to train him, and Barry had ridden him before in a maiden hurdle. Verywell had been a decent point-to-pointer and Barry thought he'd be a nice ride. He wasn't. He galloped straight through the first fence, clouted the second, where Barry lost his irons, and fell at the third. As Barry fell, he could feel the pain shooting up through his back again. He was taken away to Galway Hospital. That was on the

Saturday. His departure for Australia on the Sunday was an immediate scratching.

They couldn't determine exactly what was wrong with his back in Galway Hospital. After a couple of days of lying flat on it, he rang his dad and asked him to come and get him and take him to see Dr Shariff again in Navan. Dr Shariff found the problem: crushed vertebrae again, number five and number seven. He put him in the same body cast as he had put him in before. Later, the doctor at Galway told Barry that had he discovered that he had crushed his vertebrae he would have put a pin in his back. When a pin goes into your back, your riding days are over.

Barry returned to riding within ten weeks. Paul Carberry had taken up the job as retained rider to owner Robert Ogden in the UK, and the top job at Noel's was vacant. But if Barry thought he was a shoo-in for the job, he had to think again. There were a lot of top jockeys around at the time who were riding freelance – Dunwoody, Williamson, Swan. They were all doing it. It seemed like it was the fashionable way to go. Barry ended up riding more or less as Noel's second jockey after any one of the top guys.

Which meant that he was free to ride for me, or at least freer than he would have been had he been Noel's number one. Moscow was busy running in bumpers at the time, so Barry couldn't ride him, but I had some other nice horses around at the time, like Ferbet Junior and Slaney Native. I liked the way Barry rode, and I liked using him. It was probably his association with Ferbet Junior that cemented our relationship.

He was supposed to go to Australia that summer again, but he was leading the jockeys' championship at the time and he was going well, so he decided to stay in Ireland. Paul came back from England and Noel officially made Barry his number two. Barry was riding a bit for Willie Mullins as well at the time, when Ruby Walsh wasn't available. Then, in October 1999, Ruby broke his leg in a fall in Pardubice in the Czech Republic. It was tough on Ruby, but it meant that Barry came in for a lot of the Mullins rides. He was champion jockey that season with 84 winners.

It was also in October 1999 that Barry rode Moscow Flyer in his first ever hurdle race. And Barry will tell you today, he didn't like him at all that day at Punchestown. He might have had negative thoughts about him given that he had just dumped him on his head in the schooling hurdle. He was a leery ould fecker, Barry will tell you now. He hung like a gate.

But when Barry got the leg up on Moscow Flyer that day at Punchestown, he was getting a leg up on the express elevator to the top floor. Sure, you have to press the right buttons once you are on there, but you can't go without the elevator. None of us knew it at the time, but this fellow was about to give us all a serious lift.

CHAPTER TWELVE

TOP NOVICE

We had four runners at Punchestown on 31 October 1999. Jump for Fun in the novice hurdle, Backsheesh in the bumper, and two in the maiden hurdle – Enterprising and Moscow Flyer.

Jump for Fun was a nice horse who had finished fifth to The Bunny Boiler in a bumper at Downpatrick on his only previous start, and Backsheesh hadn't shown too much in three previous runs in bumpers. Enterprising had finished second to Hurry Bob in the four-year-old bumper at Punchestown the previous April, but he was really only running in the maiden hurdle so that he could get a handicap mark. He was running on his merits and everything, but he was only a four-year-old and he was a small horse who I thought would be better suited to carrying small weights in handicaps rather than competing off level weights in novice hurdles. Moscow was our best chance by far of a victory on the day.

Punchestown is only about half an hour's drive from Moone, so, even though the first race was at 1.15, the horses didn't have to leave at the crack of dawn. I checked the four horses in the morning. We always take our runners out in the morning to allow them to stretch their legs before they get into the horsebox to go to the races. They were all sound and well. I phoned Brian to tell him that everything was in order. There was a palpable heave of relief on the other end of the phone.

Barry was riding the favourite, Lodge Hill, for Frances Crowley against Jump for Fun in the first. I didn't mind too much. I had managed to book him for Moscow. Jump for Fun finished fifth to Vanilla Man. I was happy enough with him. It was a decent performance on his first run of the season and his first hurdle race ever. Barry finished third on Lodge Hill.

Noel Meade trained the favourite in the maiden hurdle, Young Buck, who was going to be hard to beat by all accounts and would be ridden by Paul Carberry. He had won his first bumper the previous season by ten lengths and finished a promoted second on his only other start in a hot bumper at Leopardstown. Word was that he was going well at home. We were running for places. But Barry knew him from riding him at Noel's. He didn't think he was a very fluent jumper of hurdles. If our fellow could jump well at racing pace, he wouldn't be without his chance. I knew that Moscow was well. Furthermore, Young Buck had to carry twelve stone while Moscow only had 11st 6lb. It's very easy looking back now, but even then I thought that Noel's horse would have to be good to beat us, giving us 8lb.

Nevertheless, the bookmakers made Young Buck the 8–13 favourite and sent Moscow off the 13–2 second favourite.

Brian was excited before this one. Definitely as excited as he had been since Moscow's first race. This was his first time racing over jumps. All that messing in bumpers was behind us now. This was what we bought him for.

In the parade ring before the race, I just told Barry to have him handy and allow him to see his hurdles. I don't go in for detailed instructions at all. I leave a lot of it up to Barry. But this was Moscow's first run in a hurdle race and it was important, above all else, that he enjoyed the experience. The last thing you want to do is sour a young horse against the game before he has really got going at it. I told Barry to be confident without being overly aggressive. And to watch out for markers.

The two-mile start at Punchestown is just to the right of the grandstand towards the top of the home straight. They jump one – the flight that will be the last on the following circuit – and run up past the winning post before embarking on another complete circuit of the track. Barry kicked Moscow on as soon as the tapes went up. They pinged the first and came up past us disputing the lead with David Casey on Belene Boy. I was very happy with both of them as they set off into the country.

It's sometimes hard to tell how they jump the next two at Punchestown, as they are running and jumping away from you. The trick is to watch the jockey's bottom. If the bottom remains in rhythm with the horse's gait, then you know they have negotiated the obstacles well. Barry's did, and my confidence grew.

At the fourth flight, Belene Boy made a slight mistake and Moscow found himself in front. Barry allowed him to go on and settled him into a nice rhythm at the head of the field. He could see his hurdles from a long way off and was able to measure them well. I panned back to see where Young Buck was. He was easy to spot as Paul Carberry is usually the highest thing on the racecourse. He was travelling well in fourth or fifth on the inside, but no better than Moscow was travelling in front.

Moscow winged the third-last flight and Barry asked him to go faster. Carberry sent Young Buck after him and moved into second place before the second last. But Barry still had plenty up his sleeve and kicked Moscow on again. He met the second last in his stride and got away from the back of it quickly. Carberry was all out on Young Buck in behind as the pair went down to the final flight. Jump it, and we're home.

And he did. Just as he had jumped the previous seven. My heart did a couple of back-flips as Barry just pushed him out all the way to the line. He had three lengths to spare over Young Buck, with a further ten lengths back to the third horse, our runner Enterprising, who delighted me by moving on well from the back.

It was all smiles back in the winner's enclosure. It usually is all smiles in the winner's enclosure. Barry was smiling, and Brian and Patricia were beside themselves. I was delighted for Brian. His first winner. I tried to remember my first winner and imagine how he must have been feeling. Of course I couldn't remember the feeling, but I was delighted to have been able to make it happen for him. Brian had ignored my advice and gone and backed his horse anyway. But that wasn't why he could hardly speak in the winner's enclosure: his first horse had just won his first race, and he was fizzing with excitement and pride. The fact that he had beaten an odds-on shot of Noel Meade's was an added bonus. Noel was at the very top of the sport at the time, as he is now. Brian said that it was like beating Kilkenny in the Championship.

Moscow seemed to enjoy the attention – nay, adulation – that was heaped upon him. So, this is what it's like? Winning, I mean. If I had known it was like this, I might have put in a little more effort in those bumpers. But I like this jumping lark. It's much more interesting. Much better sport.

We bounced back to Moone that evening. Backsheesh had put in the performance of his career to finish fourth in the bumper under Peter Fahey. I was happy with Jump For Fun's fifth in the novices' hurdle, and I was thrilled with Enterprising's run to finish third in the maiden hurdle.

But it was Moscow's victory that put the bounce in my step. I'm not entirely sure why, but I couldn't get rid of the smile on my face the whole way home. It may have been because of the pleasure this victory had given Brian and Patricia. Brian had made no effort to disguise his total and unbridled delight at this win. Or it may have been because this win had gone some way towards vindicating my faith in this horse. In an instant he had erased the disappointment and mild frustration we had all experienced during his bumper season. That was now consigned to the annals. It was time to look forward.

I mulled over the possible reasons for the transformation in the horse. Because it was a transformation. Maybe jumping was the key to him. Maybe the fact that they had to jump meant that he had time to catch a breather. He certainly hadn't hit the flat spot he had hit in all four of his bumpers. Or maybe he had just strengthened up during the summer and was just growing into the horse we hoped he would become. In all probability it was a combination of the two. I wasn't thinking Arkle or Champion Chase at the time – I wouldn't have dared even to begin to dream a dream so wild – but at least this horse had now begun to fulfil his potential. The potential Johnny and I had seen in him at Fairyhouse more than a year earlier. I wasn't sure where the road would lead, but at least there was a road now, and this fellow was on it.

The next task was to find a winners' race for him. Of course, as a winner he wasn't eligible for maiden hurdles any more, but he was still able to run in novice hurdles now and for the remainder of his first season. I didn't mind if I had to step him up to two and a half miles. Nothing had happened to make me think that staying wouldn't be his game.

I found a nice race for him at Down Royal the following Saturday, just six days after his Punchestown win. It was a two-mile conditions hurdle, not restricted to novices, so he would have to jump against horses with more jumping experience under their girths than he had. However, this was offset by the fact that there would probably be far fewer runners in the conditions hurdle than there would be in your typical novices' hurdle. As a consequence, it was likely that he would be able to have a clearer view of his obstacles.

The novice hurdle fields in Ireland back then, as they are now, were usually right on the safety limit. It is a problem in Ireland at present, a direct consequence of the number of horses we have in training. I am always a little nervous when one of my novices goes into the wings of a hurdle surrounded by fellow novices.

Furthermore, as Moscow was now a winner, he would be giving away weight to the non-winning novices. In the conditions hurdle in the North, the likelihood was that he would be the beneficiary of a weight concession.

The Wednesday before Down Royal, I noticed in the Racing Calendar that entries were closing for the Royal Bond Novice Hurdle – the Grade 1 race for novices that is run on Hatton's Grace Hurdle weekend at Fairyhouse, usually at the end of November. I looked at it for a little while and pondered. If you don't put him in it, you'll kick yourself if he goes and wins easily at Down Royal. If you do put him in it and he doesn't prove up to it, you can always take him out at the next forfeit stage. No harm done. Sometimes you have to take these little chances. You will never train a champion if you don't enter horses in the championship races. The downside to entering was minimal. So I entered Moscow Flyer, winner of a measly little maiden hurdle, in the monster Grade 1 Royal Bond Hurdle and smiled. This could look very stupid in a couple of days' time. Don Quixote wouldn't have a look-in. And don't tell a soul. Not even Brian Kearney.

I was also sending Ferbet Junior to Down Royal to contest the James Nicholson Champion Chase, so it made sense that Moscow would travel with him. Ferbet Junior was a very exciting chaser who had won the Kinloch Brae Chase the previous season (beating Opera Hat, trained by my brother), and he had won at the Punchestown Festival. On his only run that season to date, he had won the Powers Gold Label Champion Chase at Gowran Park, beating Amberleigh House, His Song and Imperial Call. Barry had ridden him at Punchestown and at Gowran and seemed to get on particularly well with him. He was only six, and it was his first attempt at three miles, so it was very much an experimental mission. Numbered among his opponents were Florida Pearl and Dorans Pride.

I was delighted when I found out on the Friday morning that only four horses had stood their ground in the Tattersalls Hurdle: Moscow, Celtic Project (whose only win in 26 starts had come in a private sweepstake at Sligo more than a year earlier), Dainty Daisy (who had won a bumper the previous season) and Greenstead. I was happy that we would have the measure of the other two, but Greenstead was going to be tough. He had had enough speed to win on the Flat when trained by John Gosden and he had plenty of experience over hurdles, having raced over them eight times. He had beaten Arthur Moore's Native Upmanship at Gowran and had just gone under to his stable companion Cardinal Hill in the Grade 1 novice hurdle at the Punchestown Festival the previous April. Like Young Buck six days earlier, he was trained by Noel Meade. Also like Young Buck, the punters sent him off the odds-on favourite.

Barry also knew Greenstead. It was quite uncanny the way he knew Moscow's first two major opponents from riding them at Noel's. Barry had actually ridden him at Punchestown when he was second to Cardinal Hill. He thought that Greenstead didn't have as much ability as Young Buck and was fairly confident that Moscow would beat him.

I was quite relaxed in the parade ring before the race. There was no real pressure on us. Moscow was the novice coming up against the experienced horses. We had won our maiden hurdle so there wasn't a huge expectation on us to get a win under our belt. We were second favourite and weren't expected by the pundits to beat Greenstead. I told Brian and Patricia that we would probably finish second to Noel's horse, that I'd be happy enough with that. Brian seemed happy with that as well.

I always watch the races at Down Royal on the steps on the open stand. There is good viewing there and it is rarely too crowded. As I stood there with Brian and Patricia, I noticed that Noel Meade was beside me and I saluted him. Noel put his binoculars up to his eyes and pointed them in the direction of the betting ring. 'I can't understand this betting at all,' he said to me suddenly. 'My fellow is odds-on and you're odds-against. It doesn't make sense. The horse of mine that you beat last week is a better horse than this one. My fellow shouldn't even be favourite to beat you, never mind odds-on. I'd say you'll win by a minute.' Noel is generally fairly straight up. He doesn't play down his chances unduly or hype up his geese as swans. He usually calls it as he sees it, and he is often very close to the mark. When he says that one of his is better than another, he is generally right. If Greenstead was not as good as Young Buck, and if Young Buck ran up to his best last week, then we were a shoo-in. I began to get hopeful. And as I got hopeful, I began to get nervous.

You can often get a false pace in a four-runner race. If nothing wants to make the running, they can dawdle along early on. When that happens, it can develop into a sprint finish and you can get a strange result. We thought that Moscow stayed two miles well, so we decided that, if nothing else was going to go on, we would make the running.

Nothing else did, so Barry kicked Moscow on early. He didn't set a breakneck pace, but he went a nice even gallop. Barry allowed him to settle into a rhythm and get a good sight of his hurdles. As a result, he jumped very well the whole way. Paul Carberry tracked him round on Greenstead but, to be honest, this was never really a contest. Barry gave Moscow a kick in the belly after three out and he just went further and further clear. Carberry must have been getting sick of the sight of his rear end. Moscow popped over the last two and came home by fifteen lengths from Greenstead. It was the widest margin by which he won any hurdle race, and the widest margin by which he would win any type of race until he came back to Down Royal exactly three years later to beat Kadarann in an intermediate chase.

My overriding feeling when he jumped the last, and I knew the race was in the bag, was one of quiet satisfaction. It was different to the relief and sense of vindication I had felt when he won his first hurdle race. It was also very different to the sheer ecstasy I would feel later in his career. This feeling was the clarinet in the orchestra as opposed to the double bass or the lead violin. This horse was going in the right direction. It looked like he had improved since his last run, and he had jumped like an old hand. Brian and Patricia were glowing beside me, and Brian gave me a little pat on the back. A little 'well done' pat. I quietly congratulated myself on entering the horse in the Royal Bond Hurdle. You make the wrong decisions often enough in this game, so when you make the right one you are entitled to a little bit of quiet self-indulgence. It would have been a shame now had he not been entered in it. All being well, that was where we would go next.

Before I made my way down from the open stand, I looked up at Noel Meade – the kind of look, I imagine, that a victorious tennis player gives to his or her vanquished opponent as they shake hands across the net after a match. Hard luck. You try not to look too smug or too self-satisfied. You genuinely mean hard luck. There will be other days when you will be on the receiving end. That's for sure. Noel responded with his characteristic good-natured smile. Told you so.

There were a lot of press people at Down Royal that day as it's their biggest day of the year up there. The team at Down Royal have done a great job with the course and with that meeting, and I like to support it whenever I can. It was good to have a winner there, and Ferbet Junior put in a good performance too, finishing third to Florida Pearl and Dorans Pride in the James Nicholson Chase later that day. He led for a long way, as is his wont, but just wasn't as strong over the last three fences. It was no disgrace for a six-year-old to go down to those two stalwarts of National Hunt racing however, and I was happy with his run.

I think some of the press were surprised when I told them that I had entered Moscow in the Royal Bond. It probably wasn't my style to pitch one in at the deep end, especially before he had proved that he could swim at all. Barry thought that Moscow was all right, but he wouldn't have gone overboard about him. His father, Tucker, told him after Down Royal that Moscow Flyer was a right horse, but Barry was a bit sceptical. He rides so many horses. He reckons if you get excited about every one that started showing a little bit of ability, you'd be setting yourself up for a fall every second day. He liked him all right, but not nearly as much as his father did.

We had three weeks to prepare Moscow for the Royal Bond. I usually don't like stepping horses up so dramatically in grade. We were going from a conditions hurdle, the second hurdle race of his life, straight into a Grade 1 race. But I thought he was ready for it. Only just, mind you, but ready nonetheless.

You wouldn't get excited about Moscow by just watching him work at home. He keeps plenty for himself. But I had seen him on the racecourse. Everybody had. He had impressed me a lot in both his hurdle races and there was no doubt in my mind that he was improving quickly. Even his home work in the lead-up to the Royal Bond, while still not earth-shattering, was much more impressive than it had been in October. The Royal Bond fitted in nicely with his schedule of races, and he deserved a crack at it. He was a different horse now over hurdles to the bumper horse we had trained the previous season. He was very proficient over his obstacles for a novice, and that gave him a huge advantage, especially over horses who weren't so fluent. He was a stronger horse, and strengthening by the day. He wasn't hitting a flat spot in his hurdle races and he was finishing well.

Bizarrely, the Royal Bond cut up to be another four-horse race. The Dermot Weld-trained Stage Affair was all the rage, and it looked like he had scared away a lot of the opposition. Stage Affair was a very classy recruit to hurdling, having won the Listed Mooresbridge Stakes and finished second to Daylami in the Tattersalls Gold Cup at The Curragh the previous season. He had won all four hurdle races that he had contested, all of them impressively, and three of them at long odds-on.

It was windy on Royal Bond Hurdle day at Fairyhouse and the ground was very soft. It was a pity for Fairyhouse that it was such a bad day, as this is one of their flagship days – Hatton's Grace Hurdle day, supported by the Royal Bond and the Drinmore Chase. Three Grade 1 races. They had to leave out one of the flights of hurdles down at Ballyhack as the wind kept blowing it into an upright position. I thought that conditions were far from ideal for us, but at least everyone was in the same boat.

There was drama in the Hatton's Grace Hurdle early in the day as Limestone Lad got the better of 1–7 shot Istabraq. A combination of conditions, the two-and-a-half-mile trip and the grit and determination of Limestone Lad had probably caught out the dual champion hurdler. It didn't matter that he had beaten Limestone Lad five weeks earlier at Tipperary on heavy ground on the day that Stage Affair had won his fourth hurdle race. I remember thinking that it would be too much to expect for both odds-on winners from Tipperary that day to get beaten at odds-on at Fairyhouse.

Barry was all smiles in the parade ring before the Royal Bond. He had just ridden Alexander Banquet for Willie Mullins to win the Drinmore Chase. I always think it's a good thing for a jockey to have ridden a winner on the day before he goes out to ride one of mine. It gets him into the habit of winning. Heightens his confidence.

Barry had thought a lot about how he was going to ride Moscow. He is an excellent tactical rider. He knows his horses well and he thinks about how he can ride them to maximise their strengths and exploit the weaknesses of his rivals. That's his job. This was his third time to ride Moscow in a race, and he was getting to know him better all the time. So, how to beat Stage Affair? Barry talked to his brother Ross about it the night before. He knew that Moscow stayed well, so he didn't want a slow pace, but Stage Affair could also be difficult to settle sometimes, so if he went off too quickly we would play into his hands. Barry decided that he would make it, but that he would make it a nice even gallop. Not too fast, not too slow. Then he would kick at the top of the home straight. That was where Moscow's stamina would come into play.

Fairyhouse is similar to Punchestown in that it is a right-handed galloping track, about a mile and six furlongs in circumference. The two-mile start is in front of the second-last flight of hurdles. They jump one and head off on another circuit of the track. Barry kicked Moscow out of the gate and went straight into a four-length lead. The other three raced three abreast up the home straight for the first time: Stage Affair with Tony McCoy up, Vanilla Man, Paddy Mullins' six-year-old who had won his last two, with Tommy Treacy up, and Moscow Retreat, another Moscow Society gelding, trained by Michael Hourigan and ridden by his son Paul.

Moscow seemed happy and Barry seemed happy as they went up past the stands and turned down the side of the course. Up by Ballyhack, around the top bend, and right-handed down the back straight. Not too fast a pace and not too slow. Just as Barry had said. He was doing everything easily and travelling well. McCoy sat in his slipstream in second, about two lengths behind. Stage Affair had settled OK and seemed to be travelling easily. I worried about the Flat-race speed of the Theatrical gelding as they went around. His finishing kick. Would it be too much for our National Hunt-bred five-year-old out of a Duky mare?

Moscow pinged the third last, the one before the home turn. He took about a length and a half out of Stage Affair. Barry could have kicked on then to try to make the advantage tell. A less experienced jockey might have, but Barry was sticking to the game plan. He stood up in his irons and allowed the other three to close up on him again. Then, just before they got to the home turn, Barry got into the drive position and kicked. Vanilla Man and Moscow Retreat quickly came off the bridle, but McCoy just shook the reins at Stage Affair and he covered Moscow's move.

Barry didn't look around to see where Stage Affair was. He had decided before the race that he wouldn't. If Stage Affair was going to be there at all, he figured, he was going to be up his arse going around the home turn. From there, Barry was just going to ride his race. Whether Stage Affair was there or not was not going to affect how Barry was going to ride Moscow up the home straight, so why look around and possibly betray something of your tactics?

As they came down to the second-last flight, I knew that the moment of truth was imminent. Did we have a serious horse on our hands or just a good horse who would win races? Moscow met the second last in his stride and flew it. Stage Affair also jumped it well just behind him. Barry was nearly all out now as the pair of them came down to the final flight. We would know soon. McCoy was asking Stage Affair to draw closer, but he hadn't gone for everything yet. Not by a long chalk.

Moscow got in tight to the last and landed in a bit of a heap at the back of it. Stage Affair met it in his stride. Barry had to stoke Moscow up again, and I'm not sure that Stage Affair didn't put his nose in front. Kitchen sink time. Barry gave Moscow all he had and asked for the same in return. McCoy got down to drive Stage Affair past and claim the prize. But big surprise. Not as much there as we thought. Distress signals.

Barry asked for more on the far rail. Moscow responded yet again. Flared nostrils and outstretched neck. Thou shalt not pass. Gradually and inexorably, he ground the finishing kick out of his rival. McCoy had squeezed every last drop out of Stage Affair until he had nothing left to give. Bone dry. A few strides from the line, McCoy accepted defeat. He stood up in his irons and waved the white flag. Barry didn't notice. He just kept pushing and kicking all the way through the line.

That was a turning point for me. A Moscow metamorphosis. In one instant he had turned from a decent novice hurdler into a racehorse who could potentially go right to the very top. He had won a Grade 1 race, beating one of the hottest properties in the novice hurdling ranks on either side of the Irish Sea. Indeed, Stage Affair went on that year, as a novice, to contest the AIG Champion Hurdle, where he finished second to Istabraq. He also ran in the Champion Hurdle at Cheltenham that season, although, quite remarkably, he didn't win another race until he won his beginners' chase at Punchestown three and a half years later.

It was after that race that Barry began to think Moscow could be a serious horse. He showed loads of pace and he was brave in the finish. Barry liked that combination. He reckoned he hadn't won a bumper because he was just quirky and leery. Jumping helped sharpen him up and keep him interested. He also reckoned he was a totally different horse to the one he had ridden at Punchestown just a month earlier. That could have been down to the

Punchestown factor. We know now that there is something about Punchestown for Moscow. He has never been very impressive there, either over hurdles or over fences. That said, somewhat paradoxically, he has a better record at Punchestown than he has at any other racecourse.

I'm not sure that Moscow got the credit he deserved for winning the Royal Bond. They said that the ground didn't suit Stage Affair. They were probably right, but they failed to add that it didn't suit Moscow either. He probably didn't really get much credit for beating Young Buck or Greenstead either. When an odds-on shot gets beaten, the pundits tend to look for reasons why, and treat the result with a degree of scepticism. In all of Moscow's three hurdle races up to that point, he had beaten an odds-on shot. He hadn't followed the script. As a result, people may have been a little reluctant to proclaim him as a true Grade 1 horse.

We had to think of Cheltenham after that. There was no way out of it. The press asked me about Cheltenham after the Royal Bond – standard question after the Royal Bond, I presume. Of course. We'll put him in both novice hurdles at the Festival. The Supreme Novices' Hurdle over two miles and the Sun Alliance Hurdle over two miles five furlongs. Although all his winning had been over two miles, I still wasn't going to rule him out of the longer race. I still wasn't sure that he wouldn't be even better over a longer distance.

Brian was still desperate to have a runner at Cheltenham. To be a part of it – the racecourse and the enclosures and the grandstands and the people and the parade ring. He'd love to just go and stand in the parade ring and have his horse – *his* horse – walk around the circumference. Can you imagine how that would feel? He wouldn't even have to have a chance of winning. To go to Cheltenham with a realistic chance of winning a race was just far too much even to begin to countenance. But just to be there. To be a part of it. He couldn't imagine it getting much better than that.

If we were to be ready to go to Cheltenham the following March, however, the horse needed a break. In fairness, he deserved one. He had won three hurdle races in three attempts. He had beaten three odds-on shots from the top stables and bagged a Grade 1 race into the bargain. You cannot keep a horse on the go all season without a break and expect him to perform to the best of his ability every time. Horses are just like us. They need time away from work. If you or I were to work right through the year, with no rest, at some stage our performance level would begin to dip. Horses are the same. There were good novice hurdle races to be won over the Christmas period, but it made sense to give Moscow a few weeks off at that time. It wasn't like a summer break, where we would leave him out in a field and let him get nice and fat, but it was a break from serious work just to freshen him up a bit. Then we would bring him back after Christmas with the aim of having him at concert pitch for Cheltenham. You have no business going to Prestbury Park in March if you are not tuned to the minute.

There is a good novice hurdle race at Leopardstown on Hennessy Gold Cup day at the beginning of February, the Deloitte and Touche Novice Hurdle, run over two and a quarter miles. It was ideal for Moscow for two reasons. Firstly, it fitted in perfectly with the schedule that would bring him to Cheltenham. It was far enough away so that we could let him down a little in November and then build him up again for the race, and it gave us enough time between then and Cheltenham to really tighten the screws. Secondly, the distance of the race was just right. How he performed over two and a quarter miles would give us a good indication as to whether we should go for the two-mile or the two-mile-five-furlong race at the Festival.

Before then, Moscow had his rest. We kept him ticking over, but he didn't do any serious work. Youlneverwalkalone, owned by J.P. McManus and trained by Christy Roche, won the Future Champions Novice Hurdle at Leopardstown's Christmas meeting – the race in which Moscow would probably have run. I remember thinking that he looked pretty good and wondering how Moscow would have fared against him. He would get his crack at him in time. We brought Moscow back into full work at the beginning of January 2000. We took him to Punchestown to give him a spin in a schooling hurdle on the 18th, and he went great. Just twenty days to go to the Deloitte race and I couldn't have been happier.

I had him out the following day, however, and he wasn't sound. It was a slight concern, but sometimes horses pull muscles when they do a piece of decent work and they get over them in a day or two. Then I took him out again the following day and he still wasn't sound, so I phoned Ned Gowing, the vet, and asked him to come have a look. Ned agreed that it could well be as simple as a pulled muscle and that it might be OK by Monday. If it wasn't, he'd do a scan. It wasn't. The scan revealed a hairline fracture of Moscow's pelvis. Disaster. He'd have to stand in his box for a minimum of four weeks. The Deloitte race was out. Cheltenham was out. If we were lucky we might have him back for Fairyhouse or Punchestown. If we were unlucky, he wouldn't race again.

You have to put these things into context, and in the broad scheme of things I suppose it wasn't a disaster at all. A horse misses a race – big deal. In the words of Boris Becker when he was knocked out of Wimbledon, nobody died here. We still had our horse. But it was difficult to think these thoughts as I punched Brian Kearney's number into my phone and pressed the green button.

I'm a firm believer in straight talking. I don't tend to beat around the bush too much. If you have bad news, tell it as soon as you can and tell it straight. I think people appreciate that. I know that owners do, in the main. It wasn't the prognosis Brian wanted to hear, but it was the prognosis, so he needed to hear it. That's racing.

Youlneverwalkalone won the Deloitte and Touche Hurdle. He was odds-on and was impressive in beating Sackville and Well Ridden. I watched and wondered how Moscow would have got on against him. The ground was yielding, which was more than acceptable for the time of year, and would have suited him well. I could but wonder, as I can but wonder now. We will never know, but, as we found out later on, it probably would have been a hell of a buckle between the two of them.

Moscow moved from his box to the horse-walker as Cheltenham came and went. Around and around he went every day. Left-handed and right-handed. All the while getting stronger and building up his muscles again. I had only one runner at Cheltenham that year, the Peter Queally-owned Space Trucker in the Champion Chase. He was an unbelievable horse. He won 15 times and was placed 23 times from 66 runs on the Flat, over hurdles and over fences. He finished second in a Galway Hurdle and he finished third in a Champion Hurdle. He won a Fighting Fifth and the top two-mile hurdle at Cheltenham's November meeting, which they now call the Greatwood Hurdle, where he beat that season's champion hurdler Make a Stand, giving him almost a stone.

Space Trucker will always have a special place in my heart, not only for his absolute consistency and willingness to please, but because he provided me with my first Cheltenham Festival winner when he landed the Grand Annual the previous year. He was travelling well under Shay Barry in the Champion Chase until Nordance Prince fell in front of him and all but brought him down. The race hadn't begun to develop at that stage, and he might not have been involved in one of the finishes of the season between Edredon Bleu and Direct Route anyway, but you just never know how it would have panned out.

The Noel Meade-trained Sausalito Bay won the race in which Moscow would probably have run, the Supreme Novices' Hurdle. Irish banker Youlneverwalkalone could only finish third, and a lightly raced novice of Henrietta Knight's called Best Mate ran on into second place. I was delighted for Noel. It was his first Cheltenham Festival winner after numerous attempts and much heartache. People said that once he had one, the floodgates would open and he would have many. But the following day, Barry rode Native Dara for him in the Coral Cup and went five lengths clear over the final flight, only for What's Up Boys to come from the next parish and nail him on the line. Noel said he probably would have thrown himself off a high building had Sausalito Bay not broken his duck the previous day. Remarkably, and almost unfairly, Noel hasn't had another winner at the Festival since.

Shortly after Cheltenham, Moscow was scanned and confirmed clear. We had our horse back. It was a shame to have missed Cheltenham, but sometimes things happen for a reason. We still had Fairyhouse and Punchestown to look forward to, and we just had enough time to prepare him for both.

When we started riding him out again, he was so fresh that he bucked his lad off five days in succession. I thought, 'There's feck all wrong with your pelvis if you can buck your lad off.' So we started some light work with him. As soon as we did, it took the freshness out of him and he settled down a lot. I used to ride him out a bit then, and he dropped me a few times as well. He'd just go out on to the long gallop and drop his shoulder. It was his favourite trick. And he'd stand there looking at you as you lay on the ground. What are you doing lying around then? We've got work to do!

We decided that we'd run him in a Grade 3 novices' hurdle over two and a half miles at the Fairyhouse Easter Festival. Johnny was against it. He figured that the horse had had a fractured pelvis and that the best thing would be to let him off for the season. But he seemed fresh and well to me, so I thought we had little to lose by running. Eamonn agreed with me. Also, the race at Fairyhouse would give us the opportunity to find out if he stayed two and a half miles or not.

He was like a lunatic when he got to Fairyhouse. He was impossible to saddle, he wouldn't walk round the parade ring, he charged and stopped, and he pulled Eamonn all over the place. He wouldn't let Barry get up on him in the parade ring, so we had to lead him out on to the track before we could leg him up. The signs were not good.

And he was no different in the race. Barry tried to settle him in behind, but he was having none of it. He pulled Barry's arms out in behind, so Barry let him go on at the third flight in the hope that he would settle better in front. He didn't. He pulled like crazy and galloped into every flight of hurdles. It really wasn't what he wanted to be doing on his first run back after a five-month absence and on his first attempt at two and a half miles.

He led all the way round until the home straight. I was hoping that he might keep on going, but he had expended so much energy fighting against Barry the whole way that he was a spent force by the time they got to the second last. Barry asked him to raise his effort, but there was nothing there. He had been running with the choke out for more than two miles.

Barry was easy on him after that and allowed him to come home in his own time. He finished last of the eight finishers. We were pretty despondent. Brian was fairly pragmatic, but obviously disappointed. The bubble had burst. And that's when the doubts creep in. Maybe we didn't have a top-class horse on our hands at all. He had lost his unbeaten record over hurdles, and he had lost it in style.

The recriminations started. The press and the people on the ditch of course had to have their say. Naturally you will have your post-mortems when your horse runs so disappointingly, and the recriminations were not direct, but they were reflected and they got under my skin. Was it a good idea to run him? The season was coming to an end anyway, so would it not have been better, as Johnny had suggested, to leave him off for the summer and bring him back in the autumn? Nobody said, 'Jessie, you shouldn't have run that horse,' but the understanding was there. In fairness, Johnny didn't adopt too high a moral ground. But after the race he said that we should now let him off for the summer. I didn't agree. I said we should press on and run him at Punchestown. The fact that Eamonn agreed with me gave me added confidence.

Andy Andrews used to come over from Newmarket to do my horses' backs at the time. He came over on the Wednesday after the Fairyhouse race and squared up Moscow's pelvis. One of his hips had been more forward than the other. It was just another possible reason for his dismal performance at Fairyhouse. It could have been that he was wrong behind and was feeling pain when he galloped. It could have been the fact that he boiled over beforehand, which, of course, could have been related to the pain he was feeling. It could have been down to the two-and-a-half-mile trip and that he patently failed to stay. Or it could have been down to the fact that he might have been one gallop short of peak fitness. My inclination was that it was probably a combination of all these things, and I resolved to put things right at Punchestown. In hindsight, it was definitely a risk to run him again that season. No question. The easy thing to do would have been to put him out to grass. But I was determined that he should have the opportunity to show people that he was high class. I dreaded going into the summer with business unfinished. In my guts, I felt it was the right thing to do. Sometimes you have to go with your gut feeling. There's no point in getting older if you're not going to get a little bit wiser.

Easter was unusually late that year, so Punchestown came up very quickly after Fairyhouse. There were only nine days between Moscow's race at Fairyhouse and the Grade 1 novices' hurdle at Punchestown. In that short space of time, we brought Moscow to The Curragh twice and worked him hard, once at the end of Fairyhouse week and once at the start of Punchestown week. It was a lot, but I felt it was the right thing for the horse. Guts again.

Sausalito Bay was favourite for the Evening Herald Champion Novice Hurdle at Punchestown. Justifiably so. Fresh from his famous Cheltenham win. Another odds-on shot of Noel Meade's for Moscow to take on. He was used to it at this stage. They made Minella Hotel second favourite. He was an exciting horse of John Nallen's who had finished second to Ross Moff in the Grade 2 novice hurdle at Fairyhouse. Moscow was left to run as an unconsidered 10–1 shot. Less pressure.

Or so you'd think. Actually, I felt under far more pressure before the start of this race than I had before any of his races up to that point. In the back of my mind I knew there was a chance he would run as poorly as he had run at Fairyhouse. I didn't think it was likely, but there was always that possibility. If he did trail in at the back of the field, the hurlers on the ditch would have a field day. Told you so. She shouldn't have run that horse. Sure, didn't he only crack his pelvis a few weeks ago? What was she thinking? More than that, Moscow's reputation was on the line. A poor performance here and it would have all been for nothing. It would be very easy to go back through his three wins and pick holes in them. Even the Royal Bond. The ground was all against Stage Affair. That theory was already doing the rounds. And even more was at stake. The horse's health. He had seemed fine to me at home and on The Curragh, but you never know for sure how a horse is until he races. There was a little niggle at the back of my mind. It could be back to the drawing board after this. Finish in mid-division and we'll probably have to ditch all top-echelon aspirations and start again. Add to all this my reputation as a trainer, Brian's as an owner, Eamonn's and Johnny's. So much depended on this race.

All of this flashed through my mind as I took my place in the stands. Thankfully, Moscow was much better behaved than he had been at Fairyhouse. That was very important. In truth, I didn't think we would beat Sausalito Bay, but I was hoping that we could finish second. I felt that if he ran up to his best he would finish second. I couldn't have expected to beat the supreme novice hurdler.

Sausalito Bay disputed the early running with Docklands Limo, the English challenger. Moscow settled well and tracked the pair of them in third place. With every flight of hurdles they negotiated, my confidence grew. Barry seemed happy. Moscow seemed happy. He had dropped the bit and was just cantering along easily within himself all the way along the back straight. He moved up between the two leaders over the fourth last, and flew the third last. Docklands Limo and Carl Llewellyn began to beat a retreat, and Paul Carberry got lower in the saddle on Sausalito Bay. Barry just gently asked Moscow to quicken into the second last. And he did.

He came out of it in front and set sail for home around the final bend. Sausalito Bay had no response to this injection of pace. Moscow really did quicken around the home turn, and Brian's black and white colours went clear.

I had a very similar feeling to the one I'd had at Down Royal as he approached the last. Heart all a-flutter. Just willing him over the final flight and on to the run-in. Jump it, and we're home. And just as he had done at Down Royal, he got from one side to the other without much fuss. Actually, he flew it. Barry pushed him out nice and easily. Just kept him up to his work. Aldino ran on for second place past the beaten Sausalito Bay, but that was just for the academics. There was only one horse in this race.

As I waded through the bodies in the stand on my way back to the winner's enclosure, I also waded through the menagerie of emotions in my mind. Relief and ecstasy, pride and elation. Euphoria, even. A sense of vindication of such magnitude that I had to breathe deeply just to stop my head from exploding. The win had so many implications. We had our horse back, healthy and well. He was as good as we had hoped he was. He had proved himself again and opened up so many options for himself. He could go where he liked now, compete at as high a level as we dared allow him. And we were right to kick on with him. Running him at Punchestown was the right thing to do. Hah. If I could have met the begrudgers on my way down from the stand that day, I would have stuck my finger in their eyes. Every one of them.

I was delighted for Brian, I was delighted for Barry and I was delighted for Eamonn. Not because it was a reward for Eamonn's loyalty in sticking by me when everyone else around us was saying that we should give the horse a break, but because it was a vindication of his judgement as well. Loyalty didn't come into it. He just agreed with me, independently of me, because that was what he felt as well. The fact that we both thought the same thing meant that there was a good chance it was the right course of action. And so it proved.

Thankfully.

Most of all, however, I was delighted for Moscow Flyer. He deserved this. He deserved to be reinstated as top class. He deserved to be included in the conversation when people talked about the best novice hurdlers in Ireland and the UK that season. And he deserved to go into the summer with his reputation restored. But I still don't think he got the recognition he deserved as a novice hurdler. I don't think he was accepted as a true top-class performer in spite of the fact that he won four races out of five including two Grade 1s. It didn't make sense. I suppose the fact that he hadn't been to Cheltenham counted against him. And he hadn't run over Christmas. And every time he won there was an excuse for the favourite. Remarkably, he had beaten an odds-on favourite in all four novice hurdle races that he had won. They couldn't all have had excuses.

We couldn't have been happier going into that summer, however. We knew we had a very, very good horse on our hands. Potentially a serious horse. If we chose to stay hurdling, the Champion Hurdle would be his target. If we wanted to go chasing, he would be geared up for the Arkle. That was the type of horse he was now. It was a great feeling going into the summer with those thoughts.

Autumn could not come quickly enough.

CHAPTER THIRTEEN

THE PEERLESS ISTABRAQ

Moscow Flyer spent the summer of 2000 at David Nugent's place down in Wexford. David owned Slaney Native, who had done very well for him the previous season, winning a good chase at Gowran Park and finishing second to Native Upmanship in the Grade 1 Denny Gold Medal Chase at Leopardstown at Christmas. We had sent Slaney Native to Cheltenham in 2000 where he did OK, finishing seventh to Tiutchev in the Arkle. David has a lovely place in Wexford by the banks of the Slaney river, and I felt it would be good for Moscow to go there with Slaney Native for the summer. It's very relaxed down there. I thought that the change of scenery would do him good.

He came back to Commonstown in early August and Brian came down later that month for our annual meeting. This was a very different meeting to the previous year's. Brian didn't have to ask me this time if I thought he had a good horse. The burning question this year was just how good. The other imponderable this year was whether we should stick to hurdles or send him chasing. He had been bought essentially to be a steeplechaser, but he had shown how good a hurdler he was during his novice season. It was a tough call, but it was one of those really nice decisions with which you are faced all too rarely. There aren't many nice decisions in this profession. Should we risk this horse on ground this fast? Should we try dropping that horse in grade? Should we pin-fire this one? Should we bother continuing with that one? Should we tell the owner he's just useless? These are more the norm. But this decision, hurdling or chasing with a horse who could be a champion at either, or even both? That's a nice decision. That's a should-I-have-a-Kit-Kat-or-a-Crunchie type decision. Mozart or Bach. Red or white.

There were a number of good horses going novice chasing that season. Knife Edge, who had finished third to Istabraq in the AIG Champion Hurdle the previous January, was probably going to go jumping the big black ones. Ross Moff, Al Capone, Well Ridden and Sackville were other potential new recruits to the bigger obstacles. We hadn't even schooled Moscow over a fence at that stage. Although his style of jumping hurdles suggested that he would jump fences well, it was very much a venture into the unknown. So the case for going hurdling for another season was compelling. Even if he had not received due recognition, we felt he had probably been the best novice hurdler in Ireland or England the previous season. If we kept him to the smaller obstacles, he would have to go into the big time. Take on the big guns. No hiding place in the novice ranks any more. It's like graduating from playing junior football to playing in the senior league. You compete against the best. No restrictions.

We had a close look at the top two-mile hurdlers around, and we made a list of the horses we would fear. Istabraq. Full stop. Short list. There was nothing else jumping hurdles then that we thought we couldn't beat. It was unrealistic to expect that we would be able to lower the deep green and gold colours of the nigh invincible Istabraq, but we couldn't run scared of one horse if it meant sacrificing an entire season. The triple champion hurdler's programme only took in certain races. You could name them: the December Festival Hurdle at Leopardstown at Christmas, the AIG Hurdle at Leopardstown at the end of January, and the Champion Hurdle at Cheltenham. Maybe the Shell Hurdle at Punchestown in April afterwards. There were big pots to be picked up in the races he left to the mere equines. And you never know. If we were to catch the great champion on an off day . . . Well, like I say, you just never know.

The decision was unanimous: two in favour, none against. Hurdling it was. Moscow was only six years old, rising seven, and, while he was bought to jump fences, we could afford to spend one more season jumping the smaller obstacles. If it was apparent early on that he wasn't going to be able to make the transition from the novice division, we could always go chasing with him later in the season.

It was with this attitude that we headed to Cork for his seasonal debut in late October 2000. The Grade 2 John James McManus Memorial Hurdle had been moved from Tipperary to Cork because the Limerick Junction venue was waterlogged at the time. I thought it quite ironic that the race was sponsored by J.P. McManus, owner of the one horse we feared. But although Istabraq had won the race the previous season, he wasn't in it this time; they were delaying his seasonal reappearance until Leopardstown at Christmas. JP left it up to Youlneverwalkalone to recoup his sponsorship money. The Michael O'Brien-trained Knife Edge, who would later be bought by JP, was also in the race, along with Pat Hughes' Ladbroke Hurdle winner Mantles Prince.

I was surprised that they made Youlneverwalkalone a warm favourite. Like us, he was a novice from last year having his first go in the big league. He had finished third to Sausalito Bay at Cheltenham; we had beaten Sausalito Bay out of sight at Punchestown. I presume their rationale was that Sausalito Bay was not right when he ran at Punchestown. Just like none of those odds-on shots were right when we beat them. None of the four of them. Where did they think we would have finished had we run in the Supreme Novices' Hurdle at Cheltenham? Obviously they didn't think we'd have finished any closer than third. OK, so we had to give JP's horse 3lb, but that was hardly justification for putting him in at 11–10 favourite and us in at 9–2. Perhaps they felt that JP would want to have his horse fairly straight in order that he could win his own race. But Moscow was straight enough. I didn't want to pitch him in against those experienced hurdlers only half-fit, so we had done a fair amount with him at home before his debut. I was fairly hopeful. At the very least, I thought the race would give us a good indication of where we stood vis-à-vis the more experienced horses.

Nothing went right. The plan was to kick Moscow out of the gate and have him handy the whole way. I didn't mind if we had to make the running ourselves. Some of his most impressive performances as a novice were when he made the running or took it up a long way out. Barry lined up on the tape, but something else was too keen and broke the tape. False start. They all had to come back in again. Moscow was visibly unsettled by this, and Barry wasn't happy on him at all. By the time they lined up again, Moscow was behind a wall of horses and they missed the kick. From then on it was a struggle.

Sometimes jockeys have to play the hand they are dealt. As you can never predict with certainty how a race is going to go, you can never have a rigid plan before a race. You can only plan based on how you think or how you hope a race will go. If it doesn't pan out exactly the same way, it's up to the jockey to improvise. Plan B or C, or just ad-lib. That's their job. That's what you pay them for. I don't blame Barry for missing the kick. That's just one of those things. Had there not been a false start, he probably would have kicked off in front, or very close to the front rank, as planned. But after he missed it he had a decision to make: rush him up to the front straight away and expend valuable energy, or sit and ride him from mid-division? Barry chose the latter.

It's easy now with hindsight to say that it was the wrong thing to do, but even at the time I was concerned. As the field went out on the final circuit behind Saddler's Bay and Knife Edge, I urged Barry to take closer order. Cork is quite a sharp track and the ground was not too testing. I felt that we should be playing more to what I thought was our main strength – stamina. At the third last, Youlneverwalkalone moved up to challenge Knife Edge for the lead and Moscow moved into third place behind them. But that was as far as he got. Knife Edge battled back gamely to repel the challenge of JP's horse, and Moscow kept on for third.

He was right there at the finish, only beaten half a length and three quarters of a length, but there was something wholly frustrating about the race. I felt like I just wanted to stop everything, rewind, and run the race again. My horse had more to give. Much more. It was a bit like the way I'd say the hare felt after the tortoise beat him. Not that Knife Edge or Youlneverwalkalone were tortoises. Far from it. But I just felt we hadn't got to the bottom of Moscow.

Barry got off him in the spot reserved for the third-placed horse and told me that he was very one-paced. That he was only getting going at the end. That he didn't pick up as well as he'd expected him to. I have to say that that didn't do anything to ease my frustration. Not even a little bit. What happened to the plan? What happened to riding him aggressively? Using his stamina? OK, so things went against us at the start, but you can't come in and just tell me flippantly that he was only getting going at the end after deviating from the plan like that. But I bit my tongue. There was no point. I just told Barry that I didn't think it had been one of his best rides. It was enough. Barry knew it even without me saying anything.

In the back of my mind, however, there was a nagging doubt. What if they were right and I was wrong? What if he really wasn't as good as I thought he was? What if he really should be a 9–2 shot to beat Knife Edge and Youlneverwalkalone? I had had him fairly fit for this. It was definitely disappointing. But it was only a nagging doubt. Deep in my guts I felt that we hadn't seen the real Moscow Flyer at Cork.

The Morgiana Hurdle at Punchestown, another Grade 2 race, was a month after the Cork race and provided Moscow with a chance to redeem himself, in my mind as much as in the public's. Barry was suspended, so I booked Paul Moloney for the ride. He was riding mainly for Christy Roche, trainer of Youlneverwalkalone, but we were using him quite a bit at the time as well. The Morgiana Hurdle is usually a very competitive race. It has been won by Back in Front and Limestone Lad in recent years, and Harchibald beat Macs Joy and Back in Front in the race in 2004. However, in 2000 it cut up quite disappointingly. Well, disappointing for the racecourse and the racegoers, but I suppose we weren't complaining too much.

Our chief rival according to the bookmakers was Balla Sola, trained by Willie Mullins, who had won the Red Mills Trial Hurdle at Gowran Park the previous season and had run in the Champion Hurdle at Cheltenham the previous March. Commanche Court was apparently third best, fresh from his Irish Grand National/ Heineken Cup heroics the previous spring, but obviously gearing up for a season of steeplechasing. While we didn't win the race like a 2–5 shot should have, we still won the race. As we now know, Moscow rarely does anything like a 2–5 shot should. He just goes and does it, and he usually just does enough. As much and as little as he can get away with.

We didn't really know that at the time though, and I had mixed feelings about this run. A three-and-a-half-length beating of Samapour was not the stuff of Champion Hurdle aspirants. I made excuses to myself. He had to do a lot of his own donkey work. He was on his own in front for a long way and he probably idled. Horses usually run faster when they have something to race against. Just like a human athlete. You can dig into reserves of energy you may not have thought you had if you are competing against another athlete. Also, the race was run on the inside track at Punchestown, inside the racecourse proper, and there was no atmosphere at all. That might have affected him. He is never impressive on the gallops at home. Maybe he didn't even know he was racing. In addition, the ground was soft and he blew a lot after the race. Maybe he wasn't as fit as I thought he was before the race.

There was enough in all of that to enable me to continue to think Champion Hurdle thoughts. The Champion Hurdle is run over two miles at Cheltenham in March, and it is often won by a horse who possesses as much stamina as he does speed. I suppose this is down to the fact that they go so fast in the Champion, and Cheltenham is such a tough track with all its up hills and down dales, that the race is a true test of a horse's stamina as much as his speed. Istabraq had had the stamina to win the Sun Alliance Hurdle over two miles and five furlongs at Cheltenham as a novice hurdler the year before he won the first of his Champions. They thought that the longer race would play more to his strengths than the Supreme Novices' Hurdle. And it is no coincidence that Hardy Eustace, winner of the last two Champion Hurdles, also won the Sun Alliance as a novice.

The chance to provide Moscow's stamina with the definitive test presented itself in early December. The Hatton's Grace Hurdle at Fairyhouse is a Grade 1 race run over two and a half miles. As such, it can attract both Champion Hurdle and Stayers' (World) Hurdle candidates. It also plays right into the hooves of specialist two-and-a-half-milers like Solerina. The Hatton's Grace roll of honour at that time boasted such luminaries as Istabraq, Limestone Lad, Dorans Pride, Large Action and Danoli. Indeed, it was the race in which Limestone Lad had beaten Istabraq the previous season, on the same day that Moscow had won the Royal Bond Hurdle.

Youlneverwalkalone provided the main opposition. They made him 5–4 and us 6–4; 8–1 and better the others. I thought that was about right. We were racing off level weights and it was hard to tell, based on the evidence we had, which horse was superior. It was a far cry from the 11–10 and 9–2 respectively at Cork, and nothing of consequence had happened in the interim to strengthen either of our hands. Perhaps they were just beginning to recognise my horse as a top performer. Sausalito Bay was in the line-up, but he hadn't run since we beat him at Punchestown, and the vibe from the Meade yard about him wasn't good. Dorans Pride was also there to keep us honest, but the old stager was eleven years old by then and surely vulnerable to a member of the younger brigade.

Moscow Express took them along in the early stages. He was the horse, by Moscow Society, that Hugh Williams had bred out of his Menelek mare Corrielek and sold to Tommy Wade for small money as a two-year-old. He was doing very well for Frances Crowley both over hurdles and over fences at the time. In fact, on his previous outing at Gowran Park he had fallen at the second-last fence when fighting it out with the horse with whom Moscow had spent the previous summer down at David Nugent's, Slaney Native.

Barry was back on Moscow and was happy to sit in behind the leaders. I was happy with this as well. He didn't need to be too aggressive over two and a half miles. He pulled a little in the early stages, but not too much. Conor O'Dwyer sat in last place on Youlneverwalkalone. Barry kept Moscow wide for most of the way in order to give him a sight of his hurdles. As a result, he saw a lot of daylight. He jumped well, but when he jumped a hurdle, he wanted to take off and go faster. Barry had to catch a hold of him on the landing side of every hurdle until they jumped the third last.

When they touched down over the third last, Barry asked Moscow to go on and he stretched impressively. Conor covered the move effortlessly, however. Going to the second last, Barry went for Moscow. He asked him to quicken into it in an effort to run the finish out of Youlneverwalkalone. But Conor hardly had to shake the reins. Youlneverwalkalone moved ahead on the approach to the final flight as Moscow floundered. Barry asked for everything from Moscow, but in truth he had nothing left to give. Youlneverwalkalone popped over the last and stretched away to win by over three lengths. Moscow kept on well enough to finish second, six lengths in front of Dorans Pride in third.

Barry was disappointed. Either the other horse was very, very good, or we just weren't 100 per cent on the day. He wanted to get closer to Youlneverwalkalone, and there was no obvious reason to him why he couldn't. Surprisingly, however, I wasn't too despondent after the race. Not by a long way. It is very easy to keep on making excuses for horses when they get beaten, but you really have to be as honest with yourself and with your owners as you possibly can. There is nothing to be achieved through making up excuses. Clutching at straws. You will have to face reality at some stage. Better sooner than later. If you think there is a genuine reason for a defeat, say it, and do what you can to change it for the next time. If you can see no specific reason, admit that you just weren't good enough and move on.

Moscow had looked slow from the back of the last hurdle. When a horse looks slow at the end of a race, it can be down to either a lack of speed or a lack of stamina. Either he didn't have the speed to quicken or he didn't have the stamina to keep on strongly to the line. I knew he wasn't slow; he had proved he had speed during his novice year. But this was his first real attempt at two and a half miles. The pace was strong and the ground was soft. QED. There was a good chance he just wasn't strong enough to fully stay the two-and-a-half-mile trip.

They were talking about Youlneverwalkalone as a successor to Istabraq. For me, he had beaten us in the Hatton's Grace through superior stamina. At two miles, we were travelling just as well as the winner. If he was going to succeed Istabraq, we had every right to be in there pitching. We knew that Istabraq's seasonal debut was going to be in the December Festival Hurdle at Leopardstown's Christmas festival. In spite of that, we decided that that was where Moscow should go next. There really wasn't an alternative. He belonged among the top-flight two-mile hurdlers, and the Festival Hurdle was where the top-flight two-mile hurdlers should go.

There are only a finite number of races for the top two-mile hurdlers in the run-up to Cheltenham: the Festival Hurdle, the AIG, possibly the Red Mills Trial Hurdle at Gowran Park, and then Cheltenham. After that there's Aintree, although the race there is over two and a half, and then Punchestown. The programme picks itself. Either you stay in your box or you run in those races. I was never one to leave a horse in his box when he could be running, and if we were going to go for the Champion Hurdle we were going to have to face Istabraq at some stage.

The ground at Leopardstown's Christmas festival meeting that year was atrocious. They raced on St Stephen's Day, the Tuesday, and the Wednesday, didn't race on the Thursday, the Friday or the Saturday, and came back on the Sunday, New Year's Eve, for the final day. December Festival Hurdle day. It rained and hailed all Saturday night and all Sunday morning. By the time we got to Leopardstown I was sure racing would be called off. The weather was really terrible and the ground was desperate. I would say that if it had been an ordinary day's racing, there is no way it would have gone ahead. I never really considered pulling Moscow out of the race, though. While he had never encountered ground this heavy before, he had won on very soft ground and he was very fit. I was sure Aidan O'Brien would take Istabraq out. It was his seasonal debut and he couldn't have been fully wound up. But, fair play to Aidan and to JP, Istabraq stood his ground. Our old friends Stage Affair and Mantles Prince also stood their ground, and it was race on. Remarkably, they put Istabraq in as the 1–4 favourite. No horse should have been that short on ground this bad, especially not one making his seasonal debut.

Aerleon Pete was in there to make the pace for Istabraq, but he never got to the front. Topacio took them along at a good pace for the day. You could actually see them splashing through the puddles as they went up the side of the course, across the sprint track and halfway down the back straight. This was always going to be a war of attrition. Moscow and Barry sat in third place, just behind Topacio and Aerleon Pete, while Istabraq and Charlie Swan tracked them in fourth.

At the fourth-last flight, Istabraq made a slight mistake. He almost overjumped, and Charlie became unbalanced at the back of the obstacle. It was the wrong time to make it as the pace was just beginning to quicken. It also put a small dent in the champion's shroud of invincibility. We had a chance here.

Moscow went into second place ahead of Aerleon Pete and behind Topacio. Mantles Prince and Stage Affair took closer order in behind, and Istabraq got back on an even keel. At the second last, Moscow, Stage Affair and Mantles Prince all went on from Topacio: Moscow went outside Topacio, Mantles Prince got inside Moscow, and Stage Affair went outside. As Topacio drifted off the rail, Istabraq got a dream run up the inside. Moscow was three wide going around the home turn. Far from ideal.

Topacio faded, and the four adversaries faced up to the final flight and the winning post beyond. From the rail out, Istabraq, Mantles Prince, Moscow Flyer and Stage Affair. If you stopped the video there on the approach to the last – and I have, many times since – you would think that Moscow was booked for third or fourth. Stage Affair took it up going to the last and looked to be going on strongly. Charlie was just beginning to get after Istabraq on the rail. Mantles Prince seemed to be back-pedalling, and Moscow was fourth but staying on. If you had had a large horse blanket, you could have covered the four of them with it.

I knew my horse stayed this two-mile trip really well. It looked for a few strides as if Moscow was going to be squeezed out of it as Mantles Prince and Stage Affair came close together, but Barry asked him to be strong going to the last, and he was. They were almost walking now as the ground sapped the energy out of all four of them. Charlie asked Istabraq to pick up, but he put down. Dramatically, the champion stepped on the hurdle and hit the deck. The fall of a tired horse. A huge gasp issued from the main grandstand as Istabraq rolled over just in front of it. It all happened in an instant. One moment we were fourth and looking like we might not be involved in the finish at all, a split second later we were in front. Stage Affair and Mantles Prince had both got in close to the last, and Moscow had flown it. Before Charlie had stopped rolling, Barry was stoking Moscow up the final climb.

It's a strange feeling when one of your rivals takes a tumble. Of course your competitive spirit determines that there should be a sense of joy when your chance of success is enhanced. But it is tempered with a sense of anguish. You hope they are OK. You never like to see one fall because you know what it's like yourself. There's always a danger that when something falls it will not rise again. Ideally you'd beat them on merit with no mishap. My sense of anguish was maximised for Istabraq. As was the case, I am sure, for most people at Leopardstown that day. Hence the gasp when he came down. It was at once a gasp of surprise and a gasp of concern for the champion's well-being.

I took my binoculars down and was able to alternate my gaze between Moscow slogging it out on the run-in with Stage Affair and Mantles Prince, and the stricken Istabraq. I willed Moscow on to the line and I willed the champion to his feet. By the time Moscow had got to the winning post, exhausted but elated, two lengths in front of Stage Affair, Istabraq was up on his feet. It was as if he didn't want to be seen on the ground. Not here. Not in front of the stands. In front of his adoring public. It's OK. I'm all right. Nothing to see here.

It was a great feeling to have won the Festival Hurdle. A great sense of achievement. Although it was only a Grade 2 race back then – it became a Grade 1 race in 2002 – we had still beaten the best two-mile hurdlers in Ireland at the time. Moscow Flyer had proved that he deserved his place among them, and that he deserved to be trained for the Champion Hurdle.

There was still something unsatisfactory and unfinished about the race, though. Firstly, Istabraq had fallen. We had not beaten him wholly on merit. Istabraq's fall generated more column inches the following day than Moscow Flyer's win. Even the race analysis in the *Racing Post* devoted more space to Istabraq than it did to the winner. The general vibe was that we would have beaten Istabraq anyway, but nobody was saying as much. Or if they were, they were speaking in hushed tones. Secondly, the ground really was atrocious at Leopardstown. They said that it hadn't suited Istabraq at all, and it hadn't suited Stage Affair. What they failed to realise at the time was that it hadn't suited Moscow Flyer either. He had prevailed in spite of the ground, not because of it.

Moscow was tired when we got him home that evening. Tired, but healthy and satisfied. It had been a real grueller of a race, but he had won it. You could tell as much by his entire demeanour. He walked with a positive step. They know when they win. When they have done something to make you proud. Moscow knew it that evening, and he felt very proud himself. It was a feeling he would have to get used to.

And I was proud of him. He had shown courage, tenacity, speed and stamina to get home in the Festival Hurdle. He had done it against older and more experienced horses. We were into the big league now. That was for sure. And we deserved our place in it.

CHAPTER FOURTEEN

SILENCED BY THE LAMBS

We had only three weeks after the Festival Hurdle to prepare for the AIG Europe Champion Hurdle back at Leopardstown in January 2001. But it was enough, and anyway, there was no way we were going to miss it. All the top two-mile hurdlers in Ireland would be lining up for this one. Including Istabraq, on a setting-straight-the-record mission. Brian and Patricia were going to be in Tenerife for the race, which was a shame, but they had organised the trip before they realised that it clashed with the AIG. Brian knew that there were quite a few racing pubs in Tenerife however, so at least they would be able to watch the race.

This was Moscow's chance to win his first Grade 1 race out of novice class. I remember thinking that if he won this, he would have to get the accolades he deserved, the praise that had been, up to now, somewhat unenthusiastically offered to him rather than heaped upon him as one might have expected.

He couldn't miss this one. Not if he was healthy and well.

He was. Very healthy and very well. His appetite for racing and continued soundness and well-being was something that always amazed me throughout his career. He had a little bit of trouble with his feet during those three weeks, though. He actually has four white feet. We put this special paint on his soles in order to harden them up, which seemed to work very well. We still do that. We couldn't gallop him because of his sore feet during those three weeks, so he did a lot of swimming. There are people who say that if horses were meant to swim they would have webbed feet, but I think swimming is a fine substitute when you can't gallop them. It was ideal for Moscow during those three weeks. It meant that we were able to keep him fit and look after his feet at the same time.

We decided that we would help Moscow in the AIG by running Have Merci in order to ensure that there would be a decent pace. I noted that Christy Roche had entered Aerleon Pete – JP-owned – again. He had tried to make the running for Istabraq in the Festival Hurdle, and would probably do so again. But Moscow really needed a fast pace and I thought I wouldn't leave anything to chance. Have Merci, who was owned by former Rolling Stone Ron Wood, loved bowling along in front and I had no doubt that she had the pace to lead even these top two-mile hurdlers to the second last. As a bonus, there was a chance that she would keep on well enough to finish in the first three. If she managed to do that, she would gain black type. I patted myself on the back. Such astuteness!

The plan was for Paul Moloney to send Have Merci into the lead from flagfall. Barry would track them on Moscow. At the second last, Paul would move one horse-width off the rail and allow Barry up the inside. The second-last flight of hurdles at Leopardstown is on the crown of the home turn. If Istabraq was challenging at that stage, he would have to come at least three wide. He would lose several lengths on Moscow if he was three deep. If Charlie decided not to go three wide, he would have to track Moscow through and we would have first run on him. Whichever way it panned out, it would be to our advantage. I don't know if Sheikh Mohammed was watching the AIG Europe Champion Hurdle that January, but he employed the exact same tactics later that year in the Irish Champion Stakes on the same track. Give the Slip led under Richard Hills, moved off the rail on the crown of the home turn and allowed Dettori up the inside on Fantastic Light. Kinane had to deliver his challenge three wide on Galileo. I don't know if it made the difference between victory and defeat, but Galileo sacrificed at least two lengths by going wide and there was only a head in it at the line.

The ground at Leopardstown on AIG day was not as heavy as it had been on Festival Hurdle day – I would say that few race meetings have taken place on ground as heavy as it was on Festival Hurdle day – but it was still genuinely soft. Istabraq was there all right. Two lads leading him round the parade ring. The usual. He looked fitter than he had looked just three weeks earlier. Not that he had looked big then, but his muscles just looked a little tighter today. Ready for the battle that was to ensue.

Amazingly, Stage Affair was made second favourite behind Istabraq. Moscow was only third in the betting. I often don't even notice how they bet before one of mine runs, but at Leopardstown they display the betting on a wooden board just beside the parade ring. You can't miss it. I couldn't believe that Moscow was a bigger price than Stage Affair. He'd beaten him hands down over the same course and distance just three weeks earlier. Nothing had changed in the interim. It shouldn't have annoyed me, but it did. Just a little. It all came back to the recognition that Moscow was or wasn't getting. Up to that point, we had met Stage Affair twice and we had beaten him twice, albeit on soft ground both times. There was no reason why Stage Affair should have been a shorter price. It may have been down to the fact that Stage Affair had D.K. Weld down in the trainer's column, while Moscow was lumbered with a Mrs John Harrington. Or it may have been because they thought that Moscow was only a mudlark. Some mudlark.

I have my different viewing spots at different racecourses. Lucky spots. I'm quite superstitious like that. At Leopardstown, my spot of choice is the owners' and trainers' stand. It is easy to get to and from the parade ring, and it is easy to get from there to the unsaddling area and, on the good days, the winner's enclosure. Also, it is rarely too crowded and there is excellent viewing from it. I took up my position there and watched as they lined up just to my left.

The race went exactly according to the script. Have Merci led from the start. Aerleon Pete tried to match her for pace in the early stages, but he couldn't, so Fran Berry just allowed him to stride along in second place. Moscow sat on the inside in third. Istabraq was fourth. They went down the back straight in formation. Mantles Prince, Stage Affair and Penny Rich whipped them in. Moscow got in tight to the third last and Barry had to ride him out of it. He lost some momentum, and Istabraq closed up to within a length.

Going to the second last, Aerleon Pete began to weaken. Barry sent Moscow into second place on the inside, just behind Have Merci. Paul Moloney had a little look behind. He saw Moscow on his inside, and he moved out. Just a touch, but enough to make room for Moscow between him and the inside wing of the second-last flight. Istabraq was going outside Moscow, and therefore, as Have Merci moved out, he had to go outside her as well in order to get a view of the obstacle. Just as we had planned. Istabraq was three wide going into the wings of the second last.

They were tanking along now. Probably going as fast as they go in a two-mile hurdle on soft ground. Moscow squeezed up the inside of Have Merci going to the second last. Barry saw a stride. One, two, up! In reality, he was taking off half a stride too early. If he had made it to the far side of the obstacle upright, he would have landed about two lengths clear and would have been in prime position. It would have taken a big effort from Istabraq to catch him then. If Barry had taken him back and asked him to pop the hurdle, he would have lost all momentum and probably would have come out of the back of the hurdle a half-length or a length down. It was as broad as it was long. Six of one and half a dozen of the other. And other clichés. If you are half a stride too far off for a long one, you are half a stride too close for a short one. That's the way it works. Then it's a judgement call. It's up to the jockey to decide. Long or short. You make the decision in an instant and you stick with it. Make the right one and you're a hero; make the wrong one and you're on your arse.

As it happened, in my view Barry made the right decision. The winning of the race was right there. Go long and make Istabraq use up his energy to get on terms, then kick off the last bend. Keep the inside rail. Moscow sees out this two-mile trip on this soft ground very well. It would take an exceptional one to get past. But Moscow just wasn't sure at the second last. It was as if I was watching in slow motion. I knew he was just too far off. There was a chance he wouldn't make it, but there was a good chance he would. This racing business is not an exact science. Far from it. Be brave, and fortune will generally favour you.

Not this time however. If Moscow had jumped with conviction, he would have made it. But he wasn't certain, and that made the difference. Both of his forelegs caught the top of the hurdle. Just by inches. Half a foot closer for take-off or half a foot higher and he would have sailed over it. But inches are crucial in this inexact non-science. When a horse is reaching for an obstacle as Moscow was, if he clips the top of said obstacle there can only be one outcome. Gravity will out.

It was a crashing fall. A really horrible one. The horse hit the deck, and Barry followed, Jack and Jill-like. They both skidded along the ground in unison before coming to a halt about 20 yards beyond the obstacle. Moscow got to his feet quickly. The brave ones always do. But then something unusual: he stood still. Usually they gallop off in pursuit of the others. They are herding creatures, and the majority like to gallop with companions. I stared in horror as I saw something hanging from the horse. I was sure it was his leg. That his off-hind leg was hanging off him.

You know when you think that something really awful is happening, and then it doesn't? Like if you are driving and sending a text message at the same time, and suddenly you notice that you are heading straight for the ditch or straight into the car in front of you, but you don't. You manage to break or swerve just at the last minute. Your heart gives a sudden leap of horror, followed by a just-as-sudden descent into calm, so that you actually feel a physical pain in your chest. That was what happened to me that day as I trained my binoculars on the second-last flight of hurdles.

It is difficult to see the ground after the second-last flight from the owners' and trainers' stand. There are rails in your way and there were cameramen and people all around it. But within less than a second of thinking that it was Moscow's off-hind that was hanging to the ground, I realised that it was actually Barry. His left foot had got caught in the stirrup and he was strung up for an awful moment. I have to admit that my first feeling when I realised this was one of immense relief. Relief that all four of the horse's limbs seemed to be intact. As soon as my overriding fear switched to one of concern for Barry, his leg came free and Moscow trotted off. Barry reckons that the horse was looking after him, that he didn't canter off because he knew Barry was still attached to him. I wouldn't challenge that theory at all.

By the time I came back to the present, people around me were clapping appreciatively. I looked down below me and saw Charlie beaming from ear to ear as Istabraq sauntered up to the winning line underneath him. I clapped as well. Almost in a daze. People around me were asking if Moscow was OK. I just said, 'I don't know.' He appeared to be. Was I the only one in the stand with binoculars? Mantles Prince got the better of Penny Rich for second, and Stage Affair finished fourth. Have Merci trailed in fifth. I found out later that Have Merci had almost been brought down at the second last when she tried to jump over Barry as he was fired to the ground. That was never in the plan. Fortunately, Barry was all right.

In Tenerife, Brian and Patricia had managed to find a telly in a Rangers bar that was showing the race. They were there with Paddy and Helen Cole. Just the four of them, watching the race. It was fairly traumatic for Brian. He had never seen his horse fall before, and for him to have such a horrible-looking fall on the one day when Brian wasn't at the races was difficult for him.

I was disappointed. I really was. I had thought before the race that we had a definite chance of beating Istabraq. Going to the second last I was convinced that if we jumped it we would beat him. It's hard to know now how it would have panned out. Istabraq won the race very easily. But I would have been disappointed had we not beaten Mantles Prince just as easily on the day. I am sure it would have been one hell of a tussle. Charlie Swan said afterwards that he wasn't sure. He thought he was going well, but he wasn't sure how it would have panned out. He couldn't say that he wasn't happy to see Moscow hit the deck.

But though I was disappointed, I was also terribly relieved that my horse was able to walk back into his horsebox. You hear trainers saying that they just want their horses to come back safely, and that anything more would be a bonus. Sometimes it can sound very insincere. And I have no doubt that sometimes it is. But this time I could really appreciate those sentiments. Given the chance, would I rewind time and go back to the second-last flight? Would I take the chance that he would either make the jump and land two lengths clear or land in a heap again as he did and run the risk of serious injury? The answer is an emphatic no. I would take my horse home in his box, vanquished but upright, every time.

Moscow was fairly sore when we got him home. Nothing serious at all, thank God, just generally sore and sorry for himself. Nothing that would prevent us getting him ready to run for his life in the Champion Hurdle at Cheltenham in mid-March.

We had now met Istabraq twice. One fall each, one win each. The next encounter was going to take place in the Cotswolds. There could not be a more appropriate amphitheatre for the title decider. It was going to be a home game for the title holder, that was for sure. He would be going for an unprecedented four in a row. He was going to have the home crowd and the away crowd on his side. Moscow would be the challenger, the upstart who would be trying to deprive the reigning champ of that to which he had a rightful claim. Trying to deprive everybody present of his or her own little piece of history. Red Rum v. Crisp. Ardross v. Le Moss. It would be difficult to drum up much support.

I was sitting in my kitchen when I first heard about a suspicion of an outbreak of foot and mouth disease in the UK. I very quickly realised the potential implications for the transport of humans and horses, and for racing. I vividly remembered the last outbreak, back in the late 1960s when I was going out with David and couldn't go over to England to see him.

The realisation dawned as the disease was confirmed in a number of different locations. In Ireland, it was like telling a barn full of scarecrows that there was a bush fire in the adjoining field. Anything that can potentially damage the agriculture industry is treated very seriously indeed. Correctly so. The measures and restrictions introduced in Ireland may have been draconian, but it was undoubtedly the right thing to do. Even though it was a real pain at the time, I still thought we were going about it the best way. Everybody seemed to pull together because everybody was aware that if foot and mouth got into Ireland, it would devastate so many people's lives. Even the urban community seemed to appreciate it. So many people in Ireland are dependent on farming for their livelihood.

Ultimately, the restrictions proved to be successful in preventing the disease from getting into the country. With the exception of a very small area of a Carlingford peninsula in the north-east, where it was detected very early and immediately curtailed, Ireland remained foot and mouth free. But the implications for racing were far-reaching. Racing was suspended and the transport of horses was severely restricted. There was some long and heated debate about Cheltenham. Eventually we took the decision in the trainers' association that if the Cheltenham Festival were to go ahead, we would not send any horses.

I was the trainers' representative on the board of the Irish Horseracing Authority at the time. It was an extremely difficult decision to make and to support, with a Champion Hurdle contender at home in the yard. I knew it was the right one for Irish racing – it was the only logical option open to us – but everyone was gutted. I was gutted. Brian was gutted. Cheltenham was his Holy Grail. His *raison d'ownership*. He had a horse good enough to go there that year, and the opportunity was being whisked away. In the context of the foot and mouth disease and the danger it posed to people's livelihoods, the disappointment of an owner not being able to go to Cheltenham was almost negligible. Brian appreciated that. Nevertheless, it was disappointing for all of us. It was like showing a child a box of chocolates and then putting it up on a shelf where it can't be reached.

Racing in the UK didn't stop. They suspended for a week from 27 February to 6 March and kicked on again. Rural courses like Taunton abandoned their meetings themselves, but the urban racecourses like Lingfield and Wolverhampton went ahead. The Jockey Club, rather bizarrely, deemed that racing was not contributing to the spread of the disease. Crucially, the Cheltenham Festival too was going ahead. I used to wake up with a hole in my stomach those mornings thinking of Cheltenham going ahead without the Irish. Without Moscow Flyer. It was the same feeling of frustration I'd had when I wasn't allowed go to the Moscow Olympics in 1980. Only much, much worse. People were tearing their hair out. Racing was cancelled in Ireland and people didn't really know when it would resume. I, of course, was thinking about Moscow Flyer, but the racing public was thinking about Istabraq. It was such a shame that he would not be able to go for his historic four in a row, that something else would claim his title in his absence.

Then, with six days to go to the start of the Festival, the news came through that it would be postponed. Under MAFF risk assessment guidelines, any area that had had farm animals grazing on it was considered high risk for 28 days after they had left, and Cheltenham had had a few sheep on it up until 26 days before the Festival. I remember the headline in the *Racing Post* that morning:

'Silenced by the Lambs'. It was one of the cleverest headlines of the year. It was probably not very sporting of me, but I have to say I was absolutely thrilled. It was the best news – OK, so there wasn't much competition – that I had had all spring. If Moscow wasn't allowed to contest the Champion Hurdle, I was quite satisfied that nobody else was allowed to win it. Any victory at Cheltenham that year would have been a hollow victory anyway. Like all those gold medals the Eastern Bloc countries won in 1980. Cheltenham without the Irish was difficult to imagine. Think of banoffee pie without the banana.

The Festival was initially postponed until late April, but shortly afterwards the disease was discovered within fifteen miles of the racecourse and it was abandoned completely. They were strange days. Every day you'd turn on the news and hear about a new outbreak or a new suspected case. Those pictures of the carcass pyres in the UK are difficult to forget.

We had a few dramas ourselves. We had sheep at Commonstown. I wanted to get them slaughtered in case, when we resumed racing, there would be a rule that horses who had come into contact with sheep wouldn't be allowed to travel to the races. But I couldn't get a lorry to take them to the abattoir as the lorries weren't allowed to move. Eventually I managed to get a trailer on loan and got them taken away.

Johnny had four barren mares at the time. I had heard that there was going to be a restriction on the movement of horses, so we needed to get them covered straight away. We wanted to have foals out of them the following year. You'd look pretty foolish if you had four mares who weren't in foal come next spring. How come you have four barren mares? Oh well, we couldn't cover them because of the foot and mouth restrictions. The ban was coming in at five o'clock. I remember getting into the lorry at four o'clock and driving the mares down to Rathbarry Stud to get them covered. I just left them there and stayed in a bed and breakfast down there that night. It was a bit of a rush, but at least we got the mares covered.

It was a tough time for everyone – trainers, riders and staff. There was no racing, but we still had bills to pay. I was lucky as only one of my owners took his horses home. We had to keep the horses ticking over because we weren't really sure when racing would resume. But the yard got a good old clean-up as well. We washed, painted, and gave the garden a short back and sides. And there was something unusually nice about that time as well. I had a lunch party every Sunday during the foot and mouth outbreak. There was no racing, no show-jumping and no eventing, so people were at a loss for something to do on Sunday afternoons. Life became what most people would consider to be normal for a few weeks.

And things would get back to normal for us. We knew that they would, and we had to be ready for that. That is, if normal is having one of the most exciting hurdlers in the country in your yard. If normal is planning his campaign. If normal is dreaming that he might turn out to be a racehorse that will capture people's imagination like few others have in a generation.

CHAPTER FIFTEEN

THE DECIDER

When racing resumed after the foot and mouth crisis, we still had to be very vigilant. You had to have a permit to move a horse which you had to get stamped at the police station. You had to wash the inside and outside of your lorry before you went racing, and you weren't allowed any bedding. The wheels were disinfected on the way into the tracks. It was strange going into the stables at the races seeing all these clean lorries! Interestingly, we got into the habit of cleaning our lorries before going racing, and we still do that today.

We decided that we would run Moscow as soon as we could after racing resumed. We had kept him fit enough during the foot and mouth weeks and the plan was to have him at his peak for the Shell Champion Hurdle at the end of April. Moscow was, of course, the shining beacon of the stable at the time, but he wasn't the only nice horse we had. Bust Out had won two bumpers and a maiden hurdle, and had run Ned Kelly close in a Grade 2 hurdle at Leopardstown over Christmas. He was an exciting prospect. Spirit Leader was just getting going at the time as well. She had only finished fourth in both her races up to that point, a bumper and a hurdle, but we thought she was quite nice.

The Irish racing calendar was all askew in the spring of 2001. The Easter (Grand National) meeting at Fairyhouse had been postponed until the beginning of May. That was also the year that Punchestown couldn't host their festival because they had had problems with the track. Most of the Punchestown Festival was therefore staged at Fairyhouse, with the last day – Shell Champion Hurdle day – held at Leopardstown. So we had this bizarre situation where the Punchestown Festival was run at Fairyhouse just a week before the Easter meeting was run, also at Fairyhouse.

There was a good two-and-a-quarter-mile hurdle at Gowran Park nine days before the Shell race. Ideally there would have been a longer gap between the two, but we were glad that we were at least going to get a run into Moscow. It wasn't a graded race so, as a Grade 1 winner, he had to give lumps of weight away to everything. We were giving 10lb to old adversary Mantles Prince, who looked like the main danger, although I was happy that we would be able to give him the weight. Noel Meade had a nice horse called Nomadic, who looked like he might be good, and Ted Walsh ran Colonel Yeager, who had been a top-class novice two seasons earlier but was having his first run in two years.

Moscow set out to make it all. That was the plan. I thought he was fairly straight and that we could make his class and stamina tell. No dithering around with a muddling pace that might play into the hands of some of his less-fit rivals. It can be hard to carry twelve stone on the softish, sticky ground that prevailed at Gowran, but I still thought we would win.

By the time Moscow and Barry got over the third-last flight, top weight or no top weight, they had burned off all their rivals except one. Colonel Yeager was stubbornly refusing to go away. I wasn't worried about him as they went up by the winning post for the first time, or when they went down the back straight. I did notice that he was travelling well, but it was his first run in two years and there was no way he was going to be fit enough to win this, even if we were carrying 10lb more weight than he was. Consequently, in looking for dangers during the race, as you do, I was watching the others. You can do this easily when your own horse is in front. You watch as your horse approaches the obstacle. You hold your breath. Up and over. Then you breathe a little sigh of relief and stay focused on the obstacle as the others stream over. I watched Mantles Prince and Nomadic mainly. I watched as they both came under pressure and began to retreat.

As they approached the second last, however, I began to focus on Colonel Yeager. I couldn't but. I watched him and waited for Ruby Walsh to get into the drive position. Lack of a recent run was bound to tell up the home straight. And it did. Only not on Colonel Yeager. I looked on in mild surprise and with not an insignificant degree of anguish as Barry was the first one to begin applying the pressure. Over the second last, and Barry got serious with Moscow as Ruby just nudged Colonel Yeager into the bit. By the time they got to the final flight, the game was up. Colonel Yeager had taken the lead and Moscow was treading water. Moscow clobbered the last. Tired horses do that sometimes. He did well just to remain upright, and Barry did well to stay on his back. I was thankful for that. Ruby just pushed Colonel Yeager home, hands and heels, as Barry got Moscow going again to take second spot. There were fifteen lengths back to Nomadic in third.

I was disappointed after the defeat, but I wasn't completely disconsolate. If you took Colonel Yeager out of the race, it was a very good performance, beating Nomadic and Mantles Prince by fifteen lengths and giving both of them 10lb. And Colonel Yeager could be a superstar in the making. He had finished a good fourth to Hors La Loi III in the 1999 Supreme Novices' Hurdle at Cheltenham. To go down by just over four lengths to him while conceding 10lb could turn out to be a hell of a performance.

The ground was soft, and Moscow was carrying twelve stone. The softer the ground the bigger the handicap each extra piece of lead in your saddle is. He had been off the track for three months and I had probably left him a little bit short of work for this as I didn't want to over-cook him for the Shell Champion Hurdle. So I actually left Gowran Park that day in relatively buoyant form. Especially as our little mare Spirit Leader won the last, the bumper, beating a horse of Willie Mullins' who had finished second on his only previous start by fifteen lengths. That horse was called Hedgehunter.

That Gowran race was over two and a quarter miles, and it was only in the last two furlongs that Moscow got really tired. Stop the race at two miles and he was travelling at least as well as Colonel Yeager. More and more I was coming round to the idea that two miles was Moscow's optimum distance. I didn't have to wait long to test that hypothesis, because the Shell Champion Hurdle was only nine days later at Leopardstown. Moscow was tired after his Gowran exertions, but we got him home fine and we were able to freshen him up. It would have been a completely different story had he come down at the last flight of hurdles at Gowran. At best he would have been sore. There might not have been enough time in nine days to get him ready for Leopardstown, and there were no other races for him that season. So he would have been going out for the summer with unfinished business. It would have been totally unsatisfactory. I was thankful that he was getting the chance to run again before the season ended.

If the AIG was 'Istabraq Returns', then the Shell Champion Hurdle was 'Istabraq Forever'. Not that the similarities between Istabraq and Batman ended there. Both thrived on being friends of the people and both had an air of invincibility about them. And of course, both of them had their Boy Wonders. Charlie Swan even wore green and gold, just like Robin. However the marketing people chose to present it, the Shell Champion Hurdle was the third meeting between Istabraq and Moscow Flyer in four months. One win and one fall each. Robbed of the title decider at

Cheltenham, it was appropriate that the third meeting should take place at Leopardstown, over the same course and distance as the previous two.

Moscow was up for this one. They both were. They had both been kept ticking over to be ready just in case the Champion Hurdle could be staged. Moscow had had a run at Gowran Park, but Aidan O'Brien had proved that he was well able to get one ready at home.

Somewhat unusually for the end of April, the ground was very soft again at Leopardstown. I would have loved to have taken on Istabraq on good ground. I believed that Moscow was at his best on genuine good ground, and all the indications were that Istabraq was too. But that's the way it is with racing: you have to play the hand you are dealt. We were both equally disadvantaged.

We decided that we would make plenty of use of Moscow again. He seemed to enjoy himself when he was being ridden up with the pace. He stayed two miles very well, and he had the benefit of a run under his belt. Istabraq was coming into this one without a race since the AIG at the end of January. If Aidan had left even one screw untightened, we were determined to find it.

Aerleon Pete set out to make the running, as Aerleon Pete usually did when Istabraq was competing. Barry sent Moscow up · to race with the leader straight away. It was a clever move by Barry. If he had left Conor O'Dwyer on his own in front on Aerleon Pete, he would be able to dictate the pace of the race. Invariably it would be set at a pace that would suit Istabraq. With Moscow up alongside, Barry would be able to set the pace. If Conor wanted to take him on for the lead, he would have to go at Barry's pace. If he didn't, Moscow could lead on his own. No problem. Conor did want to take us on – his instructions, I would say, were to lead and not allow Moscow to get things his own way – and the two went stride for stride down past the stands, up the side of the course and down the back straight. Charlie Swan tracked the two leaders in third place on Istabraq, anxious not to allow Moscow to get too far ahead of him. It can be difficult to make up ground when the going is as soft as it was that day. Mantles Prince and Colonel Yeager sat fourth and fifth respectively.

At the fourth-last flight, the second last in the back straight, Barry decided that he wanted to go a little faster. Aerleon Pete couldn't match the move and Moscow was in front on his own. Istabraq covered the move. Over the third last, and turn out of the back straight. Barry asked his willing partner to go faster. Moscow complied. Charlie squeezed his legs on Istabraq, and noticeably went up a gear.

I pressed my binoculars hard to my eyes as they approached the second last. Moscow in front, chased by Istabraq. The two going clear of the rest. I probably held my breath. This was the flight at which he had come a cropper in January. Just jump it. Don't stand off too far. Just pop it. Barry was going for almost everything now, trying to run the finishing kick out of his pursuer. It looked like he was meeting the obstacle in his stride.

One, two, up!

He jumped it well and landed running. I exhaled. But Istabraq had sailed over the obstacle on the outside and Charlie had barely moved. Charlie crouched a little lower, and Istabraq went up another gear. Moscow had been in top gear from before the second last. Istabraq glided around the home turn upsides. A cheer went up from the people in the grandstand as Dessie Scahill told them as much over the PA system. Could they not see it for themselves?

Moscow and Istabraq matched strides on the run to the last, Barry flat to the boards on the rails, Charlie standing up in his irons on the stands side. Charlie hadn't gone for Istabraq yet, but he hadn't sailed past Moscow either. We still had a chance. Istabraq may have gone a head or a neck up approaching the last. That was all. He looked to be travelling more easily all right, but it's a long pull from the last up to the winning line, and Moscow finds lots. There was a tiny chink of light in this one yet.

Charlie eyed up the obstacle as he approached it. It was just the same as the previous seven. In fact, they had already jumped this one first time round. Same dimensions as all the others. Same shape, same structure, same technique required to get over it. One, two, pop. That's all we need to do. There's a stride. One, two . . . Charlie went to pop. Istabraq went to pop. Then, somehow and inexplicably – these things are frequently inexplicable when they go wrong – the horse changed his mind. It may have been because he remembered falling at the same obstacle in December, or it may have been because he felt he was under a little bit of pressure from the horse to his left. Or it may have been that he just lost his concentration for a split second. Whatever the reason, he seemed to try to alter his trajectory mid-flight. Halfway through the jump, he tried to go short instead of long.

It is the worst thing a horse can do. It would be like if you were jumping over a chasm and half way through your jump you decide that you actually want to put in another stride before you take off. Only one possible result. A flight of hurdles is angled diagonally up from the ground away from the take-off side so that horses are encouraged to take off before they can get in underneath it. Istabraq's forelegs hit the middle of the obstacle. He almost stood on top of it. The hurdle came crashing to the ground and horse and jockey followed.

It was a case of *déjà vu*. We've been here before. The same gasp went up from the stands as had gone up in December. The same sensational exclamation from the commentator. I had the same sickly feeling. The same mixture of emotions. My insides were all a-whirl as Moscow scampered away up the run-in. Istabraq stopped rolling and sprang to his feet. Charlie did likewise. It could have been the Festival Hurdle all over again. As if the horse didn't want to be seen on the ground in front of the stands. Not again.

There were a few key differences between the Shell Hurdle and the Festival Hurdle, however. Whereas in the Festival Hurdle it looked like Istabraq might finish fourth, this time he was the most likely winner. No question. But post-race reports suggested that he had the race in the bag and that all he had to do was get to the far side of the last obstacle to collect. I'm not so sure about that. Charlie hadn't gone for Istabraq before they came to the final flight, but he wasn't going away from Moscow. I'm not convinced that Moscow wouldn't have got back after him up the hill. Why does a horse fall? Bad jumper? Tiredness? Lack of concentration? Too much pressure? Istabraq was not a bad jumper, so it was one, or a combination, of the last three. If he was tired, then Moscow would have come back at him. If he was being put under pressure, it was Moscow who was doing it. No other horse was able to put the champion under that sort of pressure. The second difference between this race and the Festival Hurdle was that, this time, Istabraq and Moscow were clear of the rest. Colonel Yeager finished second, seven lengths behind Moscow. Over two miles and off level weights, Moscow had beaten him hands down.

It was another unfinished chapter in the Istabraq v. Moscow Flyer saga, but we were quite understandably delighted. It was Moscow's first Grade 1 win outside of the novice division. We could only wonder what would have happened had there been no foot and mouth that year, had we been able to take on Istabraq in the Champion Hurdle. Conditions would have been completely different. Good ground, and Cheltenham. The hype, the furore, the pressure and the pace that is unique to the Cheltenham Festival. We knew at the time that Istabraq revelled in the Cheltenham cauldron. What we didn't know at the time was that Moscow would as well.

It is quite remarkable that Moscow met Istabraq three times and on none of those occasions did both horses complete the course. On the one hand, that is a wholly unsatisfactory way to leave things. On the other, however, there is something satisfying in the inconclusiveness of it all.

Moscow was the only horse Charlie Swan had feared that year going into Cheltenham. He thought he was the only thing between Istabraq and an historic four Champion Hurdles in a row. He hadn't reckoned on foot and mouth. Nobody had. In fact, Charlie has always had the utmost respect for Moscow, both while he was engaged in combat on Istabraq's back and since he gave all that up.

He says that Moscow is the best two-mile chaser he has ever seen. It is a considered opinion. Charlie won a Champion Chase on Viking Flagship.

But I am a firm believer in providence. Most things happen for a reason. Had there been no foot and mouth that year, and had Moscow gone to Cheltenham and – perish the thought – beaten Istabraq in the Champion Hurdle, we would probably never have sent him chasing. He would possibly never have scaled the heights over hurdles that he did over fences.

In the winner's enclosure after the Shell Champion Hurdle, people were asking me about plans.

'He's 40–1 for next year's Champion Hurdle,' said one of the journalists from the middle of the press scrum. 'Do you think that's good value?'

'I don't,' I said.

The pens stopped moving and the press corps looked at me intently as one incredulous, open-mouthed unit. It was as if I had told them there would be no biscuits in the press room at Leopardstown any more.

'He's going chasing.'

CHAPTER SIXTEEN

CHASING DESTINY

To be honest, I hadn't fully decided if Moscow Flyer would or wouldn't go steeplechasing in the 2001/02 season. I couldn't have made that decision on my own without talking to Brian. But that was the way I was thinking, and from our conversations that was the way I thought Brian was leaning too.

Moscow Flyer was seven years old; he would be eight the following January. While that is towards the upper end of the age spectrum for a first-season chaser, it is definitely not too old. If we spent one more season hurdling, however, he would be eight going on nine in his first season as a chaser. He would not run in the Arkle until he was nine and he would not be able to contest a Champion Chase until he was ten. That just seemed to me to be too old. Most of the best steeplechasers of modern times began jumping fences when they were much younger. Best Mate won the first of his Gold Cups when he was seven, having spent a season jumping fences as a novice. So did Arkle and L'Escargot. Little Owl, Davy Lad, Midnight Court, Imperial Call, Kicking King – all Gold Cup winners at seven. And Florida Pearl never jumped a hurdle in public. He went straight over fences and won his Sun Alliance Chase at the age of six. If we didn't go chasing in the 2001/02 season, we would probably never go chasing. And that would be a shame. After all, that was what we had bought him for. It was an embryo steeplechaser that Johnny and I had seen that June day at Tattersalls, not a hurdler.

It was going to be a tough call, however. Moscow was such a good hurdler that it would be a shame to give all that up and start again. Because that was effectively what we would be doing. The list of top-class hurdlers who never made it as chasers is about as long as the list of top-class jockeys who never made it as trainers. Just because you are good in one discipline, it does not necessarily follow that you will be good in another related discipline. The fact that Dawn Run is still the only horse ever to have won a Champion Hurdle and a Gold Cup is not a coincidence.

Moreover, I was convinced that Moscow Flyer was one of the top two two-mile hurdlers around at the time. Istabraq and Moscow Flyer. That was it. If we were not as good as Istabraq, we were not far behind him, and we were clear of the rest. Istabraq was two years older than Moscow. He would be ten at the time of the 2002 Champion Hurdle and would probably be beyond his best. Moscow would be eight and probably nearing his prime. To tell the truth, in April 2001 I couldn't see what other horses were going to be competing for the 2002 Champion Hurdle. If we stayed hurdling, and we remained healthy and well, it looked like we just had Istabraq to beat.

In spite of this, and probably somewhat illogically, I wanted to send him chasing. Deep in my guts, I thought he would be an even better steeplechaser than he was a hurdler. He had steeplechasing all over his pedigree, such as it was, and he jumped his hurdles like a steeplechaser would jump them, even though, remarkably, he had never jumped over a steeplechase fence in his life. Sometimes you have to go with your gut. Your instinct. I had been around horses for long enough and had learnt that my gut feeling about them usually proved to be correct.

I decided to pop him over a few fences before I left him off for the summer. I asked Barry to come down to school him. Not that one of the other lads couldn't have done it, but I wanted Barry to get a feel for what Moscow would be like over a fence. If he was going to be riding him in chases the following season, he might as well be the first one to school him. Also, I thought it would be good to get Barry's verdict on his jumping. Barry came down one morning in early May. Moscow had just won the Shell Champion Hurdle the previous week and we were letting him down. He was effectively on his summer holidays, but he was still fit enough to do a little bit of schooling.

We have three schooling fences down in one of the back fields at Commonstown. I gave Barry a leg up and they set off. Just the two of them. No lead horse, and nothing to compete against. They could do it in their own time. And take your time. Just do it right. And they did. One, two, up. Three times. No hairy moments, no scares. Moscow jumped the three fences as if he had been jumping fences all his life. Barry came back with one of those whole-face grins on him that he only wears these days after he wins a Champion Chase or a Gold Cup.

'He was super,' he said. 'Just lovely. A really lovely jumper.'

I was delighted that he seemed to be such a natural. Much more natural over a fence than he ever was over a hurdle. He had never been a really rapid hurdler. Not like Istabraq or Hardy Eustace, for example. He was fine when he was meeting one in his stride, but he was never as sharp to fiddle a hurdle like Istabraq could. I don't think he respected them enough. They were just finicky little things he should be able to kick out of his way. His fall at the second-last flight in the AIG was because he just grabbed at the obstacle. He didn't show it enough respect. I was thrilled that Barry seemed to be so happy with him. Both for Barry's sake and for mine. We used to joke that Barry would be coming down so that Moscow could school him over a few fences. It looked like my instinct about Moscow jumping fences was going to prove to be correct. My mind was made up: chasing it had to be.

I phoned Brian to tell him about the schooling session. I was excited about it, and I probably communicated as much to Brian. This excitement thing can be quite infectious. Brian seemed to be on the same wavelength. He was becoming progressively better versed in this whole racing business. He had done fairly well for a man who not so long ago hadn't been sure of the difference between the Supreme Novices' Hurdle and the Sun Alliance Hurdle. Already he was thinking Cheltenham thoughts. I presumed the Arkle Chase would be his target. Brian was still desperate to have a runner at Cheltenham. He often tried to hide it when we spoke about potential targets for Moscow, but he gave himself away more often than not. The Shell Champion Hurdle and Hatton's Grace and Festival Hurdles were all brilliant, but talk about a Champion Hurdle or an Arkle – that was a whole different ball game. Brian would light up. His eyes and his voice. If he spoke about the Festival Hurdle like a child would speak about Christmas morning, then the Arkle was all about meeting Santa Claus.

Moscow headed down to Wexford again for his summer holidays shortly afterwards, back down to David Nugent's with his mate Slaney Native for a well-earned break. He came back to us in late July. It seems somewhat unfair to bring them back in late July when they work so hard during the winter and are supposed to be on their summer holidays, but they need to come in that early if they are to be ready to compete in the early part of the season. And this season, in particular, it was important to get him in early if he was going to be jumping fences. I wanted to do a little bit more schooling with him before I pitched him into his first steeplechase race. Also, if we were going to be going for a championship novice chase at the Cheltenham Festival the following March, I wanted him to get as much match practice during the season as possible.

Brian came down to see his horse in early August. Moscow was quite big, but he had done a week on the horse-walker and was just getting into a little bit of light work. It is important to bring them on gradually. If you do too much too quickly, you can set them back an age. We had our planning meeting over coffee. Brian always plays down the planning meeting. He will tell you that it's only coffee and a chat about his horse. But it is very definitely an annual event, and to my mind very definitely a meeting about concocting and agreeing a plan for the season ahead. It is Brian's methodical mind applying what works for him in business to one of his primary leisure pursuits. There are no minutes taken or anything, but Brian is very deliberate, and ensures that he drives out of Commonstown with a definitive plan for Moscow for the season ahead in his mind.

To chase or not to chase – that was the question. We mulled over the pros and cons again. The Champion Hurdle was tempting, and we knew that we had a horse who had a real chance of winning it. As long as Moscow remained healthy and well, Brian's ticket to the owners' and trainers' stand at Cheltenham was secure. If we sent him over the larger obstacles, there was a chance he would not be a good enough steeplechaser even to go to Cheltenham. But the argument for going chasing was just as compelling. Even more so, as it turned out. The fact that it would not be fair to ask Moscow to learn a new trade when he was going on nine years of age was key. We agreed that we probably wouldn't go chasing if we didn't go that year. And that seemed like a waste. The complete under-utilisation of a potentially serious latent talent. It wouldn't be right. The ribbon on the package was the fact that he had schooled so well in May. Chasing it was.

I reminded Brian that we always had the option of going back over hurdles later in the season. If it didn't work out and if he really wasn't able to compete at the highest level over fences, we could shelve the chasing idea and train him for the Champion Hurdle. But though that was an option, it wouldn't have been ideal. When a horse goes jumping fences and then switches back to hurdles, he often jumps his hurdles as if they are fences. An efficient hurdler will flick through a hurdle and get away quickly from the back of it. With a steeplechase fence, you have to really jump out over the obstacle. It's a slightly different technique. If you jump over your hurdles as if they were fences, you spend more time in the air and expend more energy than you should. Consequently, it can be difficult to be competitive. There are horses who can effectively mix hurdling and chasing, but generally the top-class ones do one or the other. Moscow jumped his hurdles fairly big before he ever saw a steeplechase fence, so we would only have gone back over hurdles if all other options had been exhausted. It was an option to which I was pretty hopeful we would not have to resort.

I don't believe in schooling horses too much. School them a little, teach them the technique, teach them to respect their fences, and then let them off. I believe that you can overdo it. It's like practising putting or penalty kicks. There is only so much practice you can do. Soon the law of diminishing returns sets in, and very quickly thereafter you can actually get negative returns. If they pick up bad habits on the schooling ground, they will employ those bad habits on the racecourse. We did a little bit of schooling at home and then I took him to Punchestown to give him a try on the racecourse. Racecourse fences are generally a little bigger and a little stiffer than the ones we have at home. I wanted Moscow to see a racecourse fence and jump one on his own before he had to jump one in competition at racing pace. He went great at Punchestown. He only popped over three fences, but he jumped them like an old hand. Just as he had done at Commonstown. Barry was delighted. I was delighted. Brian was delighted.

I had it in my head that we would bring Moscow back in late October or early November, once the ground got a little bit soft. I knew that he would handle good ground, but I didn't want him having his first steeplechase race on ground that might be too firm. I didn't want him banging down on the ground and having a bad experience in his first chase. So I entered him in a beginners' chase at Fairyhouse at the end of October. A beginners' chase is a steeplechase race for horses who have never won a race over fences. The fences at Fairyhouse are quite stiff, but it's a nice galloping track and Barry would have plenty of time to organise Moscow before his fences.

Exciting times. Moscow had strengthened up again during the summer of 2001. His training had gone very well and he was fairly fit. If my instinct was correct, and he would prove to be a better chaser than he was a hurdler, we had a monster on our hands. He hadn't done anything on the schooling grounds to convince me that he would not be at least as effective over fences as he was over hurdles. Unfortunately, he was about to.

CHAPTER SEVENTEEN

THE MIGHTY FALLS

The European Breeders' Fund Beginners' Chase run on a Wednesday afternoon at Fairyhouse at the end of October would not usually feature too prominently in my diary. Indeed, it is unlikely it would feature too prominently in many people's diaries. Not even in the diary published by the European Breeders' Fund. In 2001, however, it was pencilled in from a long way out. As the race drew closer, it was written in in indelible ink and coloured over with a yellow highlighter marker. Moscow Flyer – first chase.

I was perfectly happy with him in the lead-up to the race. His training had gone without a hitch and the little bit of schooling we had done with him had been great. I don't often get excited about horses running in beginners' chases. We have so many horses running in beginners' chases, maiden hurdles and bumpers that if you were to get excited about everything that was showing a little bit of promise you'd have no energy left to brush your teeth in the evening.

But this was different. There was a definite air of excitement in the car that day on the way to Fairyhouse. It wasn't the type of excitement that makes you notice that your hands are shaking when you go to change gear, or the type that makes you drive through crossroads without yielding because your mind is elsewhere, it was more a nervous excitement. The kind you get before you play the ace in a game of whist. You almost don't want to do it. You don't want to waste it. It's nearly too much. Too powerful. You're afraid in case something goes wrong. And I was apprehensive. I suppose there is a certain amount of apprehension that goes with every degree of excitement. I remember thinking there was no upside to this escapade. Only a potential downside.

We only had to stand up to win. That's what they were saying. We were entitled – nay, expected – to win, and win easily. There would be no headlines for a win. If we made the headlines today, it would be for the wrong reasons.

I was happy that Moscow was fit enough for his seasonal debut. He wasn't Cheltenham fit, not by a long way. He wasn't trained to the minute for this. This wasn't his ultimate target. No more than an athlete or a football player, you can't have a horse fully fit for the entire season. You have to build him up gradually. That said, you can't send a horse into a race if he is unfit. If you do, you'll probably end up doing more harm than good. As well as the danger of injury being accentuated, you also run the risk of harming a horse mentally. You could push him close to or through a pain barrier that he will shy away from when presented with it next time. At least with the majority of physical ailments you can see them and treat them accordingly. The mental ones are slightly more difficult to address.

The ground was officially good to yielding at Fairyhouse on 24 October 2001. It was pretty much ideal for Moscow. It was nice safe ground that wouldn't jar his joints when he landed over his fences. At the same time, it wasn't so soft that the race would develop into a slogging match. The distance of two and a quarter miles was fine too. Horses often stay a little bit further over fences than they do over hurdles, in the same way as horses tend to stay further over hurdles than they do on the Flat. It is not unusual to see a horse who doesn't stay further than a mile on the Flat get two miles very well over hurdles. I'm sure that it is to do with the pace of the races. They go slower over hurdles than they do on the Flat, simply because they have to slow down to jump the hurdles. It's the same with a chase compared to a hurdle race, although perhaps it's not quite as obvious. Because steeplechase fences are substantially bigger than hurdles, the pace of a chase tends to be slower than the pace of a hurdle race. Hence, horses can stay further.

Brian and I met Barry in the parade ring before the race. Fairyhouse can be a fairly bleak place on a Wednesday afternoon, especially when you have become used to the crowds at the Grand National meeting and the Punchestown Festival (at Fairyhouse). Barry was his usual confident self. I just told him to settle Moscow early. It was important that he didn't run too freely. But he needed to be able to see his fences. There is a fine balance to be struck between settling a horse in behind horses and allowing him the room to see and jump his fences. I was glad that we had as skilled a horseman as Barry on our side, especially as there were fifteen horses in the race, which I thought was a lot and not ideal for Moscow's first race over fences. But Fairyhouse is a good, wide galloping track with nice wide fences. That was one of the reasons we chose Fairyhouse for his chasing bow.

Moscow ran free from the start. He was just too eager. Barry got him settled as best he could, but he was still fresh and free going into his fences. That is the last thing you want when you are running in your first steeplechase race. He was just so fresh and well and full of energy, and excited about racing again. He wanted to run as fast as he could for as long as he could. Barry said that he thought he was Muhammad Ali.

He jumped the first four fences adequately and ran up in front of the stands in third place behind Poetry Man and Draughtsman.

I was happy enough as I lowered my binoculars and took in the panorama of the entire field. There were a few stragglers out the back already, but they weren't my concern. Every time Moscow left the ground, my heart gave a little jump with him; every time he touched down on the landing side, my heart landed softly. Although he was jumping adequately for a debutant, I was getting more apprehensive as the race progressed. With each fence that he jumped, he had one less to negotiate before this first test was over. I suppose as your goal gets closer and more attainable, your natural inclination is to become more nervous in case you don't achieve it.

On the approach to the sixth-last fence, Moscow visibly quickened. In an instant, I wondered why Barry was being so aggressive going into the fence. Our plan was that he would just pop everything and learn from the experience. He didn't need to fly any of his fences; he just needed to pop. The only horse that could beat him today was himself.

Then I realised that it wasn't Barry who was asking him to quicken. He was doing it himself. He had seen a stride and was going to make this jump. It all happened so quickly, and Barry could do very little about it. He tried to take him back, but there was no communicating with Moscow. He quickly reached the point of no return and Barry had to go with him. He took off at least half a stride too early. My heart jumped higher than normal.

I needn't have worried. Horse and rider sailed over the fence, passing two horses in the air. His jump took him from fourth to second in the blink of an eye. I all but laughed out loud with relief. Barry took a tug and took his partner back. Steady now. Don't do that again.

But Moscow was an expert now. He had this chasing lark cracked. Nothing to it. Sure, they're only big hurdles and I can jump them no problem. Why are all these other losers taking so long to get over them? If you are meeting one wrong, just lengthen your stride and sail over it. Just like I did there the last time. Here comes another one.

Going to the fifth last Moscow saw another stride and quickened again. He had the revs up now. Barry saw that he was wrong and tried to restrain him. When you see that a horse is meeting a fence wrong, and you can't go long, your only option is to take a tug, take him back, get him back on his hocks and try to pop over it. Otherwise you are leaving the negotiation of the obstacle to chance and you will generally end up on your face. This is difficult to do when a horse is running too freely. Moscow was now. He had charged at the last fence and got away with it, so he probably thought that that was what you did. He was now charging at the fifth last in similar vein. But Barry had been over a lot more fences than Moscow had, and he could see that he was wrong. I had watched horses over a lot more fences than Moscow had jumped, and I could see that he was wrong. The only one who couldn't see it was Moscow. Not until it was too late.

As he went to take off, he suddenly realised that he wasn't going to make it. Oh-oh. He changed his mind. Maybe a short stride now. He tried to put in a short one just before the fence, but it was too late. He was going too fast and he was on top of the fence now anyway. My heart was up in my mouth at this stage, and Barry's was probably even higher.

Crash! He hit the birch just below the middle of the fence. It looked as if he had galloped straight into it. He had no chance. His chest lodged in the fence as his back flipped right over it. Barry was thrown forward like a pebble in a sling. Moscow's head went into the ground on the landing side of the fence, and his half a ton of body came afterwards.

It was a really horrible fall. Way beyond parental guidance. A horse has no arms that he can use to break his fall. When he goes head first over a fence, he is trusting completely to chance. It would be like you or me being pitched head first into the ground from a height with our hands tied behind our back. As Moscow's body went over his head, there was no telling which way his neck was going to go. If his nose lodged in the ground, his neck would not be able to support his body. His body and his head would be going in opposite directions. There would be only one loser in that instance – his neck. And that would be that. End of story. Bye bye Moscow.

I looked on in horror. My heart was somewhere between the top of my head and the roof of the stand. For a split second, I couldn't see his head. I didn't know where it had gone while his body was doing its somersault. Thud. I shuddered when his body hit the ground. It was as if the impact had caused the ground to vibrate and I was vibrating with it.

One moment he's cruising along and we're all very happy. The next moment he's flat on his back on the ground. It is amazing how your whole demeanour and outlook can be altered in the blink of an eye. For what seemed like an eternity, he lay on the ground, stretched out. Actually, it was only for a fraction of a second. First his head, then his shoulders and then his back came up off the ground. Nothing dangling, nothing hanging, everything apparently intact. For the second time in the space of about ten seconds, I almost laughed with relief. Moscow got to his feet, gave himself a shakedown and began figuring out his bearings. You generally have to start again after you have been upside down. He saw the other horses galloping away from him and he set off after them. Barry had bounced off the ground like a little rubber ball, but he too was back on his feet in an instant. Just as well they are both made of stern stuff, I thought. I'll settle for that, for them both being OK. I'll settle for not having to take Barry to hospital and being able to put my horse into his horsebox to bring him home. I got the double up. Barry was absolutely fine and Moscow was able to walk into his box. He would be a little stiff and sore in the morning, but everything was where it should be on him, and that was the main thing.

For the record, the Louise Wood-trained Draughtsman won that race, Ken Whelan up. Not that I saw the finish unfold, nor did I know how easily he had won. Regrettably, my attentions were elsewhere. But it could be a good one for a table quiz.

I chatted with Brian that evening. We still had our horse, which was a good starting point. I think Brian appreciated how close we had come to losing him that day. You can plan your year and dream about Cheltenham and tell your stories, but if things had gone just a little differently that day the plans would have been worthless, the dream over, the story not even half-told. Brian knew about the perils of horse racing before he got involved, but I'm not sure that he fully appreciated the fragility of it all until that day. I suppose you don't really appreciate something until you have a brush with it. One day you have a potential champion on your hands; the next day you have the insurance money.

It was also a kick up the backside for me. You deal with horses every day. You ride them out, you supervise work, you bring them to the races, you bring them home. We had about 50 horses at Commonstown at the time, but Moscow Flyer was the one who made it just a little bit easier to get out of bed in the morning. He was the one you thought of when something bad happened. If that something bad – something awful – had happened to him, it would have been difficult to swallow. Of course we would have dealt with it and kicked on, but it would have been a tough one.

I was amazed at how well Moscow was the following morning. He was a little bit stiff, but otherwise he was absolutely fine. My worry that we would have to put him on the easy list for a while did not come to fruition, and after a couple of days of some light work he was back in full training.

The original plan was to go straight from Fairyhouse to the Craddockstown Chase at Punchestown in mid-November. That was a Grade 3 race, but I had no doubt that he had the class for it. And if things had gone according to plan, we would have had more than three weeks to prepare him for it. Alas, things had not gone according to plan. I didn't want Moscow to go into a Grade 3 race against classy opponents on the back of one abortive attempt at steeplechasing. I wanted him to at least have a win under his belt before he stepped out of maiden company.

There was a two-mile beginners' chase at Down Royal just two weeks after the Fairyhouse near-calamity. They have nice fences at Down Royal and the timing was right. If he was OK – and the signs were that he would be – I thought it might be a good opportunity for my horse to get his chasing career on track and get his confidence back. The opposition was quantitatively strong but was lacking somewhat in terms of quality. That is the difficulty with these beginners' chases. There are lots of horses who have never won a chase trying to get one on the board in the early part of the season. What you gain by racing against horses who are similarly inexperienced, you lose by virtue of the fact that there are so many horses in the race.

They sent Moscow off the long odds-on favourite. Again the pressure was on. No upside. Expectations were high, and we were on a hiding to nothing. Win, and that's no more than would have been expected. Lose, and we're headline news again. And there was possibly even more pressure on this time. Anyone can be forgiven one accident, but have two and it's not an accident. It's a trend. To fall once, Mr Worthington, may be regarded as a misfortune, but to fall twice looks like carelessness. Again the plan was to settle Moscow, but to have him handy so that he wouldn't have too many horses getting in his way. Down Royal is a tighter track than Fairyhouse so it was important that he didn't have horses jumping across him or falling in front of him.

Barry had him in the first three or four throughout. They didn't go a great gallop, which suited us in a way because it gave Moscow time to size up his fences as he approached them. He and Barry worked really well as a team. They measured each fence, got the stride right and popped. Unlike the sixth last and fifth last at Fairyhouse, Moscow heeded Barry's instructions. It was as if he had succumbed to the fact that the rider knew a little more about this game than he did. In a strange way, I think his fall at Fairyhouse actually helped him. He knew how sore it was to go down on the ground, and he didn't want to do it again. As a result, he wasn't too brave at Down Royal.

There is a happy medium to be struck between being too brave and being too cowardly. Any horse can get from one side of a fence to the other. But in order to be an effective steeplechaser you have to negotiate each obstacle with a certain degree of speed. There was a chance that the Fairyhouse fall would have dented Moscow's confidence irrevocably. It didn't. But it did teach him to respect his fences, and that is rarely a bad thing.

Because they had gone a moderate gallop early on, the pace picked up appreciably approaching the third last. Moscow was right there in the front rank, but they were really sprinting by the time they got to the third last, so he needed to meet it right. He did. I would say more by judgement than by luck, but of course there was a little bit of luck involved. In fact, he met the last three bang on. Paul Carberry on Noel Meade's Royal Jake went for home from the second last, but Barry hadn't moved a muscle on Moscow and he tracked him the whole way down to the last. One, two, up. He popped over it, Barry just shook the reins at him, and they bounded clear.

I exhaled. I wasn't sure for how long I had been holding my breath, but I had been. Brian gave me a little hug where we stood on the open-topped stand up from the winning line. I couldn't tell if he had been holding his breath or not, but he was breathing now, and that was the main thing.

It was nice to be standing in the winner's enclosure waiting for Moscow and Barry to come back in, rather than chasing around the racecourse trying to catch him and wondering if Barry is OK. The smiles were smiles of pure relief. You're probably not entitled to be too gleeful when you win at 2–5, but we were allowed this.

The press were all at Down Royal as it was the first day of their big meeting up north. Where to next? The Craddockstown Chase at Punchestown and then the Denny Gold Medal Chase at Leopardstown I delighted in telling them. It's easy when you have the programme mapped out before the season starts. Now at least we were back on the rails. The Craddockstown was just a week after Down Royal. Again, in an ideal world we would have had a little longer between races, but the Down Royal race had not been in the original schedule. We had had to improvise a little. That was just the way.

In the eight days between the two races, we did very little with Moscow. There really wasn't sufficient time to let him rest after his northern exertions and build him up again for Punchestown. So we just kept him ticking over and hoped that he would still be fit enough. We didn't even pop him over a fence. I don't bother if their jumping is OK. You can't replicate racing conditions at home anyway. Schooling fences are easier than most racecourse fences, and you don't jump them at racing pace. And Moscow's jumping had been more than OK at Down Royal.

Unfortunately, the ground at Punchestown on Craddockstown Chase day was soft. Moscow had proved that he could handle soft ground, but I was fast coming to the idea that he was at his best on good ground. Especially over fences. He seemed to jump his fences well off good ground and he was able to make his hurdle speed tell. Also, if he was less than 100 per cent fit after a week of less than full-on training, soft ground and Grade 3 opposition could find him out.

He had only three opponents at Punchestown. I'm not sure why that was as the Craddockstown usually commands quite a respectable number of runners. It is well positioned in the early season and, as a Grade 3 race, is usually contested by horses who have already won a beginners' chase or a novices' chase over two miles. It may have been that Moscow scared a lot of them away.

I saw Grimes as the main danger. He was far more experienced over fences than Moscow, having contested his first steeplechase race in 1999. Remarkably, although he had won the Galway Plate against seasoned handicappers the previous August, he was still a novice. I expected that Grimes would make the running. He had been prominent throughout in the Galway Plate, and had stayed on well to win that, and that was over two miles and six furlongs. He was far more experienced over fences than the rest of us, and I suspected that he would try to run and jump us into the ground. If he did, I was happy for Barry to let him off. We didn't want to get into a jumping competition early on with a horse who had won a Galway Plate.

Sure enough, when the tapes went up Paul Carberry bounced Grimes away. Barry settled Moscow in last place and concentrated on getting him jumping. But it wasn't working. He wasn't fluent. When it looked like he was meeting one in his stride, he would put in a short one. He didn't look like falling or anything, but he was losing ground at his fences. Careful, if you were looking on the bright side. A little deliberate. Downright sticky and over-cautious, if you were being realistic. Maybe it was the soft ground. Maybe he didn't like the loose ground under his feet when he was going into his fences. Maybe he was feeling the effects of a race just eight days ago. Maybe he had forgotten how to jump fences. Maybe he had lost his confidence. Maybe it was a right-handed thing.

All these thoughts went through my head as they went up the side of the course. At the third fence, Grimes cried enough. He wasn't happy either. It was probably the ground for him. He was a much better horse on top of the ground. He began to back-pedal as Moscow took closer order. Moscow's jumping began to warm up as they went down the back straight. It looked like it was all coming back to him now, or he had figured out how to jump out of this soft ground. At the fourth last he took it up from Penny Native and went on. His jumping was better now, but it definitely wasn't up to championship standard. He kicked clear at the second last and went on to win his race.

He only won by four lengths in the end, from Masalarian. It was a win, but it was unimpressive. Barry had had to keep him up to his work all the way to the line. And he wasn't happy. He dismounted without the smile he usually sports when he dismounts in the winner's enclosure.

'He was bone idle when he got to the front,' he told me. 'He wasn't doing a stroke for me. I don't know why. He was a different horse today to the one I rode at Down Royal.'

I didn't know what to make of it. Perhaps it was the fact that this was a Grade 3 race and these were Grade 3 horses. But Masalarian? He would have picked him up and carried him had they been racing over hurdles. It didn't make sense.

In hindsight, it was probably the Punchestown phenomenon. Barry says that Moscow always hangs to his left up the home straight at Punchestown. He doesn't help you at all. I don't know what it is. He doesn't do it at any other track. It's not a right-handed thing, as some of his best performances have been at right-handed tracks. It's something that is unique to Punchestown.

I had him checked out when we got him home. Everything was fine. I had mixed feelings when I heard that. On the one hand you are delighted that there's nothing wrong with the horse. On the other hand, you would like to have found a reason why he had run so moderately. If that was as good as he was, then we had no business thinking about the Arkle Chase. If he was only four lengths better than Masalarian off level weights, then we should go back to jumping hurdles.

In reality, I never considered going over hurdles again. Not seriously anyway. Although the Craddockstown had probably been a weak race, he had won it. He was probably only just doing enough. If another horse had come to him, he would have found more. I put it down to the ground and the proximity of his previous race, and looked ahead to Leopardstown.

Christmas is busy at Commonstown, as it is at any yard. As well as the usual Christmas things that you have to do, Christmas Day is the day before one of the busiest periods of the entire season. My brother John and I take it in turns to host Christmas dinner. Actually, my sister-in-law, Chich, and I take it in turns to host Christmas dinner. Alternate years. It was my turn in 2001. Of course Emma and Kate were there, and James and Tara, and their families. David Nugent was there that year too. We could have sixteen or seventeen people for dinner. It's great fun, but there is a lot of work involved in catering for that number of people.

Of course the horses don't know it's Christmas Day, and they need to be exercised in the morning just the same as any other morning. Sometimes the horses that are running later in the week need to go to The Curragh to do a decent piece of work up the Old Vic. Because racing begins so early over the next four days it's impossible to do it on any of those days before you go racing. If they need to go, then they need to go. That's just the way it is, Christmas morning or not. I try to be as fair with staff as I can. I try to let as many of them as possible go home for Christmas. Some of the foreigners go home and some stay around. That's fair enough.

We had several high-profile runners that Christmas. Bust Out was going in the December Festival Hurdle – the race Moscow had won the previous year – against Istabraq. He had only had one run back after almost a year off the track, but we were hopeful that he would run well. Space Trucker was going in the Paddy Power Chase. He hadn't won a race in a year and a half, but we were pleased with him at home and the Paddy Power didn't look like it was going to be that strong a race. In fact, there was quite a dearth of top-class two-mile chasers in Ireland at the time. Knife Edge appeared to be the best of them, but he was some way off the top horses in the UK, like Flagship Uberalles, Tiutchev and Edredon Bleu.

Moscow was well during the run-up to Christmas. His race, the Denny Gold Medal Novice Chase, was on St Stephen's Day (Boxing Day). I expected him to win it, and I really hoped that he would. They were talking about him now as Ireland's main hope for the Arkle Chase at Cheltenham, and that scared me a bit. Until the lead-up to Christmas 2001 I had always been a little bit miffed that he didn't seem to get the credit he deserved. I still believe he never got due recognition for his exploits, or indeed for his ability, as a hurdler. But now I felt they were talking him up too much. In three steeplechases, he had fallen once, won an egg and spoon race at Down Royal, and won a Grade 3 four-runner race unimpressively where his main rival had not run up to form. I was allowed to plan his season quietly with the Arkle as his primary objective, but it was crazy that they were talking him up as a likely Arkle winner. It was only because there were no other likely contenders in Ireland.

Youlneverwalkalone had begun the season over hurdles, but after he was beaten by Limestone Lad in the Morgiana Hurdle they switched him to fences. He had been beaten when odds-on for his beginners' chase at Fairyhouse just four weeks before Christmas, which was hardly the ideal preparation for a Grade 1 chase like the Denny. Colonel Yeager was also in the Denny line-up. He had been brought down early on in his only chase to date. Indeed, it was the only race he had run since he had finished second to Moscow in the Shell Champion Hurdle. All things considered, Moscow was entitled to be favourite. He had won two chases while his two main rivals were still maidens over fences. And he was. Clear favourite.

He travelled like a favourite all the way down the back straight, and stretched the field like a favourite when he took it up at the second last. Youlneverwalkalone moved into second on the run to the final fence, but this bird had flown. Moscow jumped the last well and kept on all the way to the line. He only had two lengths to spare over Youlneverwalkalone, but I was beginning to realise that that was just him. He really didn't want to do too much more than he had to. Especially on this soft ground. I was sure that if something else had come at him up the run-in, he would have picked up again.

Barry told me afterwards that he choked on the run-in. Just in the last 100 yards or so. He just cleared himself out and kept going. He's done it a few times since as well, when he was running at less than peak fitness or on heavy ground. I thought that he had been a little sticky at one or two fences down the back straight, but Barry was delighted with him. He was wrong at those fences, Barry told me later, but he was happy with the way the horse put himself right. The way that he'd adapted his stride and negotiated the fences belied his inexperience. He hadn't been flamboyant at his fences, but he hadn't needed to be. He was now the undisputed best two-mile novice chaser in Ireland. Mission accomplished.

Bust Out ran the race of his life to finish second, beaten a head, to Istabraq in the Festival Hurdle. He might even have beaten the reigning champion had he not been hampered by the fall of Liss A Paoraigh. Everyone was telling me I should run him in the Pierse Hurdle, that he was so well handicapped he would be a certainty in that. But I didn't want to run him in a hurly-burly race like the

Pierse. That race is always run on the inside track at Leopardstown, and it can get very tight. I was thinking more in terms of AIG Hurdle, Champion Hurdle. I thought he had the class to go that route. As it turned out, it was all academic. He went wrong shortly after that and we had to leave him off for almost a year.

Spirit Leader was driving us mad at the time. She had run in five hurdle races and had finished second in all five. It wasn't that she was ungenuine or anything. She just always seemed to come up against something that was better than her on the day. We brought her to Down Royal shortly after Christmas for a mares-only maiden hurdle. I just wanted her to get a win over hurdles under her belt and kick on. I thought that a mares-only maiden hurdle at Down Royal in the middle of January might not take that much winning. As ill luck had it, Sean Treacy had had the same notion for his smart mare Be My Belle. Spirit Leader was runner-up again. Six seconds in a row. I threw my hat at it and said I'd put her away and wait for better ground. Be My Belle went on to beat Boss Doyle and Sackville at Gowran Park next time out. She would win the Thyestes Chase the following year as a novice chaser.

Meanwhile, we were preparing Moscow for the Baileys Arkle at Leopardstown at the end of January 2002. Baileys Arkle, Arkle Chase at Cheltenham – that was the plan. There were seven weeks between the Baileys Arkle and Cheltenham, which was a bit of a stretch, but it would allow us to get him ready at home.

Everything was going according to plan until the week before the race. Barry was involved in an incident in the maiden hurdle at Fairyhouse on the Sunday, exactly a week before the Baileys Arkle. Timmy Murphy's horse Darbys Bridge fell at the third flight. Barry was coming behind on Robert E Lee and was brought down, along with six other horses. It really was a horrible incident. Darbys Bridge was killed instantly and several of the jockeys were injured. Timmy was stood down for seven days with concussion, and Barry and a claiming rider, John O'Loughlin, were stood down for two.

At first we thought that Barry had just bruised his back, and that the two-day sabbatical was only precautionary. The following day, however, he had a pain in his elbow and went to get it X-rayed. Hairline fracture. Disaster. He was out for at least three weeks. Well, disaster is probably a little too strong. Disaster would be a hairline fracture of Moscow's elbow. But this was a good runner-up. Barry's knowledge and understanding of Moscow Flyer was invaluable in a race. Barry had ridden him in his four steeplechase races to date. With each race over fences their mutual understanding was noticeably growing. Each performance had been an improvement on the previous one. It was not ideal to have to change the rider of a novice chaser for his fifth chase, just one race before we were going to send him to Cheltenham. But Barry couldn't ride him, so our only other option was not to run him, and that wasn't really an option as this was the ideal race for him. It was our last chance to test him against Grade 1 opposition, and to test his jumping in Grade 1 conditions, before sending him to Cheltenham.

Paul Moloney was the obvious deputy. He had ridden Moscow to win the Morgiana Hurdle and, outside of his bumper days, he was the only other man to have ridden him in a race. Paul came down on the Thursday to have a sit on Moscow again. He popped him over our three fences at Commonstown. Although I didn't tell either of them at the time, this was more for Paul's benefit than for Moscow's.

It was another day of very soft ground at Leopardstown. I know that the majority of Leopardstown's big National Hunt days take place in the depths of winter, but there was never any respite for Moscow. It seems that whenever he ran at Leopardstown, either over hurdles or over fences, the ground was bottomless.

Truth to tell, the Baileys Arkle that year was not a strong race. Ferdy Murphy was due to send Truckers Tavern – unbeaten in three chases – over from England, but he decided during the week to keep him for the P.J. Moriarty Chase over two miles and five furlongs two weeks later. That suited us fine. As far as I saw it, we only had to stand up to win. There really wasn't anything else in the race that could have had Arkle aspirations. Maybe Mantles

Prince, but we had beaten him so many times in the past, both over hurdles and over fences, that we couldn't fear him.

Johnny couldn't go to Leopardstown that day as he was laid up in hospital trying to come to terms with his new hip. He had had arthritis in the old one for a little while and was resigned to the fact that he would have to have it replaced. His thinking was that if he had it done after Christmas, he would be right for Cheltenham. He might not be fit to run in the Mildmay of Flete, but at least he would be mobile. His thinking, of course, was that he would be there to see Moscow.

There were good friends of mine over from America and staying with us at the time, Russell Jones and Donna Sharpe, who have just got married there in the summer of 2005. They went hunting during the week, and I said, 'Well, you'd better stay back now and go to Leopardstown to see Moscow run on Sunday.' Alas, they didn't see what I expected them to see.

Paul Moloney was fine before the Baileys Arkle. If he was nervous, he didn't show it. It had rained a lot on the day and the ground was very soft down the back straight. The plan was to get Moscow settled early, but to have him handy if we could. We had so much in hand over the others that we should win easily with normal luck. But we didn't have normal luck. Not even close to it. Moscow was a bit keen early on as they raced up past the stands first time. I don't know if he was uncomfortable with his new partner or with this new pair of hands on the end of the reins that held the bit in his mouth, but I doubt it. He had settled well for Paul in the Morgiana. It was probably just a case of the pace not being fast enough for him. Paul let him stride on up the side of the course to our right and he eased into second place behind Barry Cash on Phariwarmer. He jumped the fourth – the first in the back straight – in a clear second place, and they headed on down to the fifth.

I was happy enough at that stage. He had jumped the first four OK and he seemed to have settled a little better. He and Paul had gone through the getting-to-know-you-again stages and were warming to the task of racing. He seemed to meet the fifth OK too.

He definitely wasn't too long at it. I suppose if anything he was a little tight, but no tighter than at a lot of the fences he had just popped out over in the past. He went to pop this one as well. Just a routine pop. Nothing too extravagant. Not a leap that would gain a lot of ground or win a race. Just a functional pop that would get him from one side to the other. But for some reason he didn't get high enough. His concentration might have wandered momentarily, or he might have been getting a little complacent at these fences. He had jumped plenty of them now and there was nothing to it. Just pop over. Nonchalant as you like.

He clipped the top of the fence. It was a clip you would get away with at Down Royal or Gowran, but not at Leopardstown. Not when the fences are so big and stiff that you have to really jump out over them. He was off balance as he descended on the landing side. As the ground neared he visibly struggled to get his front legs out in front of him into landing position. It was a bit like an aeroplane trying to get its wheels out as it descends to the ground. It's not the way you want to do it ideally, but if you can get the wheels out on time, you get the same net result. Moscow got his landing gear out all right, but only just. As his forelegs landed on the ground, they skidded away from him on the soft surface. Where his front legs go, the rest of him follows. Gravity dictates. His body was almost eased down on to the ground, Paul was detached, and the two of them slid along for a couple of yards.

There followed a millisecond of total panic. You would have thought I'd be almost used to it by this stage, but I wasn't. You just don't get used to seeing your horses fall. You can't watch them fall and not worry desperately about their well-being. Again, the panic hardly lasted long enough for me to react to it in any way. Moscow was on his feet, Paul was on his feet. No real harm done.

Paul got a bit of a hard time in the press afterwards. I suppose it had to be expected. A new jockey gets on a high-profile horse and the horse falls – there are bound to be questions asked in the papers. And you ask the same questions yourself. It's natural. A horse ends up on the floor, you have to go back and have a look at the incident and see why it happened. See if the fall could have been prevented.

The answer was, of course it could. Had Paul known that the horse was going to fall by him sitting still and allowing him to pop it, of course he would have done something different. When a horse ends up on the floor, something has gone wrong. If you knew that he was going to fall, you wouldn't have ridden him into the fence the way you did. It's the same thing when a horse gets beaten: if you knew he was going to get beaten given that you rode him the way you did, of course you would have ridden him differently. But I couldn't criticise Paul. He didn't put Moscow on the floor. Far from it. Moscow might not have fallen had Barry been riding him, but he might have. It's just one of those imponderables the answer to which we will never know.

And there were many silver linings. As falls go, it was a soft fall. Neither horse nor rider was in any way the worse for it. OK, so we hadn't won the Baileys Arkle, which had been at our mercy, but we still had a horse. You learn to appreciate that any day you bring a horse to the races in a horsebox and bring him home with you in a horsebox is a good day.

Strangely, although you never want to fall, I think that this fall helped Moscow later on. He never fell again. He made mistakes and he got rid of jockeys all right, but he never ended up on the ground himself again. He always seemed to find a leg.

On the downside, however, Moscow Flyer was now three wins and two falls from five starts over fences. It was hardly the ideal record for an Arkle Chase contender on the face of it. The critics were out. The 'dodgy jumper' tag was dusted down and applied from certain quarters. We would just have to prove those people wrong all over again on the biggest stage of all.

CHAPTER EIGHTEEN

ARKLE HERO

While Moscow was blotting his copybook in Ireland, across the water there was a horse who was busy beating every two-mile novice chaser in the land. Seebald was a German-bred horse that Martin Pipe was training for the two Liverpool footballers Steve McManaman and Robbie Fowler. He had been just below top class as a hurdler the previous season, but this season as a chaser he was proving to be something of a revelation.

Seebald contested seven chases between May 2001 and January 2002. He won them all. Every single one of them, and all very impressively. He first came to my attention when he beat Fondmort and Armaturk in the two-mile novice chase at Cheltenham's November meeting. Fondmort was travelling well when he slithered to the ground after jumping the second last that day, but Seebald may have had his measure anyway. He was favourite for the Arkle, the one they were talking about as the most likely winner. I couldn't help feeling that we would have his measure. The fact that he had won a decent race at Cheltenham was definitely in his favour, but Moscow had been a much classier hurdler than Seebald. Seebald jumped fences well, but I knew that, contrary to popular opinion at the time, so did Moscow.

I toyed with the idea of giving Moscow another run over fences before Cheltenham. It wasn't in the plan to have another run, but neither was falling at the fifth fence in the Baileys Arkle. It definitely wasn't ideal to be going to Cheltenham on the back of a fall, and the best plans are those that can be amended as conditions change.

But I only toyed with the idea. For the same reasons behind our decision at the start of the year to go straight from Leopardstown to Cheltenham, I decided against giving him another run. There wasn't really another suitable race that was sufficiently far in advance of Cheltenham so that we wouldn't be in danger of leaving the Arkle behind us. An over-reach or a hard race close to Cheltenham, and that could be that. I was happy that he was a good jumper, and I was confident that we could prepare him for the Arkle at home.

Strange thing. If we had won the Baileys Arkle, we would have been challenging Seebald for favouritism. There is no doubt about that. But as we had failed to complete at Leopardstown, we went largely unconsidered in England. As well as Seebald, Nicky Henderson's Fondmort was well fancied. So was the Tim Easterby-trained Barton, who had been a Sun Alliance Hurdle winner a couple of seasons earlier but who had plied his chasing trade in small races in the north of England that season. The English didn't seem to want to consider Moscow Flyer. Two falls in five races. Dodgy jumper. I couldn't believe that they were quoting our horse at 8–1 and 10–1. You never know how things would have panned out, but had Moscow stood up, he probably would have won the Baileys Arkle. If he had, he would have been a 3–1 or a s4–1 shot. And we knew he was a good jumper who had just been unlucky at Leopardstown. It didn't make sense.

Although Seebald had form at Cheltenham, I was happy that the track would hold no fears for Moscow. He is a well-balanced horse. If you are well balanced, it doesn't matter what type of track you race on. Flat track, uphill, downhill, left-handed, right-handed – they're all the same.

I was very busy in the lead-up to Cheltenham that year. As well as looking after the horses, I had all these pre-Cheltenham evenings to do. These are events where a panel of so-called experts – that includes me apparently! – sit up at the top of a function room and go through all the races at Cheltenham, telling a wholly attentive audience what will win each race. They can be good fun, but I seriously question the real value punters get out of them. I had been doing one or two every year since 1997, when Space Trucker had finished third in the Champion Hurdle, but it seemed to be pretty manic in 2002. It may have been that Moscow was becoming very popular in Ireland, or it may have been that pre-Cheltenham evening fever had gripped the country. I suspect the latter.

Barry was on one or two panels with me. When I was asked about Moscow Flyer's chances of winning the Arkle, I diluted my real thoughts significantly. I talked about Seebald and the good English horses. 'And don't rule out the other Irish ones either. Assessed won the Baileys Arkle well, you know, and Moscow only beat Youlneverwalkalone by two lengths at Christmas. Moscow is well, though, and deserves his chance. I'm hopeful.' But Barry didn't hold back. Both barrels. Barry said a lot of what I thought but dared not say. Moscow was his banker for the meeting. People had forgotten how good a hurdler he had been. He was rated far higher than Seebald ever was over hurdles. The only way Seebald would be able to beat him would be if he was a better jumper of fences than Moscow. And Moscow is not a bad jumper. 'Listen to me. Moscow is not a bad jumper. He was unlucky to fall at Leopardstown. He is one of the classiest hurdlers to go novice chasing in a long time, and I think that whatever beats him wins.'

A friend of Barry's rang him just before Cheltenham and told him he was going to have a few quid on Moscow each-way. Barry told him not to – have the whole lot on to win. He showed remarkable confidence for a jockey who had never ridden a winner at the Festival. I suppose if there is one thing of which you could never accuse Barry Geraghty, it is a lack of confidence.

Brian chewed his nails in the weeks leading up to Cheltenham. If not literally, then definitely metaphorically. Brian isn't one of those owners who is on the phone every day wondering how his horse is. As I have said before, once he has employed someone to do a job, he just leaves them alone to do it. There's no point in having a dog and going to the shop yourself to get the paper. But during the build-up to Cheltenham in 2002, I am sure he teetered on the brink. He and Patricia went to Tenerife for a week just before the Festival. That was probably a good idea as it stopped him wondering if he was going to get there. If I wasn't on the phone to him, it was good news. No foot and mouth this year. No ailments. No stones to step on. No injuries from which to recover. It was looking good for Brian's first venture to Cheltenham as an owner. The realisation of the dream that he had bought into almost four years earlier. Just to stand in the middle of the parade ring and watch his horse walk around it. That was all he wanted. Winning was hardly even a consideration. Just to be there. Just to be a part of it all. That was the dream.

Moscow's preparation for Cheltenham could hardly have gone more smoothly. He was absolutely fine after his Leopardstown mishap. We gave him a little break out in the field for a week and then we began to build him up again. He schooled once and well, as if to reassure us that he was, in fact, a good jumper. We didn't do anything different with him just because it was Cheltenham. We got him race-fit again and aimed to have him ready to run for his life on the day.

When Eamonn drove out through the gate of Commonstown on the Sunday morning, two days before the Arkle Chase, with Moscow in the back of the horsebox with Soltero – our runner in the Supreme Novices' Hurdle – for company, my job was done. There was nothing more I could do. It was up to Eamonn to get him there safely and get him settled in well at Cheltenham. It was Moscow's first time outside Ireland and it was important that he didn't get himself worked up. Then it would be up to Moscow and Barry.

I concentrated on getting myself there. Johnny and I usually stay at Seven Barrows in Lambourn with Nicky and Diana Henderson during the Cheltenham Festival, and 2002 was no different. Well, it was slightly different in that we wouldn't be rooting for Nicky's horse in the Arkle, and he wouldn't be rooting for ours. The craic was good at Seven Barrows on the Monday night. A couple of glasses of wine settled my nerves a little. Because I was nervous. Nervous and excited. If I had thought we had little chance of winning the Arkle, I wouldn't have been nervous at all. But I was nervous in case something went wrong. If nothing went wrong, I genuinely thought that Moscow Flyer was the most likely winner of the race. Nicky really fancied Fondmort. And with just cause. He had come out after his mishap at Cheltenham against Seebald and won the Henry VIII Chase at Sandown, and the Wayward Lad Chase at Kempton at Christmas. He was touted as one of the best jumpers of a fence in the novice ranks, and Nicky thought that he had him spot on.

I left Johnny and the Hendersons at Seven Barrows on Tuesday morning and drove to the course with my daughter Emma. Johnny had recovered well from his hip operation and was able to get around OK with the aid of a crutch. He would have slowed Emma and me down, however, so we thought it best to leave him in the capable hands of the Hendersons.

We got to the course at about ten o'clock. Moscow and Soltero had travelled over without incident and Eamonn had already had them out for a stretch of their legs in the middle of the course. Everything was sorted, then. All in hand. Then I began to walk my box. No matter how many times I go to Cheltenham, I always get to the course way too early on Tuesday. I'll never learn. Too much time for box-walking. If I was a horse, you'd have to hang a couple of tyres in the box with me.

The Arkle is the second race on the first day of Cheltenham. That's the thing about Cheltenham – you're straight into it. And once you're into it, there is no let-up until you're out of it. I thought that, with the fourth day in 2005, there would be some dilution of the freneticism with which it all takes place, but there wasn't. It's still 100 miles an hour the whole way.

As it happened, Soltero was going in the first race, the Supreme Novices' Hurdle. He was a nice young horse without being top class. He had won a decent little novices' hurdle at Thurles on his previous outing, beating Jimmy Mangan's horse Monty's Pass, on whom Barry would win the Grand National the following season, and a young horse of Dusty Sheehy's called Rathgar Beau. Only a bit-part player at the time, the same Rathgar Beau would assume one of the main supporting roles in the Moscow Flyer story.

Soltero liked good ground and was owned by a syndicate who were dying to go to Cheltenham. We figured that he had earned his travel expenses with his win at Thurles, so we said we'd let him take his chance. He was a 50–1 shot so we weren't expecting too much, but he ran well enough to finish in mid-division.

Going to the final flight in that race, Ruby Walsh and Adamant Approach looked to have the prize in the bag, but the horse stepped at the hurdle and came down. This left the path clear for a protracted uphill duel between Christy Roche's Like-A-Butterfly and Martin Pipe's Westender. If the Irish roar at Cheltenham is worth a head or a neck, it made the difference between victory and defeat for Charlie Swan on Like-A-Butterfly. They didn't stop cheering him until he had left the winner's enclosure to weigh in.

The Cheltenham treadmill was running now, and we were on it. Well before they make the presentation for one race at Cheltenham, they are parading for the next. The next was ours. Our reason for being here. The race our whole season had been leading up to. I was very glad that Soltero had been running in the first race, as it took my mind off the Arkle for half an hour or so. It did no harm for Barry to have had a spin around the track either, before he got the leg up on Moscow. It didn't matter that the first race was over hurdles. It was more for him to get the first-race nerves out of the way than for him to learn any more about the actual track. He had been over it often enough on foot and on horseback before.

I went to the unsaddling area after the first to make sure that everything was all right with Soltero before making my way to the weigh room to collect Moscow's saddle. I took it to the pre-parade ring. Moscow was in it before me, ambling nonchalantly around as if he was out for an afternoon stroll, Eamonn just to the left of his head.

Brian and Patricia were already in the parade ring when I got there. We exchanged cheek-kisses and pleasantries. This is it. Brian was drinking it all in. This is the parade ring at Cheltenham. The grass in here really does feel like the surface of a billiard table. The Arkle Challenge Trophy Chase. And there's my horse. He was savouring the moment. Lapping it up and appreciating every instant. This was the dream, and he was living it. A runner at Cheltenham. Who would have thought it would come to this? That the day Shean Town won at Leopardstown and he told Arthur Craigie to ask his trainer to get him a horse would lead to today? The parade ring at Cheltenham. Not in your wildest imagination.

There were television cameras around the parade ring, honing in on anyone who looked like they might have something vaguely interesting to say. Derek Thompson was there with his microphone. I was hoping he wouldn't approach me. I could really do without coming across as a bag of nerves on national television. My wish was granted. He didn't. I mustn't have had one of the fancied runners.

Barry bobbed over and nodded his hellos. Calm as you like. You would never have thought that he hadn't ridden a winner at the Cheltenham Festival before, or that he had told everyone who would listen to him that Moscow Flyer was going to take a hell of a lot of beating in the Arkle. If his heart was beating twice as quickly as normal, his demeanour didn't betray it. A duck's feet.

To be honest, I can't remember what we said to one another as we all stood there. It didn't matter anyway. All the talking was done. The instructions were simple, just the same as they'd been at Leopardstown, Punchestown, Down Royal and Fairyhouse: get him settled, have him handy, ride him with confidence.

The bell sounded, and Barry and I went to find our horse. Number six. The good-looking one with the noseband and the little white blob in the middle of his forehead. We didn't speak on our way over. I didn't want to communicate any of my nervousness to him. Eamonn had the stirrups down by the time we got there. Moscow began to do his usual little tight circles as I went to leg Barry up. Good luck. Ride your race.

I stood in the parade ring and watched as they made their way around once more, the three of them – Eamonn, Barry and Moscow. It was a strange feeling. A mixture of nervousness and helplessness. I couldn't do any more. It was a bit like how a parent feels before seeing her child perform on the stage. You rehearse with them at home, you will them to perform to the best of their ability, but there is nothing more you can do once they go backstage. Even if your child were to fall on her face in the middle of the stage, you couldn't jump up and help. You are powerless. And in horse racing terms, this was the greatest stage of all. This was Broadway.

Cheltenham is the only racecourse at which I don't watch Moscow's races with Brian. I have always gone to Jim Wilson's box. Jim rode Little Owl to win the Gold Cup in 1981, and he is still the last amateur rider to win a Gold Cup. Call it superstition or call it routine, it's just what I do, and I wasn't about to change it when I had a real chance of winning the Arkle. Brian and Patricia headed off for the owners' and trainers' stand. Meet you back here afterwards.

My heart pounded as they circled at the start. Please let them off soon. The sooner they start the sooner it will be over and the sooner we will know. Just stay clear of incident. If he is beaten, let it be on merit. I didn't know how I would handle the frustration of being beaten without getting a fair crack at it.

And then they were lining up. Brian's black and white silks towards the outside, towards the left as you looked at them. The cheer began in the belly of the stands, just as it had for the first race, and grew louder as the twelve runners walked in. A tingle began in the base of my spine, ran all the way up to the back of my neck and all the way back down again. The starter lowered his flag, pressed the lever and released the tape.

The two-mile start at Cheltenham is one of the furthest points on the course from the stands. It must be all of five or six furlongs straight down the track. As a result, if you watch the start of the Arkle through your binoculars from the stands you see them coming head on, straight at the first fence, and it is hard to see if they are meeting it in their stride or not. Moscow seemed to be away OK with them. I alternated my gaze between the racecourse and the big screen to my right. They seemed to be going a fierce gallop. Much faster than Moscow would ever have travelled over fences in Ireland. He would have to meet the first fence right. There's no time to warm up here. Not in the white-hot heat of an Arkle. It's do it now or else be lost.

As they approached the first, I watched the screen. He seemed to be meeting it on a good stride. Barry crouched. One, two, up. He pinged it, landed running, and settled into his rhythm.

I had expected the noted trailblazer Ei Ei to take them along, but he couldn't get to the front. That's how fast they were travelling. The Simon Sherwood-trained Il'Athou was leading from Ei Ei and Armaturk. Barry had settled Moscow in mid-division on the outside as they passed the winning post on the first circuit. It wasn't difficult to get him to settle given how fast they were going, but he had now jumped the first three well, and I was happy.

Halfway down the back straight, Barry asked Moscow to get closer. The frantic early pace was beginning to take its toll on the leaders. Il'Athou and Ei Ei were starting to back-pedal, and even

Armaturk was showing signs of distress. As Moscow made his move, however, I quickly noticed that McCoy's all-white, streamlined figure was also making progress on Seebald in behind. although he was under pressure to do so.

You don't want to be wrong at the open ditch on the far side, the fourth last. The open ditches at Cheltenham are as wide and as stiff as you will find on any racecourse anywhere in the UK or Ireland. A horse can get scared in mid-flight at this fence, drop his hind legs in it in an effort to correct himself, get his midriff stuck and catapult his pilot into orbit. If you do manage to keep the partnership intact, at best you have lost ground and momentum at a crucial stage of the race. Moscow was meeting it a little long. Barry saw that a long way off and kicked him into it. Three long strides and jump. They flew it and landed upsides Fondmort in second place.

Armaturk took them down the hill to the third last. I hate the third last. It is downhill just as they are starting to race, and horses are usually travelling into it too quickly. Moscow was tracking Armaturk, Fondmort had switched outside Moscow, and Seebald was just getting going in behind. But Barry was the least animated of the four jockeys. In fact, he looked to be going easiest of the whole field. The realisation began to dawn that this race was in our grasp. My heart began to pound. Just get over the third last. Just get to the far side of it upright.

My binoculars were shaking now. They were shaking so much that I didn't know if he met the third last in his stride or not. I just saw him approach the fence, and then I saw him on the landing side. Upright. I couldn't even tell if he had jumped over it or run right through it. I heaved a huge sigh of relief and took my binoculars down. They were sacked.

Barry squeezed Moscow down the hill and on to the second last. McCoy had been after Seebald for a while now. Armaturk and Fondmort had cried enough, so now it was a duel. Seebald v. Moscow. McCoy v. Geraghty. England v. Ireland. The stands exploded. I think I muttered something under my breath. Something barely audible and completely incomprehensible that began in my head as 'Just jump it!' And he did. Actually, he didn't. He fiddled it, but that was enough. He had enough in hand. Seebald jumped it well, but the advantage was definitely with Moscow.

Around the home turn and down to the last, it was ours to lose. Seebald was keeping on valiantly, but vainly. Only then did I start to shout, though the difference I made to the overall decibel level was negligible I'm sure. I could hardly even hear myself. At the last, Barry asked Moscow for one last exact leap. Moscow didn't disappoint him. Just as he hadn't disappointed him at any of the other eleven obstacles. He sailed over it and set off up the hill. He pricked his ears as if to tell us that he had much more energy left if it was needed. Barry just encouraged him the whole way until fully 25 yards before the line, when he stood up in the irons and saluted the stands. The stands responded in kind, and the roof just about stayed on.

A kaleidoscope of emotion welled up inside me and got stuck somewhere between my rib cage and my throat. Elation, relief, ecstasy, vindication, even a hint of nationalism. But ask me what my overriding feeling was then, and still is today, and I'll tell you, 'Pride.' I was proud of Barry, who had just put in a riding performance that absolutely belied his Cheltenham maiden status. I was proud of Eamonn, for the way he had looked after the horse. Proud of Johnny, for believing in me and believing in Moscow. But most of all I was proud of Moscow Flyer. I was so proud of him that I felt like jumping off the stands, running down to him on the racecourse and flinging my arms around his neck. Most inappropriate.

It was an unbelievable feeling. It was one of those feelings you will remember for the rest of your life. If you could put that feeling into a bottle and let a little bit of it out when things weren't going so well, you would. But you can't, so you just have to savour all of it in the present. Drink it in in the here and now, and cherish every drop.

I made my way through a sea of hugs, kisses and back-slaps

down to the bottom of the parade ring where the horses come in to unsaddle. It seemed as if everyone on the racecourse had got there before me. I couldn't get close to my horse, but I didn't mind. I just walked in behind Eamonn, Barry and Moscow and left them to it.

Barry lapped it all up. He was entitled to. It was his first Cheltenham winner. I had been lucky enough to train Space Trucker to win the Grand Annual in 1999, but, while that was brilliant, it was nothing like this. Eamonn was nearly in tears. And as he led Moscow and Barry into the most coveted winner's enclosure in National Hunt racing, Barry waved his whip, grinned his grin, stood up in his irons and stretched himself so that he couldn't have got any higher without standing on Moscow's back. The crowd loved it. They cheered and clapped and bayed for more.

When they call 'horses away' in Cheltenham's winner's enclosure and the horses are led back to the stables for a well-earned wash and rest, they are usually replaced in the enclosure by a throng of press people. And then the interviews begin. Delighted with him. Great for Barry. Great for Brian. Great for Eamonn. Yes, we might go to Punchestown. We'll see how he is when we get him home. Don't ask me about the Champion Chase next year. Let's enjoy this for now.

When you are up on the presentation stand at Cheltenham, and about 30 steps full of people in front of you are applauding your achievement, you just don't want it to end. You don't want to get down from the podium. It doesn't matter that the Champion Hurdle contenders are parading behind you. This is your moment, and you are going to have it. Eventually you get down and you walk out of the winner's enclosure on the same air on which you walked in.

As the *Irish Independent* sponsored the Arkle, and still do, they invited us up to their box for a drink. That was nice, as we had somewhere to go just to have a quiet drink together. Brian and Patricia, their son Conor, Johnny and me. We were able to watch the race again with our hearts beating at a normal rate. You see so much more when you are not shaking like a pneumatic drill. We had another drink with Brian and Patricia at the racecourse before we went back to the Hendersons' and had a right party. Poor Nicky. Even though Fondmort had finished lame, he was still delighted for us and for Moscow, and he insisted on having a celebratory party for us.

I could hardly keep the smile off my face for the rest of the meeting. Even though I was probably severely hung over on the Wednesday, I didn't notice, and I didn't really care. The congratulations flowed all week. People I knew and people I didn't know. Irish and English. It didn't seem to matter, and as I said, I didn't really care. People are so nice. It was a fantastic feeling. I probably wouldn't have needed an aeroplane to take me home at the end of the week. I'm sure I could have floated over the Irish Sea myself.

But while it's important to celebrate and appreciate your horses' achievements, it is also important to keep some kind of perspective. Fairyhouse and Punchestown were coming up at home, and we had to consider if we were going to go to either or both. We now had the Arkle winner. The best two-mile novice chaser around. It was important that we got the rest of the season right.

CHAPTER NINETEEN

HOME WIN

The Powers Gold Cup at the Fairyhouse Easter Festival is a logical next port of call for the Arkle winner. A two-and-a-half-mile Grade 1 novice chase, with a lot of prestige and a good prize fund, it would have been ideal for Moscow. However, Easter came quite quickly after Cheltenham that year and I thought it would be unfair to ask Moscow to race again just over two weeks after running his heart out in the Arkle. I actually took him out of the Powers Gold Cup at the forfeit stage so that I wouldn't be tempted to run him on the day.

Punchestown was seven weeks after Cheltenham. That gave us enough time to give Moscow a little break and get him ready again. People were saying that I should run him in the BMW Chase – the two-mile championship race. Their thinking was that the two-mile championship division was a weak division that year and that, even though Moscow was only a novice, he would have a great chance of beating the more experienced horses. I'm not sure if they were the same people who had been saying that he was a dodgy jumper. That he didn't jump well enough to win an Arkle. But they might have been. I didn't even consider running Moscow in the BMW, even though the Champion Chase winner, Flagship Uberalles, was going to Sandown, and runner-up Native Upmanship was going in the Heineken Gold Cup over three miles instead of the BMW over two. I figured that, while Moscow was a novice and eligible to run in novice races, he should stick to novice races. The Swordlestown Cup was the race for him at Punchestown. All going well, there would be time enough to take on the big guns the following season.

Nor did I really consider roughing him off for the season after Cheltenham. He had run only six times that season, and he had fallen twice, so really he'd had only four full races. That was a relatively light campaign. Of course, if he had been showing signs of weariness when we began to train him for Punchestown, I would probably have sent him straight out into a field. But he was bouncing.

To tell the truth, we didn't do that much with him coming up to Punchestown. We had had him super-fit for Cheltenham, and I didn't feel that he needed to do too much. I thought it would be a relatively easy race for him anyway. None of the English horses were coming over, and we had beaten all the Irish two-mile novices easily when we had stood up before. Mantles Prince was in there pitching again. I'm sure his trainer Pat Hughes was sick of the sight of Moscow Flyer. And Assessed, the horse who had won the Baileys Arkle after Moscow had fallen. He had run quite a good race in the Arkle at Cheltenham in spite of the fact that he hadn't jumped too well. I thought he might give us most to do, but with normal luck, even if Moscow was only 90 per cent fit, I was fairly confident we would win.

Nicky and Diana Henderson came over to stay with us for Punchestown that year. They usually come over to stay with us for . Punchestown. Nicky loves Punchestown, and we have to reciprocate the Cheltenham deal. Nicky brought a couple of horses over for the meeting. Barry was riding Lord of the River for him in the Pat Taaffe Chase on Swordlestown Cup day and Landing Light in the Emo Oil Champion Hurdle on the Friday. We had a mid-Punchestown party at Commonstown on Wednesday night, so most of us were a little the worse for wear on Thursday.

Cathal Ryan always has a big brunch at his Swordlestown Stud before racing on Thursday, Swordlestown Cup day. As the trainer of the odds-on favourite for the race, I should have been there from early on. But we were late getting away in the morning – we were late starting, but so much has to be done at home before you can leave for the races – and we didn't arrive at Swordlestown until the brunch was almost over. I'm not sure Cathal was too pleased. In fairness, we should have been on time. Those Hendersons are a bad influence.

Punchestown is generally a more relaxed meeting than Cheltenham, but there was still a fair amount of pressure on Moscow to perform. He was expected to go out and win the Swordlestown Cup easily. It was nothing like the pressure of Cheltenham, not by a long way, but I was still anxious that he go out, put in a clear round, and come back to us safely. Barry had him handy from the start, travelling easily and jumping well. At the fifth last he gave Moscow his head and allowed him to stride on. By the third last he had gone clear. Race over. Bar a fall.

He wasn't too clever at the second last, though. I wasn't sure if he lost his concentration or if he and Barry just got their wires crossed. He never really looked like coming down, and Barry never really looked like he would come off, but it definitely gave cause for a moment's anxiety. If there had been a challenger within hailing distance at the time, it could have been a concern. After that, he coasted over the last and coasted up the run-in. The Punchestown crowd gave him a really warm reception. They appreciate their good horses at Punchestown. I probably didn't realise it fully beforehand, but people were very appreciative of the fact that I had allowed Moscow to run. They appreciated the opportunity to see the Arkle hero compete on home soil. It meant that those who weren't at Cheltenham could come and see him in the flesh. I was glad that I had let him run, and I heaved a huge sigh of relief when he crossed the line.

We got him into the winner's enclosure, washed him down, put him in his horsebox and brought him home. Just half an hour down the road. And that was it for the season, on Thursday, 25 April 2002. He had had his first race that season on 24 October 2001. It had been a long and eventful six months.

I thought back to that day at Fairyhouse when our horse was lying prostrate on the ground after taking the mother and father of all falls. If you had told me at that moment that we would have him home with us but he would never win another race, I would have settled for that. If he had fallen a little awkwardly that day, that would have been that. But now here we were, six months later. An Arkle Chase in the bag, a Swordlestown Cup and a Denny. Three Grade 1 races. Already they were talking about Moscow Flyer as a live candidate for the Champion Chase the following year. It was a lot to take in. We had an awful lot for which to be thankful. For my own part, I was relieved that we had got through the season. Very relieved. And delighted that he had proved himself to be the class horse I knew he was.

Still, it's a big step up from novice class to championship division. There are more Arkle winners who don't make it against the experienced horses than Arkle winners who do. So I played down talk of the Champion Chase. He's only a novice. Let's get through the summer and then let's see how he goes. We just don't know yet if he will prove to be up to it.

Deep down, however, I suspected that he might be. Truth be told, I was excited as hell about the season ahead.

CHAPTER TWENTY

CHAMPION CHASER

The summer of 2002 was one of content at Commonstown. Spirit Leader had finally won her maiden hurdle and was looking like she might be a bit better than average. Bust Out was off with leg trouble since his defeat by Istabraq, but he was going over fences that season and looked like he might make up into a top novice chaser. We had another nice young hurdler called Intelligent, who was going chasing. And, of course, we had the best two-mile novice chaser of the previous season in one of the fields down the back. Time would tell if he would be able to hack it in the Premiership.

Moscow didn't go down to David Nugent's that year. There was no real scientific reason for keeping him at Commonstown. We just figured that it would be as handy to keep him and he would be as happy with us as he would be down in Wexford. He just ambled around his field, bucking and kicking his merry way through the summer.

He was becoming quite a character. As he began to realise that he was often the focus of attention, he began to develop his own little idiosyncrasies. For example, he wouldn't leave his box to go out into the field if it was raining. He'd just stand by the open door looking up at the sky. You don't expect me to go out in that, do you? He realised he could get away with being a little different. We were in danger of spoiling him. I suppose when you have one as good as him, you don't mind spoiling them a little.

We brought him in, as usual, at the beginning of August, got his shoes on him and put him on the horse-walker for two days. I don't like to leave him on the walker for too long because, if we do, he gets very fresh and starts bucking people off when we start to ride him. Two days is enough. Then we trotted him around the gallops for about three weeks before easing him into his work. Once he is working, he is happy. Once the freshness goes out of him he settles into his work and doesn't engage in his second favourite pastime – bucking people off.

Planning with Brian that year was easy: start at the Champion Chase and work backwards. Like I said before, it is easy to plan a campaign for a good horse. It's the bad ones that are difficult. There was a Grade 2 chase at Leopardstown at Christmas that would fit in nicely, and we'd probably find a race somewhere for him between Christmas and March. I also had it in my head that I'd like to bring him over to Sandown for the Tingle Creek Chase in early December. That would give us a chance to take on the big boys like Cenkos and Flagship Uberalles, that year's Champion Chase winner. Moscow deserved his shot at them, and at least then we would know where we stood. Brian was excited about the prospect.

As a starting point, there was an intermediate chase at Down Royal that November over two miles and two furlongs. It was an ideal race for Moscow's seasonal debut as it was restricted to second-season chasers – horses who had been novices the previous season. It would allow him to get in some match practice without having to compete against the very top two-milers. Don't take on the experienced horses until you have to.

As it happened, Moscow scared away a lot of the opposition and was left with only two opponents: Fiery Ring, who was trained by my brother John and who I thought would make the pace for us, and Kadarann. Kadarann had been well behind us in the Arkle, but he had won three races in the interim, including a decent handicap chase at the Ayr Scottish National meeting. Paul Nicholls, who trained Kadarann, liked to have a winner at the Down Royal meeting, so he wasn't travelling to the North for the cheap diesel. Furthermore, the conditions of the race dictated that we had to concede 8lb to him. I remember complaining to Noel Meade before the race about the lack of runners. I wanted Moscow to gain more experience of jumping among horses before he stepped into the big time. Noel laughed. As long as he won, what did it matter how many runners there were in it? I suppose he had a point.

Fiery Ring made the running. He was meant to make the running for longer than he did, but he just didn't go fast enough for Moscow. Barry allowed Moscow to stride on at the second fence past the stands. Kadarann went with him, but by the third last Moscow had pulled right away. He won by twenty lengths. I was very happy with that performance. He would have only been about 75 per cent fit and the ground was quite soft. Kadarann was a fair yardstick, and we were giving him a lot of weight. Then we started training Moscow. If he was going to have a date with Flagship Uberalles and company at Sandown, he was going to have to look the part.

Spirit Leader and Intelligent had both run at Down Royal as well. Intelligent had won the beginners' chase Moscow had won the previous year, although in 2002 it was run over two and a half miles instead of two. Spirit Leader had finished third in a valuable handicap hurdle. I thought that we would send all three to Sandown together. Spirit Leader was so highly rated that she was always going to be carrying big weights in handicap hurdles in Ireland. I figured that those big two-mile handicap hurdles in England always attract classy horses who would be much higher rated than her, so there was a chance she could get into something like the William Hill off a nice weight. And there was a nice three-mile intermediate chase at Sandown on the Friday that I thought would suit Intelligent well.

Eamonn drove the three of them over on the lorry. They got lost on the M25, which was not ideal for a man used to driving down main street Moone where rush hour is when a tractor and a trailer go down the street together. He did get his bearings, however, and the four of them got to the course safely. Everything intact. I flew over on the Friday morning with my daughter Emma. Sandown looked after us very well. In fact, Sandown have always looked after us very well. They gave us lunch in the royal box on both days, which was greatly appreciated. They couldn't do enough for us.

Intelligent was the outsider of four in the GQ Future Stars Chase. Among his three rivals was Valley Henry, a young horse of Paul Barber's, trained by Paul Nicholls, who was being touted as a future Gold Cup winner. When they said that the race was well named, I don't think they were referring to our horse. Barry had ridden Valley Henry when he had won at Ayr the previous April, and he was asked to ride him again. In fairness, I couldn't blame him for riding Nicholls' horse instead of mine. His was one of the top staying novice chasers of the previous season who was being geared up for a tilt at the Gold Cup, while mine was a youngster who had just won his first chase.

Barry was riding a good bit for Nicholls at the time. In fact, he could have joined Nicholls the previous summer. He rode a little bit for him towards the end of the 2001/02 season and was given the opportunity to join him full-time during the summer. Some of his mates told him that he would be mad to turn it down. They said he should at least go and try it for a year, and if it didn't work out, he could just come back. But Barry didn't think it was something he could try for a year. He felt that he couldn't just up and leave, be gone for a year, and then expect to find everything as he had left it if and when he came back. People move on. It can be a fickle business. He was probably right. It was a tough one for Barry. He had the opportunity to join one of the most powerful yards in the UK as first jockey, but he would have had to have moved to the UK and give up Ireland. He had a good set-up in Ireland. He was riding for a lot of the top yards, the prize money was good, and there was a tax exemption for sports people.

One of the main determining factors in his decision not to leave was an eight-year-old bay gelding by Moscow Society out of a Duky mare with a white blob on his forehead and a thin white streak running down his face. Barry didn't want to miss out on anything to do with Moscow Flyer. Not a beat. And if he needed confirmation that he had made the correct decision, he got it the following spring when he rode five winners at Cheltenham and won the Grand National on Monty's Pass. That December he became the first jockey ever to be voted Irish Sports Personality of the Year.

I had an able deputy for Intelligent in Mick Fitzgerald. Mick had actually ridden Valley Henry to win on his first run that season at Exeter. Intelligent ran well and finished second to Valley Henry. They didn't go a great gallop, but our horse ran on nicely. He had two decent horses in Haut Cercy and Maximize behind him. Mick got off him and said that he was a real Grand National type. I thought that we might try to emulate Miss Orchestra's Midlands National win in the interim.

We stayed with the Hendersons in Lambourn on the Friday night and went back to Sandown the following morning. Barry was on *The Morning Line* that morning being his usual confident-verging-on-cocky self. There is a fine line between the two. I'm not quite sure where it is exactly. I suppose people use hindsight to determine it. If the horse wins, you were full of confidence; if he gets beaten, you were being cocky.

I had the usual Moscow Flyer nerves that morning and did the usual box-walking. I was very happy that the horse was well. He had travelled over well and seemed to be in good form on Saturday morning. This race would be the litmus test of where we stood. It would tell us if we had a realistic chance of winning the Champion

Chase, or if we were being stupid even considering going for it. It is the natural progression for an Arkle winner, but it is still a huge leap up in class. The fact that he was already nearly favourite for the Champion Chase was largely irrelevant as far as I was concerned. John Francome reckoned that Moscow would have to improve by up to 12lb to be involved in the finish of the Tingle Creek. Cenkos and Edredon Bleu were both front-runners, so we knew there would be a nice fast pace. There were only six runners, so the chances of meeting trouble in-running were slim. He was as well as we thought we could have him, and we were as confident and as hopeful as you can be when you are stepping into the big league. On the downside, it was going to be difficult to think of an excuse if he got beaten. That made me nervous. If he got beaten, it would be difficult to think anything other than that he just wasn't good enough.

The two-mile start at Sandown is way down to the right of the stands, at the top of the home straight. They jump two and go up past the winning post before setting out on a complete circuit. Barry settled Moscow in second-last place on the outside, but not too far off the leader. I was happy enough as it was a small field and a strong pace. He jumped the first two well and settled into his rhythm past the winning post, around the top turn and down the side of the track.

You often see horses clipping the top of the third fence and coming down too steeply. Moscow met it fine and popped over it. All well. Partnership intact.

Over the first in the back straight, and there was no let-up. Cenkos had been harrying Edredon Bleu for the lead from tape-fly and was still at it. Let me lead. Go on. Let me lead for a little while. You've been in front from the start. Come on. I'll be your best friend. Moscow was a little slow over it, and Barry asked him to get closer.

Going to the second fence in the back straight, Moscow and Barry were tracking Flagship Uberalles and Richard Johnson. I was happy enough with that. Flagship Uberalles was favourite for this and was the reigning champion chaser. He set the standard by which Moscow had to be measured. Moreover, in twenty steeplechase races up to that day, Flagship Uberalles had never fallen or unseated his rider. He had hardly made a mistake.

Up to that day.

The favourite seemed to jump the fence OK, but he stumbled on landing. Moscow jumped it about a length and a half behind. When Flagship stumbled, he lost all impetus and all but came to a standstill. Moscow was heading straight into the back of him. He had to take evasive action. Almost in one movement, he landed and jinked to his left. Of course Barry went straight on. This was a wholly unexpected development. The jockey was left grasping at fresh air. He nearly landed on Flagship Uberalles' back. Partnership dissolved.

The ground was fairly soft so Barry had an easy landing. Or as easy a landing as you can have when you unexpectedly fall off something that is over five feet from the ground. Moscow galloped on with the rest of the field. I watched him as he jumped every fence with them except for the third last, the Pond Fence, which he adeptly evaded and hoped that nobody would notice. He tracked Cenkos over the last two fences and chased him all the way up the run-in so that Ruby Walsh rode a finish on the winner even though he was miles clear of the next horse with a rider. He could see this white noseband out of the corner of his eye, and he knew it was Moscow. He just didn't think to check to see if Barry was on him. Moscow stretched his neck out on the line and got up by a short head. He couldn't understand why he wasn't led into the winner's enclosure.

Brian and Patricia were disappointed, but they were great, as usual. These things happen. The horse is all right and Barry is all right. As long as they are all right. I was disappointed and frustrated. The not-knowing was the most difficult part. We had travelled to Sandown to find out if what we suspected was true – if we had a Champion Chase candidate in our care. We left Sandown none the wiser. He hadn't even started racing by the time he lost Barry. I thought, how stupid he was, to jink so suddenly. He gave

Barry no chance of staying with him. But that's him. He's sharp like that. He notices the slightest of things and reacts to them. Before I left the owners' and trainers' stand, I had come around. Moscow seemed to be OK and Barry seemed to be OK. As Brian had said, that was the main thing. All being well, we would find out another day. And there would be another day.

I watched as Moscow cantered up past the winning post below me and straight up to the shoot that leads back to the stables. This was his first time at Sandown, but already he had figured out where the exit back to the stables was. I watched as Eamonn picked him up and led him back in. He seemed to be fine.

It's funny the way these things work out. Half an hour later, Spirit Leader went and won the William Hill Handicap Hurdle under Norman Williamson. *Thuas seal, thíos seal*. What could have turned out to be a disastrous weekend actually hadn't worked out too badly. It depended on your perspective. Looking at it from the sunny side, Spirit Leader had won a £40,000 pot, Intelligent had run a really nice race, and Moscow was still in one piece. That was the way I was thinking coming home that evening.

We gave Moscow a fairly easy time when we got him home. He had three or four days in a field. Quite literally, we let him off in the field in the morning and put him back in his box in the evening. We didn't ask him to do any work for a week. Not a stroke. Fortunately, he was none the worse for his Sandown exertions, so we were able to train him for Christmas. In fairness, he had had no more than a canter around Sandown, but sometimes even the travelling can take it out of them. Moscow came back fresh and well, and ready to go again.

The Paddy Power Dial-a-Bet Chase was the two-mile conditions chase for him at Leopardstown's Christmas Festival. It was another wet December and the ground was atrocious. So much so that one of the days had to be cancelled at Leopardstown that year and the Paddy Power race was put back a day. Even then the ground was so bad that two fences had to be omitted. Although conditions were desperate, I never really considered not running him. If he was to be a serious Champion Chase contender, he needed as much match practice as he could get. If it was flat out the whole way in the Arkle against novices over National Hunt's sprint distance, what would it be like in a Champion Chase?

The bookmakers still had him in as favourite for the Champion Chase, in spite of the Tingle Creek mishap. I was slightly bemused by this. The one time he had competed against experienced two-mile chasers, he had failed to complete. It was quite the opposite to their attitude towards him when he was jumping hurdles. I certainly thought he had the potential to be that good, but he still had to prove it.

Knife Edge, Alcapone, Arctic Copper and Go Roger Go lined up in the Paddy Power. The usual suspects. In truth, I would have been very disappointed had we not been able to beat them well, but there was still a fair bit of pressure on Moscow to perform – weight of expectation again, mainly. Specifically, there was pressure on him to complete.

It wasn't a satisfactory race. Conditions were so bad that Moscow couldn't get into his rhythm at all. I doubt if any of his competitors found it a satisfactory race either, but they weren't my concern. Moscow jumped around adequately and won by five lengths from Knife Edge. Job done, and we got in out of the rain.

Flagship Uberalles ran in the King George at Kempton that Christmas. I thought it was a strange move to run the reigning two-mile champion chaser in the King George over three miles. He was only eight years old at the time, and before running at Kempton he had looked like the one who would set the standard at Cheltenham. Best Mate won that King George, with Flagship Uberalles pulled up before three out. He simply didn't stay, and he never ran over three miles again. I don't know if he ever recovered his real two-mile speed after that.

The next race for Moscow on the list of engagements was the Tied Cottage Chase, a Grade 2 two-mile chase run at Punchestown in mid-February. This race had disappeared from the calendar for three years and only returned in 2003. I had been complaining that there was no race in Ireland that was suitable for Moscow as a prep race for Cheltenham. We had no race here, like the Game Spirit Chase at Newbury, for Champion Chase aspirants. We had the Newlands Chase at Naas in late February, but that was just a little too close to Cheltenham. A hard race or an over-reach there, and you could leave your Champion Chase behind you in Naas. I don't know if the Irish race planners had Moscow Flyer in mind when they reintroduced the Tied Cottage race, but I was delighted to see it on the calendar. It was ideal for him.

He went to Punchestown as the long odds-on favourite. Commanche Court ran in the Tied Cottage that year, and Killultagh Storm, and my brother's horse Fiery Ring. In truth, however, Moscow was head and shoulders above any other two-mile chaser in the country at the time. Again the ground at Punchestown that day was far softer than we would have wanted, but it didn't matter. Moscow jumped past Copernicus at the fifth last and just coasted clear. All was well until he came down to the last. Remember, this was Punchestown. He rarely leaves Punchestown without giving us at least a moment's anxiety. This time the moment came at the last. It was possibly down to a lack of concentration as he had been out on his own for so long, but he just blundered his way through it. He never really looked like falling, but I was glad when he got to the far side of it on all fours.

We had exactly five and a half weeks between the Tied Cottage Chase and the Champion Chase at Cheltenham. That was just about ideal. Enough time to let him down a little bit and build him back up again. We planned to have him at concert pitch on Champion Chase day, and hoped that nothing would happen in the interim to upset that plan. Nothing did. Moscow Flyer is the most remarkable horse. Throughout his career, it has been so easy to plan his campaign because he has remained so sound. Apart from the hairline fracture of his pelvis, he has hardly ever missed a day's work through injury.

There was a little more pressure on us in the lead-up to Cheltenham 2003 than there had been in 2002. He was the Arkle winner and, more importantly, the Champion Chase favourite. I still wasn't sure that they had it right in putting him in as their 5–2 favourite, but I suppose I couldn't really argue against it. There wasn't one rival in the field I feared.

Spirit Leader was also on her way to Cheltenham to contest the County Hurdle, the last race of the meeting. Since her win at Sandown she had been beaten in the Pierse Hurdle at Leopardstown under a big weight, but had gone back to the UK and won the Tote Gold Trophy – I still call it the Schweppes – at Newbury. She had won two of the biggest two-mile handicap hurdles on the calendar in the UK. It was a bit much to expect her to make it three in the County Hurdle. Wasn't it?

I worked the two of them together at Leopardstown just before Cheltenham. Of the two, Spirit Leader impressed me most. I was delighted with her, and at the same time far from disappointed with Moscow. He only ever does as much as he has to.

The first thing that struck me when I arrived at Cheltenham on 11 March was that we were here again. It was quite surreal walking into the enclosures on the Tuesday morning thinking that we were back. I remember thinking that even to be back again was an achievement. So much can go wrong with a racehorse. Excluding the mishap at Sandown, Moscow hadn't put one foot out of place in twelve months. It was quite extraordinary. It was great to be back.

I was afforded the luxury of a day with no runners and no panic. The grey horse Rooster Booster won the Champion Hurdle impressively. He had come up through the handicap ranks, having finished second in the Tote Gold Trophy and having won the County Hurdle the previous season. No reason why Spirit Leader couldn't make up into a Champion contender. Although we'll see how Thursday goes first.

Also on the Tuesday, the Arkle was won by Paul Nicholls' horse Azertyuiop. He trounced what looked like a very good field of novices that included Impek, Hand Inn Hand, Farmer Jack and Isio. Azertyuiop had been a good hurdler, but he had been a revelation since being sent over fences. This was his fourth steeplechase race and his fourth impressive win. He may have had a strange name – the top line of a French typewriter keyboard – but it looked likely that he would be looking for a seat at the top table the following season.

Once Wednesday morning arrived, the luxury was over. No more swanning around enjoying the racing. No way. There was work to do and pressure to bear. Now, I don't wish to downplay the Arkle Chase in any way. To win the Arkle in 2002 was absolutely fantastic. But this was a little different. This was the Champion Chase. This was one of the three championship races of the Festival. Gold Cup, Champion Hurdle, Champion Chase – that's the golden triangle.

There was a sense of *déjà vu* in the parade ring beforehand. We were all here again. Brian and Patricia smiling nervously. Me with the same mad pangs of nervousness and excitement. Barry nodding nonchalantly from beneath his helmet. No worries. Johnny shaking hands with just about everybody. All that was missing was his crutch. It was Conor Kearney, Brian's son, who was on crutch duty in March 2003 after breaking his ankle. If we win this, I thought, we might have to arrange for someone else to be on crutches next year. I bade my farewells and went off to Jim Wilson's box. If Brian and Patricia had thought that was strange the previous year, they were fully prepared for it this year.

I saw Tiutchev as our main danger. He had won the Arkle in 2000 when trained by Nicky Henderson and had just joined Martin Pipe at the beginning of that season. On his last outing he had won the Ritz Club Chase at Ascot. The noises emanating from the Pipe yard were positive ones, and McCoy was riding. Outside him, I didn't think we had too much to fear. Edredon Bleu appeared to be on the descent from his peak, and Flagship Uberalles was on a recovery mission after trying and failing at three miles in the King George. Cenkos had been beaten by Kadarann in the Game Spirit Chase, and Moscow had beaten Kadarann out of sight at Down Royal. Willie Mullins was trying Florida Pearl over two miles, and Native Upmanship was having another go, but, to be honest, I thought that with normal luck Moscow would win.

We probably had slightly better than normal luck. Not that we needed to be lucky; we just needed to avoid ill-luck. Edredon Bleu took them along in the early stages. Moscow travelled well and jumped well in the middle of them early on and gradually moved up to fourth or fifth going down the far side. He got in a little close to the water jump, but hardly lost any ground. Going to the fourth last, his favourite, Barry took a little tug. Not yet. At the fence he was a little long. Barry asked him to stand off it. Moscow wasn't sure. He almost changed his mind going over it, but he didn't. Even so, he just about made it to the far side. Back of the saddle and buckle of the reins time for Barry. He lost a little momentum, but not too much. He recovered his position on the rails as my heart recovered its position just inside my rib cage.

After that he looked home, bar a fall. He was travelling by far the best going down to the third last. Tiutchev had fallen at the fifth and everything else, with the possible exception of Seebald and Latalomne in front, was off the bridle. Barry pulled him out from behind the two leaders. He sensed that they were flagging and didn't want to get caught in behind them. You just don't know what tired horses are going to do. Best-case scenario, you are on top of them before you know it and have to take evasive action; worst-case scenario, they fall in front of you. That is why you want to have a jockey on your side. Too many would-be jockeys in the stands judge the standard of jockeyship by what they see when the whips are flailing in a finish. But there is so much more to it than that. Barry pulled out because he sensed it was the right thing to do. No real explanation. He decided to do it and did it all within a fraction of a second before you could say house-of-cards.

Call it luck or gods on your side or horsemanship, but that manoeuvre probably made the difference between winning the Champion Chase and crying over what might have been. Moscow was disputing the lead jumping the second last, Latalomne and

Seebald to his left. Moscow jumped the fence well and landed running away. Neither of the others did. Both of them got in a little too tight to the fence, both of them clipped the top of it, both of them landed too steeply, and both of them crumpled to the floor. If Norman Williamson and Vinnie Keane had not been wearing different coloured silks, you would have thought you were looking at one horse and rider combination and its reflection. Synchronised falling. When you watch the video replay, it's difficult to focus on Moscow and Barry tram-tracking around the home turn and not watch poor Vinnie Keane in the background thumping the ground and then diving headlong into it in disgust. It was the second time in two years that he and Latalomne had fallen at the same fence when leading in the same race.

Native Upmanship was forced a little wide in order to avoid the sprawling Latalomne, but it was academic. Moscow and Barry were facing up to the last fence again. Same requirements as last year for the same result: jump it and we win. And he did. Impeccably. He jumped it almost without touching it. Puissance wall-like. He didn't need Barry's continued urgings to climb the hill. He knew this one well. The crowd-cheer lifted him and carried him up it. Moscow pricked his ears and acknowledged his adoring audience as Barry waved to it. Conor O'Dwyer hugged him, Ruby gave him five, and Paul Carberry and Jim Culloty shook his hand even before they had pulled up. It was just a taster for what was to follow.

I couldn't believe that he had done it. That Moscow Flyer had won the Champion Chase. I really hadn't been able to see what could beat him beforehand, but when he actually won it I found it hard to come to terms with it. Moscow Flyer – champion chaser. It had a good ring to it. I hugged Jim Wilson and I hugged Emma. I probably hugged everyone in Jim Wilson's box.

Moscow was all but carried shoulder-high into the winner's enclosure. It was all Eamonn could do to stay at his head and lead him. Truth to tell, he didn't need to be led. He knew his way into that enclosure by now. Barry did his flying dismount. I don't think he had planned to do it. It just seemed like a good thing to do at the time. He must have been watching too much Flat racing. While he remained upright, he wouldn't have got more than 4.5 or 5 from a gymnastics judge. Frankie Dettori he ain't!

Princess Anne presented the prize that year. That was nice as I knew her from eventing. And just like the previous year, we didn't want to get down from the podium. There was a slight difference, however. The Champion Hurdle was the race that followed the Arkle in 2002, and once the Arkle presentations were complete, attention immediately focused on the Champion Hurdle. This time we were the feature event of the day. Take as long as you like.

We were back up on it after the last race, the County Hurdle, after Spirit Leader had battled her heart out to hold on by a neck and a short head from Balapour and Through the Rye. It was quite amazing. Everyone was saying that she couldn't win with 11st 7lb on her back. She was 18lb higher than she had been when she won the William Hill at Sandown. It was the first time any horse had won those three top two-mile handicap hurdles in the UK – the William Hill, the Tote Gold Trophy and the County Hurdle. I wouldn't be surprised if it was never done again.

Barry had ridden three other winners to be top jockey at the Festival. There were eighteen races in which professional jockeys were eligible to ride at the Festival and Barry had won five of them. It was a great achievement. I had brought two hopefuls to Cheltenham and come home with two winners. It was quite an amazing three days.

I floated home across the Irish Sea on Thursday night. I had probably celebrated enough on Wednesday night to cover Spirit Leader's win on Thursday as well. Johnny didn't subscribe to that notion. He stayed to celebrate on Thursday as well. But I had to go back. I had been away since Monday and I generally don't like being away too long. I had declarations to do for the weekend and I had to see Intelligent before he went to Uttoxeter for the Midlands National the following Saturday. I thought he had a great chance in it, but it would have been far too much to expect him to win that as well after the Cheltenham we had just had. But he did. He and Robert Power just got the better of Martin Pipe's fourth string, Akarus, in a gruelling finish. Robert claimed 5lb off Intelligent, just as Barry had claimed 5lb off Miss Orchestra when she won the same race five years earlier.

Intelligent's win put the raisins in the rum and raisin ice cream that was the second week in March 2003. It was a week you wouldn't even dare to mention if you were asked to talk about your wildest dreams. If I were to train racehorses for another 60 years I could never again have a week like that.

Emma got all the press cuttings from the week and put them into a folder. I got the photographer Caroline Norris to come down and take a photo of the three heroes together – Moscow, Intelligent and Spirit Leader – and I used it on the Christmas cards that we sent out that year. Regrettably, by the time we were sending out the cards, Intelligent was dead. Like I said before, you have to appreciate the good times in this game when they are around. There are enough bad times waiting around the corner to whack you on the head with a crowbar and steal your purse.

We thought about taking Moscow to Aintree for the two-and-a-half-mile chase, but decided against it. We didn't need to go there. Although I still had it in my head that he would stay further than two miles, we didn't need to find out if he would or wouldn't. Not yet anyway. He was the best two-mile steeplechaser around, so why go after something when you don't need to? We brought him home and kept him for Punchestown.

He wasn't as revved up for Punchestown as he had been for Cheltenham, but he was still fit enough to be able to win his race. We had nothing to fear. Flagship Uberalles and Latalomne represented the Champion Chase form. We had beaten them well just six weeks earlier. And then there were the usual Irish two-milers of the era: Arctic Copper, Killultagh Storm, Knife Edge. Roll call complete.

Moscow didn't jump the first fence very well at Punchestown, but he quickly settled into his rhythm. Barry got him nicely switched off going down the far side. By the time they got to the fourth last, Barry decided that they weren't going fast enough for him so he went on. He went about six lengths clear around the home turn. As they came down to the second last, he began to idle – his usual on-the-way-to-the-second-last-at-Punchestown antics. Flagship Uberalles was closing on him on the far side. I was anxious, but I still felt confident that he would raise his game again between the last two when the other horse came to him.

I never got to find out. He didn't pick up at all at the second last. He seemed to be meeting it spot on. Barry asked him to jump it in his stride, but at the last minute Moscow decided that he wanted to put in a short one before it. He did, but then he didn't seem to try to jump over it. He hit the middle of the fence with his chest and just about managed to get his forelegs out in front of him. That was no use to Barry, though. He was already out of contact with the saddle. On his way out over Moscow's head he tried to grab on to his neck, his mane, his ears. Nothing stuck. Barry went over the top, landed on his head, and rolled 180 degrees before coming to a halt.

It was a disappointing end to the season. There is no question about that. I was a little sad for the horse, that he had blotted his copybook on his seasonal swansong at home after achieving so much during the year. And I was annoyed that it had happened. Nobody was to blame. It was just one of those things. But it left a little bit of a bad taste in my mouth after what was a truly unbelievable season.

And it gave the knockers fodder. You never want to give the knockers fodder. There are always one or two. The people who pick holes in your achievements. The ones who said that the Champion Chase wasn't that strong a race and that the Arkle that Azertyuiop won in 2003 was a stronger Arkle than the one Moscow had won in 2002. That hypothesis would soon be put to the test. Going into the summer of 2003, however, Moscow Flyer was the champion chaser and unquestionably the best two-mile steeplechaser in training.

CHAPTER TWENTY-ONE

DETHRONED

People were beginning to comment on the pattern that was emerging on Moscow's CV. The three-wins-and-a-fall pattern. He had fallen in his first ever steeplechase race. Then he won three, then he fell. Then he won three more, then he unseated his rider. Won three more, unseated rider. One way of looking at it was that he failed to complete every fourth race. Another way was that he had never been beaten when he completed the course. I didn't look at it either way. When people asked me about it, I just said that Moscow couldn't count.

Had he been able to, he would have counted four mates in the field with him in the summer of 2003. That was a particularly wet summer. It was so wet that Moscow got rain rash the whole way from his withers to his tail. He was an awful sight when Brian came down to see him in August, but there was nothing to worry about. Rain rash is only cosmetically displeasing. It doesn't affect them at all. Moscow didn't have a mirror, so he didn't mind. That was the only issue with him that summer. His feet were fine because we knew how to treat them. He had no injuries or mishaps, coughs or runny noses. Frightfully boring. But I guess boring is good when you're talking about training a racehorse.

We couldn't go North with him in November as he obviously wasn't eligible for the beginners' chase or the intermediate chase. But there was a nice race at Navan, the Fortria Chase, that would be an ideal way to ease into the season. After that, the races picked themselves: Tingle Creek, Paddy Power, Tied Cottage, and back to Cheltenham for the Champion Chase. Then we'd see. We had the option of Aintree or Punchestown. The race for him at Aintree was the Melling Chase, run over two and a half miles. The race that Arthur Moore's Native Upmanship had made his own over the last two years. I had it in the back of my mind that I would like to try him over two and a half miles that year, but our planning meetings rarely looked beyond Cheltenham. After Cheltenham, we could have a planning update.

Only three rivals took us on in the Fortria. My brother John was having another crack with Fiery Ring. John was quite adept at placing Fiery Ring in these top-class races and picking up place money. He won over €100,000 in prize money in his career and only won four races. Glenelly Gale was also taking us on. Quite remarkably, he had won the James Nicholson Chase at Down Royal the previous day over three miles as the outsider of four runners. Arthur Moore packed him up and brought him down to Navan to run over two miles less than 24 hours later.

If there was a danger, however, in my view it was Rathgar Beau. He was trained by Dusty Sheehy and was a decent two-mile novice chaser from the previous season who was stepping up in grade. He had won two novice chases in the spring before being sent to Aintree for their Grade 1 two-mile novice chase. He was well backed there but fell four out. Rathgar Beau had finished third to Bust Out in the Baileys Arkle at Leopardstown the previous January. Regrettably, Bust Out had gone wrong again after that when we were preparing him for the Arkle at Cheltenham. He hasn't run since, though I am hoping that we can bring him back during the 2005/06 season. He will still be only nine years old and has very few miles on the clock. If we can keep him sound, I still believe he is potentially top class.

Moscow was a little way off full fitness for the Fortria – his main early-season target was the Tingle Creek, and I wanted to have him spot on for that – but we decided that we would let him make the running. He had made the running before, and with only four runners and John not agreeing to allow Fiery Ring to set the pace, we figured that he would have no problem making it again. He was at his most vulnerable with a muddling pace and a messy race. By making the running, he could set his own pace. And he did. He set a steady gallop early on and gradually quickened the tempo. As he did so, he began to warm to his task and have a cut at his fences. Unusually for Navan in November, the ground was quite fast, which suited Moscow well. They had new fences in Navan that year as well which were very well presented.

I had it in my head that Rathgar Beau wasn't the best of jumpers. He was only a second-season chaser and he had fallen at Aintree. Best make a decent pace and test his jumping. He made a mistake at the fifth last that put paid to his chances. Barry had to get after Moscow a little between the last two as Glenelly Gale looked like he would mount a challenge, but that challenge dissipated quickly and Moscow coasted home. It was really nothing more than a hack around in the end. He had a good blow afterwards, which is always an indication that they are not fully fit, and we were delighted. Job done. Minimal fuss.

We had unfinished business in the Tingle Creek. It would have been easy to stay at home and keep Moscow fresh until Leopardstown at Christmas, but we were anxious to put the record straight in the Tingle Creek. All our old friends would be there – Flagship Uberalles, Cenkos, Seebald – and one new one: Azertyuiop. That's the thing about the two-mile division. It doesn't tend to change that much from one year to the next. Maybe the

Arkle winner will be a challenger, but you don't get too many new Champion Chase contenders who come along with a real chance of making an impact. By all accounts this fellow was going to make an impact.

His debut in the major league, however, had been fairly inauspicious. Five days before Moscow got the new season off to a flyer at Navan, Azertyuiop had got rid of Mick Fitzgerald at the first fence at Exeter, in his first steeplechase race out of novice company. Poor Mick. It was the only time in his career that he rode the horse in a race and he didn't get beyond the first fence! Unusually, the excuses for Azertyuiop were being bandied about before the Tingle Creek. If he gets beaten, that'll be because he won't have had a run. Effectively, he's having his first run of the season in the Tingle Creek. If he gets beaten, it will probably be through lack of fitness or lack of match practice. You'll see a better horse after Sandown. I wasn't surprised at the excuses. We all make them. Usually, however, we make them after a horse has been beaten, not before he runs. I felt like saying, 'Well, if Paul Nicholls can't get a horse fit enough at home, then nobody can.' But I didn't. I bit my tongue and said that we were going there fit and well. We could only worry about our own horse.

I took three horses over to Sandown that year: Moscow Flyer, Green Belt Flyer (no relation) and Intelligent. Eamonn and Galway went over with them in the lorry. Kate and Johnny came over with me and we stayed with the Hendersons as usual. Emma joined us on the Saturday.

Green Belt Flyer went in the two-and-a-half-mile novice hurdle on the Friday. I thought he'd stay, but he didn't. He finished down the field. That race was won by Inglis Drever, who went on and won the World Hurdle in 2005. An hour later Intelligent ran in the intermediate chase – the same intermediate chase in which he had finished second to Valley Henry the previous year. No Valley Henry this time, and only three rivals, but we would have to see off the attentions of Impek, who had finished second to Azertyuiop in the previous season's Arkle.

As it happened, however, we never got the chance to see him off. With a circuit to go, Intelligent got in a little close and came down. It looked like a fairly innocuous fall, but whatever way he fell, he broke his neck and was killed instantly. I was gutted. Really gutted. He was such a lovely horse. I used to ride him out myself at home most of the time and I had grown particularly attached to him. He would jump through a brick wall for you. He was only seven years old and had his entire career ahead of him. When you lose a horse, it affects you. It affects some people more than others, but you would have to be made of stone for it not to affect you at all. When I woke up on the Saturday morning, I thought I just wanted Moscow to come back in one piece. Winning goes out the window at that stage. It genuinely does. All you want is your horse back.

When we went to saddle Moscow before the race, he was really horrible. He pushed us into every corner of the saddling box and didn't want to be saddled at all. I still don't know why he did that. It was highly unusual. He may just have been playing with us, or something may have been troubling him. Once we got him saddled and down the shoot to the parade ring, however, he was fine. There was something unusual, too, about Barry when he came out of the weigh room. Brian's colours looked a little different on him. A little cleaner or something. It turned out that the secretary had packed the wrong colours: white with black chevrons as opposed to black with white chevrons. Barry hadn't noticed. The clerk of the scales hadn't noticed. We put our heads down and said nothing. At least he had the correct cap. It could be for luck.

Eskleybrook started playing up at the start. He was digging his toes in and didn't want to line up. He was a 100–1 shot and had no chance anyway, but there was a danger that he could upset the others. I had visions of awful things happening at the start. Of Moscow whipping round or dropping Barry when the tape went up. It was turning into one of those weekends. But he did neither. He jumped off with the rest of them, and I heaved a sigh of relief. Eskleybrook didn't. He got left twenty lengths.

Moscow jumped the first on the outside of Cenkos in second place and settled down nicely. At the first fence down the back straight, he jumped a little to his left and cannoned into Le Roi Miguel. My heart gave a little flutter. Just a little one. Once he jumped over the fence at which he had come to grief the previous year, I settled down. We're further now than we've ever been in a Tingle Creek.

There are seven fences down Sandown's back straight: an open ditch, a water jump and five plain fences. The last three, the Railway Fences, come very close together. Miss the first one, they say, and you will miss all three. Moscow pinged the first one, and by the time they had jumped the third one and started the swing around for home, he was in front. He flew the Pond Fence, flew the last two, and flew up the hill, Azertyuiop and Flagship Uberalles in his wake. To be honest, I didn't notice either of them until Moscow was bounding up the Sandown hill four lengths clear. I was just watching my horse throughout. And I can report that he was almost flawless.

We had a bottle of champagne at Gatwick airport that evening on our way back to Ireland, and we had dinner at Rathsallagh House Hotel when we got there. It was a nice feeling, to hold the Champion Chase and the Tingle Creek titles at the same time. We had beaten them all, and we had beaten them again. Including the young pretender.

Of course the excuses were trotted out, as expected. They were even louder now than they had been before the race. Moscow Flyer had had a run; Azertyuiop hadn't. It would be a different story at Cheltenham. We just kept our mouths shut and prepared for Leopardstown.

Our horses weren't exactly sparkling in the run-up to Christmas that year. They weren't sick or anything. Or at least, not sick in the sense that you could pinpoint what was wrong with them and treat it. And they weren't running so badly that you would be justified in putting them on the easy list for a while and letting them down. They weren't falling in a heap in their races when the pace quickened. But they just weren't in top form. Still, Macs Joy had won his maiden hurdle at Down Patrick just after the Tingle Creek, and Green Belt Flyer had won a novice hurdle at Gowran just before Christmas, so I wasn't that worried about them. And Moscow seemed to be fine. Not absolutely jumping out of his skin, but still fine.

Native Scout was the latest new Irish kid on the block. Barry had ridden him when he had beaten Ross Moff in a handicap chase at Fairyhouse at the end of November, and he was going to take us on in the Paddy Power Dial-a-Bet Chase at Leopardstown over Christmas. Barry thought he was decent, especially on soft ground. He shouldn't get close to Moscow – he was rated 33lb inferior to Moscow at the time – but he would probably prove to be the best of the rest. And so it proved. Moscow won well without being overly impressive. Native Scout looked like he might be dangerous until they jumped the second last, but then Moscow quickened away. I was happy enough, although I just didn't think he was zinging. We hadn't done a huge amount with him since the Tingle Creek, and perhaps being just short of full fitness told on the soft ground.

The Tied Cottage Chase was an option as his final race before Cheltenham, and I also had a look at the Game Spirit Chase at Newbury. But, to be honest, we were considering not running him at all between Christmas and March. He had had quite a hard race at Sandown, and I thought we might just keep him off the racecourse that year and prepare him at home. As it happened, our hand was forced.

Moscow got a bit sick after Christmas. Again, it wasn't anything serious. He just got a bit of a runny nose and wasn't quite himself. When they are like that you can do a lot of harm by running them, so we decided to skip Punchestown and Newbury and bring him back for Cheltenham. It was really the sensible thing to do. We made the decision quite soon after Christmas, which was good, as that meant we were able to take it easy with him from early January 2004. A few weeks after Christmas he started to come to himself again and we were able to do some work with him. From there,

Moscow and Barry land an incredible 2005 Queen Mother Champion Chase.

Moscow gets a congratulatory ear-tug.

Well played Ruby – bad luck.

Barry, Brian and Moscow are head and shoulders above the rest.

A worm's eye view at Aintree.

How would you like me to hold my head? Is this OK? [© Healys]

Brian with Moscow – proud as punch. [© Healys]

The famous photo finish. Whose nose is on the line? [© HRI]

Envying Ridgewood Pearl's vantage point on The Curragh.
[© Caroline Norris]

Win or come second to Moscow Flyer
at Gowran Park.

A momento from 2005's
Champion Chase.

The three-year-old Moscow Society gelding in Meelick in June 1997.

From left to right: Intelligent [Midlands Grand National], Spirit Leader [County Hurdle] and Moscow Flyer [Champion Chase]: three big winners in just a few short days. [© Caroline Norris]

Strolling in the woods with Moscow Flyer, and Toffee.
[© Irish Independent]

Do I look good with my ears pricked like this? [© Caroline Norris]

A quiet moment together. [© Caroline Norris]

we were able to follow the tried and tested pre-Cheltenham programme. Canter for a couple of weeks, do a bit at home, down to the Old Vic gallop on The Curragh, do another bit at home, pop him over a fence or two, then off to Cheltenham.

We tried to fit in the television cameras and the journalists. There were a lot of them that year. I suppose that is to be expected given that we had the champion chaser who was going back to Cheltenham to defend his crown. Moscow loved it. He basked in all the attention. He would greet the television cameras with glee. Any sight of a camera and he's straight over to it. Oh, so you want to take a photograph of me, do you? Well, OK then. Which way would you like me to hold my head?

In the meantime, Azertyuiop was busy staking his own claim. He ran twice between the Tingle Creek and Cheltenham. In the Victor Chandler Chase at Ascot, he just failed to beat that high-class chaser of Nicky Henderson's, Isio, giving him a stone and 5lb. Then he went and won the Game Spirit Chase doing handsprings. He really was impressive. You say that you can't do anything about the opposition – and you can't – and that all you can do is concentrate on your own horse, but it is difficult not to keep an eye on your likely main dangers. And Azertyuiop was definitely a danger. The bookmakers and the pundits made the Champion Chase that year a two-horse race between him and Moscow. It was difficult to disagree.

Johnny and I take separate routes to Cheltenham. Johnny takes his car over on the boat and has a couple of days touring around England visiting old friends and clients. I usually fly over at around lunchtime on Monday and hire a car at the airport. I visit my sister on the way to Lambourn, where I call into the Walwyns' for a drink before heading on to the Hendersons'. Johnny and I meet up at the Hendersons' on the Monday evening for a good supper with Nicky and Diana and whoever else happens to be there. Eamonn goes with Moscow. He always has done. He goes over in the box with him and whatever other runners we have. And he normally leaves with Moscow directly after his race. We try to get them home as quickly as possible. If we want to run them at Aintree, we want to give them as much time between the two meetings as we can.

Moscow was very well in the run-up to Cheltenham 2004. He really was bouncing. He loves the spring. He loves to feel the warm weather, and he loves the good ground that it brings. He hadn't had a run since Christmas so he was dying to get out and expend all this pent-up energy. He was one of three defending champions going back to the Festival. He was defending the Champion Chase, Rooster Booster was defending the Champion Hurdle, and Best Mate was defending the Gold Cup. All three were favourites for their respective races, and all three looked to be the most likely winners.

Everything is very easy in hindsight. If we had known that Moscow was going to be this good, we would have had to pay a lot more than 17,000 guineas for him. If we had known that he was going to be this good over fences, we would have sent him chasing years before we did. In hindsight, Moscow was probably too fresh going to Cheltenham that year. I half-blame myself for that, and I half-blame Moscow. If he hadn't been ill after Christmas, he probably would have run in the Tied Cottage Chase. That had taken the freshness out of him the previous season, and it probably would have done so again. But I suppose I have to share some of the blame. Given that he missed his prep race, I probably could have worked him harder just to take that fresh edge off him.

It's true to say that I was more worried about Azertyuiop in 2004 than I had been about any rival in 2003. He was in the same place as Moscow had been the previous season – the young pretender, challenging the might of the establishment. It was a different feeling. Moscow was now the establishment. The old guard. The reigning champion who was shouldering the pressure that invariably accompanies the champion's mantle. Eamonn said that when Moscow got to Cheltenham that year, he knew exactly where he was. He knew what was in store. And he was his usual self, barging about and giving an outward display of his inner well-being. This was his third time at Cheltenham and he knew exactly where he was going. No need to show me. I'm the boss.

Barry had a different build-up to the race. Whereas the previous year he had won on nearly everything he sat on, this year was different. He was brought down on Pizarro in the Sun Alliance Chase, the race directly preceding the Champion Chase. I'm not sure if it affected Barry's confidence at all. I'm sure it didn't. Even so, it's not the ideal way to prepare for a Champion Chase.

The game plan for the race was the same as always: get him settled, get him into a rhythm, have him handy. Barry didn't like going around the inside on him; he thought it better to go around the middle. What you give away in ground you make up for in momentum and in being able to see your fences.

Moscow set off towards the back, just on the outside of Azertyuiop. He jumped the first three well – particularly the third, where Barry asked him to stand off and he made about two lengths in the air. Going down the far side, he disputed fourth place with Azertyuiop behind a scorching pace being set by Ei Ei and Cenkos. Then he started to race a bit keenly going downhill to the first in the back straight, and Barry had to take him back a bit. Over the water jump. We don't have water jumps in Ireland and we never school Moscow over one, but he always jumps them well when he encounters one in the UK.

Going to the fifth last, Ruby Walsh and Azertyuiop got a dream run up the inside as Ei Ei dropped back. They flew the fence as Moscow didn't meet it on a stride and just kind of popped it. Suddenly, going around the turn at the top end of the course, Azertyuiop was in front on the rails while Moscow disputed fifth place on the outside. He was only three lengths behind, but if there was a run of the race going with one of the main protagonists, it wasn't with Moscow.

About eight seconds later, however, the run of the race suddenly became irrelevant. Moscow and Barry had been over the ditch at the top of the hill twice before, once in the Arkle and once in the previous year's Champion Chase. They jumped it well in the Arkle, but in the Champion Chase they had attained less than full marks for negotiation skills. This was in the back of my head as they approached it this time. When I watch Moscow race at Cheltenham through my binoculars, I can barely see the race as my hands are usually shaking too much. They were shaking again as they approached the ditch. I saw him take off and I thought he was fine. I didn't really see the mistake. In fact I didn't know that he had gone until Jim Wilson's exclamation – 'Oh!' – as if someone had punched him in the stomach.

'Bad luck.'

I looked and I saw the loose horse with the noseband.

'Oh no.' I think I said it out loud. 'He's gone.'

I couldn't believe it. I watched as Moscow cantered away riderless just behind the main group of horses. I looked back and saw Brian Kearney's black and white silks on the ground just after the fourth last, with Barry in them. And then I felt the same punch. Right in the solar plexus.

When I was coming down from the stands, I heard a punter behind me giving out about the jockey – Barry Gravity. Of course I asked Barry what had happened. He just said, 'I didn't win.' It's difficult to know what went wrong. No matter how many times you replay it on the video, you still get the same result. Barry could see that he was meeting it wrong and tried to take him back and get him to pop it. But Moscow wasn't listening too well. He doesn't when he is so fresh. He just wants to get on with it. When he wasn't coming back on his hocks, Barry had to change his strategy. He had to change it just a stride before the obstacle. Go on then. By then Moscow realised that he was too far off. He tried to put in a short one, but there wasn't enough turf left between him and the ditch. He actually put his front feet into the ditch, put his chest on the fence, almost touched the ground on the landing side with his head and somehow managed to get his forelegs out in front of him to stop him from falling down. Even if you watch the manoeuvre in slow motion on the video, it is still difficult to tell exactly how he managed to remain upright.

Barry landed on the floor and looked around for Moscow. He

feared the worst. It could have been a horrendous fall. But when he looked on the ground beside him, no horse. He looked behind him. Still no horse. The last place he looked was at the rest of the runners as they thundered away from the fence. He couldn't believe that Moscow was with them. He couldn't believe that a horse could remain on his feet after making such a bad mistake.

There was indecision there. Possibly by Moscow, possibly by Barry, possibly by both. Maybe the horse made a mistake, maybe Barry made a mistake. Again, it happens. There's no point in getting cross about it. I'm sure Barry has gone over it a thousand times in his head. Should he have done this, should he have done that. Maybe if he had kicked him into the fence he would have pinged it. Or maybe if I had given Moscow another gallop he wouldn't have been so fresh and would have come back on his hocks when Barry asked him to. When a horse ends up chucking his jockey on the deck, you know that something has gone wrong. It's difficult to isolate one thing. It's probably a combination of several things.

Moscow continued to gallop around with them and jumped every jump. He's unbelievable. As the crowd roared for Ruby and Azertyuiop when they jumped the last, Moscow was endeavouring to catch Flagship Uberalles for second place. He didn't know that they weren't cheering for him. I was the only one cheering for him. He seemed to be OK. He seemed to be galloping freely. We wouldn't know for sure though until we got him home.

Eamonn got him where they pull up and brought him to the little unsaddling area at the side. That's where you go when you don't finish in the first four. It is the loneliest place in Cheltenham. I met Brian there, and we checked Moscow out. He seemed to be OK. It's always a good day when your horse is OK. I remarked to Brian that it would be far worse if he was being brought back to us in the Blue Cross trailer. Brian agreed, as I knew he would. We still had our horse. We took the saddle in and went for a drink. There wasn't much more we could do.

It was disappointing, for all of us. Of course it was. We had planned for this day for a year, and it had all gone pear-shaped. Everybody feels it, and it was hard to read the headlines the following day. The ones proclaiming a new champ. The king is dead, long live the king. I just kept thinking, 'We'll come back and win it next year.' I still believed that Moscow was the best horse. But even if he was the best horse at the age of ten, would he still be the best horse at eleven? Barry thought he would be. He kept on saying that it wasn't the following year he was worried about, it was the year after that. Even so, I thought we should try something a little different. He has lost his Champion Chase crown, so let's take him to Aintree if he's OK and see if he stays two and a half miles. That way, I thought, if he is not the best horse over two miles next year, at least we'll have another option.

We got him back to Commonstown and he seemed to be fine. No stiffness, no soreness. There were only two weeks and two days between the Champion Chase at Cheltenham and the Melling Chase at Aintree that year, so if he had been feeling any effects of his mishap, it might not have been possible to go to Aintree. You can't dwell on the past too much, you have to continue to look forward, so we got over Cheltenham quickly enough and focused on Aintree. We didn't do a huge amount with him at all during those two weeks. We just kept him ticking over. He had been super-fit for Cheltenham, so he really didn't need to do that much. He spent a lot of time out in the field just enjoying himself. Barry came down and popped him over three fences, just to keep his eye in.

I was dying to try him over two and a half miles. I still believed that he would stay. I talked to Barry about how to ride him at Aintree. I thought that he might race a little keenly, going at two-mile pace instead of two-and-a-half-mile pace. Barry had no doubt that he would stay and had no fears about riding him aggressively.

There is a totally different atmosphere at Aintree to that at Cheltenham. Aintree is much more relaxed. On the Friday the Liverpool ladies dress up in their best and, teetering on their high heels, walk for about three miles to the racecourse. It doesn't matter what the weather is like, they are all bared down to their tits with their fake tans and their skirts up to their waists. It's unbelievable. I'd been to Aintree before with Space Trucker and Brockley Court, but I'd never noticed that before.

Nicky Henderson was there, giving out to me. He had deliberately side-stepped Cheltenham with Isio in order to avoid Moscow and Azertyuiop and go to Aintree fresh. And then Moscow shows up. He said that it shouldn't have been allowed. Arthur sent Native Upmanship again, seeking the hat-trick and the trophy for keeps, and Paul Nicholls fielded Cenkos and Le Roi Miguel.

Moscow and Isio went clear going to the third last. They had dropped Native Upmanship at the cross-fence. Moscow got in a little close to the third last and Isio went on. Barry just squeezed his legs and Moscow ranged upsides. They jumped the second last together.

When you run from the second last to the last at Aintree, you run right across the Grand National course. There is a vast space there – nothing to race against – that tired horses don't like. They can very easily down tools on the run to the last. It was at that point that I thought, 'We'll find out now if he stays or not.' He had to stay to keep tabs on Isio, who was a classy individual and had won over two and a half. And he did. He ran away from Isio between the last two fences, jumped the last, and won easing down. It was a great feeling. It didn't fully make up for Cheltenham, but it was a fair consolation prize. It proved that he still retained his ability, and that he stayed at least two and a half miles. It gave us more options, too. I immediately began to think of the King George over three miles. Why not? His pedigree was all about stamina. At least we had the option. But that was all for next season. This season we still had Punchestown to go.

I didn't really consider roughing him off for the season after Aintree. He had had only five races that season, one of which he hadn't completed. Four and a half races is not a particularly busy campaign, especially not for a two-mile chaser, though it might be enough for a three-mile horse. It's a bit like a 100-metre athlete versus a marathon runner. You can run a lot more 100-metre races in a season than you can run marathons. I thought it would also be good for the Irish racing public to get to see Moscow. Of his five races that season up to that point, three of them had been in England. Moreover, I like to support Punchestown – my recently acquired son-in-law is racing manager there – and the prize money is good.

To be honest, I hardly trained him at all after Aintree. There were less than four weeks between Aintree and Punchestown, and I figured that it would be better for Moscow to relax a little rather than be trained hard for his final run of the season. The ground was good on the day, which helped him a lot, and he jumped the second last well, which helped him even more. Rathgar Beau did challenge him between the last two, but he was never really getting to him, and Moscow won handily enough. It was a nice way to end the season. Actually, bar the Cheltenham mishap, it was probably his best season so far. He had raced six times, won five races – three Grade 1s and two Grade 2s – and got rid of his rider once.

Just to put the cinnamon in the porridge, we were invited to London for the newly instigated National Hunt awards. This is now the National Hunt equivalent of the International Classifications on the Flat, where the British and Irish National Hunt handicappers come together and agree ratings for all the top National Hunt horses. I went over on my own, not expecting anything. Brian was away on business, and Johnny just didn't want to go to London.

Moscow and Azertyuiop shared the award for best two-mile chaser. Apparently the Irish and British handicappers had had a fierce argument about which of them had been the best that season. Azertyuiop had won the Champion Chase all right, but Moscow had won the Tingle Creek and just about everything else. I was happy to be rated joint best. It was probably a fair reflection of the season. Moscow was also rated the top two-and-a-half-mile chaser, and I wasn't expecting that. To be honest, I hadn't really thought of him as a two-and-a-half-mile chaser. But that run at Aintree was apparently the best performance any chaser had put in over two and a half miles that season. I was thrilled. So I came staggering back from London laden down with two trophies, and nobody with me to help me carry them.

I wasn't sure how many trophies we would get to carry home the following season. It was going to get even tougher, there was no doubt about that. Moscow was going to be ten years old, rising eleven, while Azertyuiop was only seven rising eight. In theory, Moscow would be on the wane while Paul Nicholls' horse would be improving. I consoled myself with the thought that Moscow didn't conform to many theories, so why should he conform to this one?

CHAPTER TWENTY-TWO

STILL THE BEST

I lay in my bed one morning in early August 2004 and thought about the season ahead. There was much to look forward to. In my guts, I still felt that Moscow had been the best two-mile chaser of the 2003/04 season. I didn't voice my opinion out loud, as it would probably just have been seen as sour grapes after our Champion Chase escapades, but I genuinely thought we were better than Azertyuiop.

There was another new kid on the block, however. A young German-bred horse of Martin Pipe's called Well Chief had won the Arkle on only his second ever start over fences. He was only five years old and already they were talking about him as a champion chaser in waiting.

And, of course, there could be another new dimension for Moscow this season. He had proved that he stayed two and a half miles, so we had the option of stepping him up to three and seeing if he would get that trip. His pedigree screamed stamina, and he certainly hadn't been stopping at the end of the two and a half miles at Aintree. The King George is run over three miles at Kempton on St Stephen's Day. Kempton's three miles is as easy a three miles as you will find anywhere in Ireland or the UK. It's a flat track with no undulations, which means that it doesn't put a premium on stamina. It is also a very well-drained track, so the ground is normally a lot better there over Christmas than it is at, say, Leopardstown. If Moscow was going to stay three miles anywhere, he would stay it at Kempton. I have to say, the prospect of running Moscow in the King George excited me a lot.

Armed with these thoughts, I met up with Brian for our annual conference. There was a little bit more to discuss this time. Moscow wasn't getting any younger. Do we step him up to three miles this season or not? It was almost like the year when we decided to send him over fences. If he hadn't gone over fences in 2001, he probably would have spent his entire career jumping hurdles. It was a tough one, but after some discussion we decided that we would start off on the usual path. Fortria Chase at Navan in early November, then Tingle Creek. Then we would know. If he didn't retained the speed to win the Tingle Creek, we would step him up in distance. If he did, we would probably go down the Champion Chase route with him again. I was very comfortable with that, as was Brian. It made complete sense.

The danger when you step a horse up in trip is that he won't settle. The pace of a two-mile race is obviously a lot quicker than the pace of a three-mile race, with the result that when you step a two-miler up to three miles, he wants to go faster than he should, simply because he is used to going faster. If he struggles against his jockey early and fights for his head, then it's unlikely he will have enough energy left at the end of the race to mount a challenge. But I was fairly sure that, although Moscow was a specialist two-miler, he would have no difficulty settling at three-mile pace. He is generally fairly co-operative. You set him at the speed you want and, after a little pull and a tug, he'll settle at that speed. Oh, all right, he'll say. So this is the speed at which you want me to go. Fair enough. Cruise control.

I have to say that, deep down, before Moscow began to do serious work that autumn, I felt it was more likely than not that he would be running in the King George. The Azertyuiop vibes were so strong. The Nicholls team were so bullish. He was the reigning champion, and he had never been better, by all accounts. Bang on track for the Tingle Creek. He was only seven and looked like he had improved over the summer. And then there was this Arkle winner of Pipe's coming up, who was also going for the Tingle Creek. Moscow was ten, and past it. If you listened to some people, we were booked for third place in the Tingle Creek.

The funny thing was that from the moment Moscow came in to start work in August, he seemed to be better than ever. It may seem stupid to say that at the age of ten he seemed to be better than he had ever been before, but he did. I couldn't believe it. Eamonn couldn't believe it. You couldn't put your finger on it. He just seemed to be doing everything a lot more easily than he had in seasons gone by. He was easier to get ready too. Maybe he was just getting more sensible as he grew older.

Azertyuiop made his seasonal debut at Exeter five days before the Fortria Chase. It could have been a game of chess. He was white – his move first. It was a Tuesday afternoon and I was at Tattersalls Ireland, at the November sales. They had SIS there so I stopped looking at horses to watch the race. Of course I did. You couldn't not. And he was impressive. No doubt. He was giving lumps of weight away all round and he completely annihilated good two-mile chasers like Seebald, Kadarann, Flagship Uberalles and Edredon Bleu. He was reported to be 12kg heavier than his ideal racing weight and the ground was much softer than ideal. The reports about his well-being were true after all.

Our move.

It came at Navan that Sunday. I was very happy with Moscow going into the Fortria Chase. We did all our preparation at home. Barry came down to school him over our three fences – or rather,

Moscow schooled Barry. Barry would go one, two, up, but Moscow would go no, no, no, we go one, two, three here. We still have a laugh about that. They just jumped the three fences once. If Barry hadn't been happy, they would have gone again. But he was. There's only so much you can teach your grandmother about sucking eggs. The race went well. Moscow settled in second behind Arctic Copper, took it up at the fourth fence, and strode out. Rathgar Beau came to challenge between the last two, but Moscow had everything under control. Rathgar was trying so hard to bridge the gap that he unshipped Shay Barry at the last. It was a real ejector-seat fall. Shay was thrown into orbit. Thankfully, he was none the worse for it.

Moscow came back after Navan delighted with himself. He continued to surprise us. You would really have thought that at his age he'd begin to stiffen up a little after his races. But there was not even a hint of it after the Fortria. He gobbled up all his food and was bouncing out of his skin the following day. We were all on track for the Tingle Creek. Azertyuiop had impressed on his debut, Moscow had impressed on his, and Martin Pipe was preparing Well Chief for the race behind closed doors at Nicholashayne.

During the build-up to the Tingle Creek, I received a phone call from Weatherbys. 'Do you want to enter Moscow Flyer in the King George or not?' In all the furore, I had forgotten that entries were closing that day. Had they not rung, I would have missed the entry deadline and Moscow wouldn't have been able to run in the King George. I suppose, because Moscow was such a high-profile horse, it was in their interest to have him in the race. Even so, it wasn't very clever of me. All my talk in the press about running in the King George, and I would have missed the deadline. Yes, of course! Put him in! Quickly!

Apart from that, Moscow's build-up to the Tingle Creek could not have gone better. He continued from where he had left off before the Fortria. Everything just seemed to be so easy for him. Barry came down and popped him over our three fences again. He zinged. He was ready.

We had no other runners at Sandown over the weekend, so Moscow had no equine company. He, Eamonn and Galway got there on Friday morning; I flew over with Johnny, Kate, Emma and her fiancé Richie Galway on the Saturday morning. Sandown sent a taxi to collect us at Gatwick. We spent a short while trying to find the taxi man, but a few frayed nerves later he found us and took us to the royal box at Sandown. That was nice, but it was also a little strange. We were all there: us, Brian and his people, the Azertyuiop people and the Well Chief people. Paul Nicholls was there. He told me that his fellow was absolutely spot on. I said, 'Hmm. Well, I hope mine is too.' He wished me good luck and I wished him good luck. The same way as you shake hands with your opposing number before a hurling match. Before you go and whack him on the legs with your hurl.

John Hales was there too, Azertyuiop's owner. He is the man who made his fortune by securing the rights to sell Teletubbies merchandise. He also owned that top-class grey horse One Man, who won a Hennessy, two King Georges and a Champion Chase before being so tragically killed at Aintree in 1998 in a race my brother won with Opera Hat. I got chatting to him and his daughter after lunch. I had met John that summer at the Dublin Horse Show. He owned the horse Arko III on whom Nick Skelton went clear in the first round of the Olympics in Athens. The gold medal was his to lose in the second round. Unfortunately, he did lose it – he had three or four fences down. I commiserated with John. I told him I'd thought the gold medal would be his, that if there was one person I thought wouldn't go to pieces, it was Nick Skelton. It was good to have something else to talk about, because John was very keen on Azertyuiop. I avoided talking about the race. I knew that they fancied their horse and I didn't want to hear any more about how well he was.

The truth was, if I had been asked to nominate Moscow's main danger, I would have pointed to Well Chief. The way I looked at it, we had beaten Azertyuiop before. The only reason he had beaten us the last time was because we didn't complete. I thought he would be tough, but I thought we would have his measure. Well Chief was different. We had never met him, so we didn't know how he compared. He'd really impressed me when he beat Kicking King in the Arkle, and he was equally impressive when he won at Aintree. He was only five years old and probably improving at a rate of knots.

There is a lovely weigh room at Sandown. They have an open fireplace there and it's really old-fashioned. I met Barry there and gave him the saddle so that he could weigh out. Then I went down to the stables to Eamonn and Moscow.

Moscow knew he was back at Sandown. Horses aren't stupid. He knew what was afoot. When he stopped on the path at the junction where you go left to the racecourse and right down into the parade ring, he might have been thinking, 'Hold on a moment, the racecourse is over there.' Or he might have been playing to the gallery. Heightening the sense of anticipation before his trumpeted arrival into the parade ring.

Brian and Patricia had had lunch with us in the royal box, so there was nothing left to say in the parade ring. We all knew that this would be a defining moment in Moscow's career. Did he still have the speed? Was he still the fastest? It was a lot to expect of a ten-year-old. But we did expect. And we would know soon enough.

As I've already described, it was one of those races where nothing went wrong for anyone. Moscow got in a little tight to the third fence and to the second of the Railway Fences, Well Chief was a little novicey at one of the ditches, and Azertyuiop ran a little freely turning down the back straight. But, in the main, the race couldn't have gone better for any of the three of us. Moscow took it up going out of the back straight, and going to the third last I was a little worried. Both Azertyuiop and Well Chief were travelling easily in behind and Moscow was meeting the obstacle wrong. But he is so fast away from his fences. He just popped over it and immediately quickened. Three strides later and both of his pursuers came under pressure. When Moscow jumped the second last two lengths in front, I knew he would win. They just don't come from behind him. They never have done. He had just proved that he still had the speed to lead them over the second last, and I knew he had the stamina to see it out all the way up the hill.

It is difficult to describe the feeling when Barry stood up in his irons and saluted to the grandstand. It was similar to the feeling I'd had when he won the Arkle, or when he won the Champion Chase. Those two were unbelievable. Really unbelievable. But this was unbelievable plus. Of course there was the pure, unbridled joy of winning the Tingle Creek. Of winning such a race. But this was more than just victory in a race. This was proof that Moscow was still as good as ever, that at the age of ten he still had the speed and ability to beat two of the best young two-mile chasers we had seen in a generation. I could have cried. Not only was he telling us he was still the best two-mile chaser in the business, he was also telling the world. He had won one of the highest-quality two-mile chases staged in living memory, and he had won it on merit. Nobody could think of an excuse for any runner beforehand or afterwards. The people who had scratched him off their lists – and there were many of them – were scrambling for the crayons.

John Hales was one of the first people to come up to me in the winner's enclosure and congratulate me. Paul Nicholls and Martin Pipe did too. In fairness to them all, they were quite magnanimous. It was a pity that John had a bit of a go at Ruby for not kicking on earlier on Azertyuiop. In fairness, the press probably turned that molehill into a rather large hillock. But I think everybody realised that it wouldn't have mattered what Ruby had done. Unless he could have started before Moscow, he wouldn't have beaten him that day.

Moscow's victory wasn't a turning point, it was more a confirmation that we were going down the right road again. It would be hard to go for the King George now. Why would you run the best two-mile chaser in a Grade 1 race over three miles? No reason. You couldn't justify it. It would be like winning a gold medal over 1,500 metres and then running in the 10,000 metres.

Ironically, Kempton racecourse had arranged for a team of press people to come to see Moscow the following Monday. They were promoting the King George. I had a chat with Brian at Sandown. He said that it would still be nice to go to the King George but that he would leave it completely up to me.

Looking back on it now, it was foolish even to consider going for the King George. But with the press gathered in my kitchen that Monday morning, I told them that I hadn't made up my mind yet. And I hadn't. I wasn't stringing anyone along. I suppose that, since I had been so excited about the prospect of running in the King George, a seismic shift in my way of thinking was required. I talked to Johnny later that week, I talked to Brian again, and I talked to Barry. It was fairly unanimous once the dust had settled: we have beaten them at Sandown, so what we want to do now is go and beat them at Cheltenham. Claim the Champion Chase crown back. And if we were going to do that, running over three miles at Christmas would be of no assistance whatsoever.

It's a strange thing. When I bought this horse I thought there was a possibility that he would turn out to be my Gold Cup horse. I never thought he would be a Champion Chase horse. Everything about him screamed stamina. And I still felt that he would stay. But he was a horse with whom we never got to experiment. He was so good at two miles that we never got to try him over longer distances. Who knows? He might have been just as good over three miles as he was over two. Look at John Hales' horse One Man. Even though he won a Hennessy and two King Georges, it turns out that they were running him over the wrong distance all his life. They only tried him over two miles because he wasn't getting home in his Gold Cups over three and a quarter miles. He won the Champion Chase at the age of ten, on his first try over two miles since his very first race in a novice hurdle at Hexham. How many Champion Chases would he have won had they trained him as a two-miler from the beginning? Probably lots.

Deep down, I had been looking forward to trying Moscow over three miles. I really thought he could be at least as good over three miles as he was over two. Especially now that he was getting on a bit in years. And then he goes and wins the Tingle Creek. Beats them all. Ruins all my plans.

The irony is that, even if we had decided to send Moscow to Kempton on St Stephen's Day, as things turned out he wouldn't have gone. Some of my horses were a little under the weather that Christmas. In fact, it seemed that there were few stables in Ireland that could boast a full clean bill of health. We had a good few runners over the Christmas festival period, and we scoped all of them on the morning of their races. We scoped Moscow on 26 December, and he was clean. We scoped him again the following morning – the day of the Grade 1 Paddy Power Dial-a-Bet Chase. Surprisingly, he scoped dirty. He didn't have much in him. Just a little piece of mucus. You could have got away with it, but I wasn't going to risk him. Not Moscow. If you ran him and he was a bit sick, you could have made him a lot sick. It was the first time since his bumper season that Moscow Flyer had been declared for a race and hadn't run. He was the cheapest horse on entry fees you could possibly have had. We entered him, we ran him. That was usually the way it worked. It was disappointing, but it was the correct decision. No debate. The Champion Chase was our objective, and we weren't going to risk leaving that one behind us at Leopardstown. And we still had something to celebrate that Christmas. Macs Joy beat Brave Inca and Hardy Eustace in the December Festival Hurdle – the same race Moscow had won in 2000.

Moscow was on antibiotics and the easy list for a little while. If he had to get sick, it was the ideal time for him to do so. We were going to be able to get him back in time for the Tied Cottage Chase again at Punchestown. If he had run at Christmas, I'm not sure if we would have run him at Punchestown as well. Fortunately we didn't have to make that decision. Providence dictated.

So he got to Punchestown at the end of January in one piece. Probably a little or a lot less fit than was ideal, but he got there. And he scrambled home by two and a half lengths from Steel Band. Steel

Band was a novice who had one win over fences to his name in five attempts. He was rated 58lb inferior to Moscow Flyer. To beat him by two and a half lengths, apparently all out, is not Champion Chase form. It's not Champion Sports form. I wasn't jumping over the moon, but I hadn't expected fireworks. He gurgled and everything during the race. He had been off for a while and was a long way from peak fitness. He blew a lot after the race and we knew he would come on a lot for it. But he needed to. Barry was happy with his jumping. I suppose he jumped well given that it was Punchestown.

We had six and a half weeks between the Tied Cottage Chase and Cheltenham. It was enough. It had been enough on the previous three occasions, so there was no reason why it shouldn't be enough this time. We didn't do anything different with Moscow just because he was eleven. We worked him at home, we schooled him at home, and we worked him up the Old Vic gallop. We thought about taking him to Leopardstown ten days before Cheltenham and giving him a school on the racecourse, but the ground was too heavy and we feared we might do him more harm than good. He didn't need to go. He knew what was going on. His last piece of work up the Old Vic was superb. He had rarely worked as well before.

I suppose, in a funny way, I was fairly confident that he would win the Champion Chase. Or at least I was a lot more confident than I had been on either of the previous two occasions. I'm not sure why that was. It was probably because he had beaten them all at Sandown. But it seemed strange. Eleven-year-olds don't win Champion Chases. Still, Moscow definitely seemed to be more settled this year. More professional. For some reason I also felt that he was under less pressure than before. He had already won an Arkle, a Champion Chase and two Tingle Creeks. He didn't really have anything left to prove. He was just back to claim what was his by rights.

Moscow went over to Cheltenham on the Saturday night with Eamonn, Ulaan Baatar, Macs Joy and Colca Canyon. Eamonn thought he would appreciate the time to settle in. He was right. Eamonn is seldom wrong when he talks about Moscow.

On the Tuesday morning I did a press conference with Barry and some of the other Irish trainers and jockeys. The same old questions that I had been fielding by telephone for the previous six weeks. He's as well as ever. I can't see why he won't win. Normal luck. The usual stuff.

On the Tuesday afternoon Macs Joy finished fifth to Hardy Eustace in the Champion Hurdle and Ulaan Baatar finished down the field in the Arkle. The ground was just too quick for Ulaan Baatar, but I was happy enough with Macs Joy. It was an amazing Champion Hurdle in terms of quality – Irish quality – and he was the only one of the leading contenders who hadn't been to Cheltenham before. He missed the second last. He's not a very big horse and it just knocked the stuffing out of him.

Eamonn took Moscow out for a leg-stretch on Wednesday morning, and I did my usual routine. Left the Hendersons' in the morning with Kate. Got to the racecourse too early. Did a little bit of box-walking, although not as much as usual. I was a lot calmer than normal. It was a calmness that came from either confidence or old age. When Barry was asked by a journalist if he felt any pressure, he said that pressure was for tyres. I tried to avoid being interviewed in the parade ring before the race, as I always do. Brian Gleeson had collared me at Aintree the previous year. It was awful. I just wanted to get away from the camera into my privacy. Monosyllabic answers. Just let me go. I don't mind being interviewed after a race, but beforehand I just want to be left alone.

Well Chief and Azertyuiop were there as well. It was the Tingle Creek all over again, except it was at Cheltenham, and this time Moscow was favourite. Both of our main rivals had had a busy time of it since the Tingle Creek. Well Chief had fallen in the Castleford Chase at Wetherby before winning the Victor Chandler Chase under a big weight. Azertyuiop had run in the King George at Kempton on St Stephen's Day.

It is very unusual for a Champion Chase horse – a specialist two-mile chaser – to be aimed at the King George. It is almost unprecedented for two Champion Chase horses to be aimed at the King George. Looks like carelessness, as Oscar Wilde might say. Strange thing: I had heard no talk of Azertyuiop going for the King George before I told the press that we were thinking of going. Only then did I hear that Azertyuiop was going. They may have been thinking about it all along. I just hadn't heard any mention of it. Moscow didn't go and Azertyuiop did. That's the way it worked out. He finished third to Kicking King. It is hard to say that a horse who finished third in a King George didn't stay three miles, but he probably didn't. It might not have done his preparation for the Champion Chase much good, in the same way as it wouldn't have done Moscow's preparation for the Champion Chase much good. In fairness to Azertyuiop, he did bounce back to beat Well Chief in the Game Spirit Chase at Newbury just over four weeks before Cheltenham. But again, I don't think that race did either of them any good. I didn't think either of them jumped particularly well. Azertyuiop was giving 4lb to Well Chief and he beat him well. It was a good performance, but they both had fairly hard races.

Eamonn led Moscow and Barry on to the course. They had been here before. Nothing new to see here. As Eamonn was letting them go to canter down to the start, he gave Barry a thump on the leg. 'Pop the ditch! Pop the ditch!' Barry didn't have to ask which ditch. He knew the one Eamonn meant – the fourth last. The one at which he lost Moscow from underneath him in 2004. The one at which he had made a mistake in 2003. 'Just make sure you pop it. You don't need to fly it. You're on the best horse in the race. Just get to the other side.'

Moscow and Well Chief travelled well in the early stages of the race. Azertyuiop didn't. Even before he made his mistake at the water jump, he wasn't really travelling. Not as well as you need to travel if you are going to win a Champion Chase. It was a strange mistake that he made at the water. He didn't drop his hind legs in it, but he still seemed to lose his hind legs at the back of it. That was the final nail.

Early leader Kadarann was already back-pedalling as they approached the fourth last. Paul Carberry on Dessie Hughes' Central House had taken it up. Barry swung along on Moscow on the outside, and Timmy Murphy on Well Chief stalked the pair. Barry said afterwards that he could still feel the pain in his leg from Eamonn's thump as he approached that obstacle. Pop the ditch! Pop the ditch! And he did. He wasn't foot perfect – far from it. He actually lost about half a length on Central House. But he was over it. I heaved a sigh of relief. Now that that was out of the way, he could concentrate on going on and winning the race.

Moscow took it up from Central House on the way down the hill to the third last. His compatriot just wasn't going fast enough for him. It was plenty early enough to be taking it up, more than half a mile from home, I thought. But Barry knows what he is doing. He knows at what speed Moscow is most comfortable. He's happy just dossing away out in front. Let them come and get him.

Well Chief tried. Timmy Murphy tried to cajole his partner into a challenging position. Moscow flew the third last and the crowd cheered. Moscow flew the second last too, and the crowd cheered again. I cheered with them. He could have been a matador. Around the home turn, the race was over. Just as the Tingle Creek had been over when he'd come round the home turn at Sandown. They don't come from behind him up these hills. I took my binoculars down and watched the finish with my naked eyes. They'd been no good anyway. Kept on shaking.

Barry looked around. This was a functional look, not a fashion item. He wanted to see where Well Chief was. Content that he had him beaten – 'Moscow was taking the Mick' – he put his head down and measured the last. The crowd had reserved the biggest cheer for this one. I had no cheer left in me. My insides jumped up and down though. Moscow pricked his ears and gobbled up the hill. Barry did his usual salute three strides from the line. It may not be the prettiest salute in the world, but I love to see him do it. Well

Chief finished a gallant runner-up, two lengths behind, but if Well Chief had found those two lengths, Moscow would have found two more.

This really was amazing. Moscow had won the Champion Chase again at the age of eleven. Not since Royal Relief in 1974 had a horse reclaimed the Champion Chase title after losing it. There was immense satisfaction in this. I just swooned around the winner's enclosure, taking it all in. Accepting the congratulations and basking in the afterglow. Brian smiled lots and shook the hand of whoever wanted to shake his. Barry did his usual flying dismount and ended up on his backside. You would think he'd have perfected it by now. He needs to take lessons in elegance.

Nicky Henderson had a winner that day as well, so we had a double celebration back at Seven Barrows that evening. But before I left the racecourse I'd had a chat with Brian about the rest of the season. There were just over three weeks between Cheltenham and Aintree, and another two and a half weeks between Aintree and Punchestown. We could do both. Moscow had had a fairly light campaign. Moreover, he wasn't getting any younger, and in all probability – although you really never do know with Moscow – he wouldn't be any better at the age of twelve than he was at the age of eleven. While he is well in himself, let's run him instead of wrapping him in cotton wool. It makes sense. All agreed. Now, let's have a drink.

He went to Aintree and put up one of the most impressive performances of his career, beating Le Roi Miguel by sixteen lengths. It could have been 66 lengths. Bar a slight mistake at the second fence, he was foot perfect. He just pricked his ears, jumped from fence to fence, and had the race in the bag well before he swung for home on his own. He really does thrive in the spring, when he feels the sun on his back. It was as if he was getting better with age.

We had one more stop before we wrapped it up for the season, the Kerrygold Champion Chase at Punchestown on 26 April. Five wins from five runs that season to date. A win at Punchestown would make it six. More than that, after Aintree, Moscow was nineteen wins from nineteen completions over fences. Punchestown would make it a round twenty. I'd always said that his unbeaten run would come to an end at some point. I just hoped that it wouldn't be in our back yard.

CHAPTER TWENTY-THREE

PHOTO FINISH

There has always been a lot of talk about Moscow Flyer's aversion to Punchestown. He has rarely been impressive there. Not as impressive as he has been at, say, Sandown or Cheltenham. Barry says that he doesn't ride half as well at Punchestown as he does at other courses. He can't put his finger on it. It's not a right-handed thing. Sandown is right-handed, Down Royal is right-handed, and he is very good at both of them. Punchestown is no stiffer or no easier than other tracks at which he has excelled. Barry simply says that he doesn't seem to help himself much at Punchestown. Everything is just a little more difficult there than it is anywhere else.

It is quite remarkable, then, that Moscow has won more races at Punchestown than he has won at any other track. As we prepared for Punchestown in April 2005, his record there was almost perfect. Eight wins from nine races. Five chases and three hurdles. And one unseated rider. It would not convince you that he didn't like the track.

There was no question of not going to the Punchestown Festival in 2005. The Kerrygold Champion Chase was tailor-made for Moscow – a Grade 1 chase over two miles where they all carry level weights. It was there for the picking. And I do like to support Punchestown. The fact that my daughter is now married to the racing manager there was an added dimension. I probably would have been excommunicated if I hadn't let Moscow run.

We hardly did anything with Moscow between Aintree and Punchestown. He had only run five times that season, but he had effectively been on the go since October 2004. Six months. I didn't want to give him a hard time, and he was fit enough anyway after Aintree.

No overseas raiders came to take us on. This was a wholly indigenous contest. Rathgar Beau was the only danger, I felt. He was the second-best two-mile chaser in the country. There was very little doubt about that. Dusty Sheehy had toyed with the idea of letting him contest the Champion Chase at Cheltenham, but had decided in the end to run him in the Daily Telegraph Trophy instead. That was the new race over two miles five furlongs. He finished third to Thisthatandtother in that after looking like he would win it going to the last. I was also running Colca Canyon in the Kerrygold race. He had run a cracker in the Mildmay of Flete at Cheltenham under a big weight. He was probably below Grade 1 standard, but he was as worthy of his place in the line-up as most of the others.

Moscow, the 1–4 favourite, pulled for his head on the approach to the first fence, but he jumped that well and settled OK, on the outside of Central House. Robert Power allowed Colca Canyon to stride on around the turn away from the stands and over the second fence. I wasn't sure why he was allowing Colca Canyon to go on. He wasn't in the race to make a pace for Moscow Flyer and he was usually ridden from behind. Perhaps the horse wasn't settling in behind, I thought, and Robert thought that he would settle better in front. Robert is a good horseman with a good head on his shoulders, and I trusted that he was doing whatever he thought was the right thing. That is all I ask of any of my jockeys.

Moscow settled in third, behind Colca Canyon and Mossy Green. Central House and Rathgar Beau followed him. Moscow got in a little tight to the first fence down the back straight, but it was nothing to get worried about. At the last on the far side, he jumped up alongside Colca Canyon. Barry looked around. Nothing there to be too worried about.

Going to the fourth last as the pace increased, Colca Canyon began to struggle and Barry found himself in front. Shay Barry rushed Rathgar Beau up from fifth to second and took up the box seat just behind Moscow. At the third last, the last fence before they turned into the straight, Moscow was tight, but he fiddled it well. Barry asked him to stretch around the home turn.

He did stretch, but Rathgar Beau stretched with him. Before they swung in, as I watched them side on, it looked like Moscow was going away from Rathgar, but only gradually. When they swung in, I only had a head-on view, so I couldn't really tell. It looked like Moscow had the upper hand, but only just. It was time to get a little worried. The usual Punchestown jitters.

I thought he was at least two lengths clear going to the second last. Just pop the second last and he should be home free. But he didn't. The second last at Punchestown and the fourth last at Cheltenham. He just doesn't do either of them easily. Of course he knows them. Of course he remembers. It looked like he was meeting this one on a stride. Barry asked him to pick up, and he did. But then he dived at it. Almost as if he changed his mind in the middle of take-off. Oh-oh, this is the second last at Punchestown! Like a pilot would decide that he's not going to be able to lift off halfway down the runway. He hit the middle of the fence. Barry sat tight. Moscow went through the fence. His momentum just about got him to the landing side. Barry was still on board when he got there, but they had lost all momentum. Barry had to get him going again.

By the time he did, Rathgar Beau had gone a length up on the near side. He was still at least half a length up when they jumped the last. Moscow on the far side, Rathgar on the near side. Barry and Shay driving and pushing and flailing and urging. Every last ounce of energy required. Halfway up the run-in, I thought Moscow was going to get up. He was going to maintain his unbeaten record, but only just. We had got away with it. A hundred yards from the line, I thought Rathgar was up. Moscow was going to be beaten. I couldn't believe it. Two strides later, I just didn't know. I think I was screaming at the top of my lungs.

Ten strides from the line, their heads bobbed in unison. By the time they got to the line, however, the synchronisation was lost. When Moscow's head was up, Rathgar's was down. When Rathgar's was up, Moscow's was down. They flashed past together. This would be decided by the bob of a head. Whoever's head had been down at the exact point at which they decided to draw the line would be the winner.

I rushed down from the stands so that I could catch Eamonn and Barry as they came in from the racecourse to the unsaddling enclosure. I walked down the long walkway with them. Barry didn't know who had won. Eamonn didn't know. Shay Barry on Rathgar Beau just behind us didn't know. Nobody knew.

Eamonn led Moscow and Barry back into the parade ring. The unsaddling area reserved for the winner is up at the top end of the parade ring, but Eamonn wouldn't bring them up near it. He began to walk around in circles at the opposite end. Rathgar Beau's lad did likewise. Neither Barry nor Shay dismounted. They would wait for the result. We all would.

As the minutes ticked by, the thoughts went through my head. It was a strange feeling, thinking that he might have lost. This would be a new experience for Moscow, to have finished a race over fences and not won it. It would be a new experience for all of us.

Five minutes now since they passed the post. It must be a dead heat.

It would be a shame if the record were to go. Twenty wins from twenty completions would be a fantastic achievement. But I had always told myself, and anyone else who would listen, that the record would go at some stage. How bad would it be if it were to go here and now? At least then the pressure would be off. They wouldn't be able to talk about it any more. And they might stop talking about his jumping as a result.

Eight minutes.

It has to be a dead heat. What can they be doing? The photo-finish technology is so good these days that they can usually call the result in less than a minute. Even tight ones.

Eleven minutes now.

Maybe it was because I was involved, but I cannot remember a photo finish that took longer.

And then the announcement came. Result of the third race. I checked Moscow's saddlecloth again. Number four. Rathgar was number seven. A hush descended not only on those in and around the parade ring, but on the whole racecourse. It felt like a hush had descended on the entire country. I expected the next words over the PA system to be 'a dead heat for first place'. I really did. Everybody on the racecourse did. Everybody watching on television did. The announcer delayed for what seemed like an eternity. I don't know why. I suppose he did because he could. He had the power that comes with information.

Then it came. 'First . . .' I was shocked. There was going to be a winner. They had managed to split them after all. Another pause. More dramatic effect. 'Number seven.'

A whoop issued from the racecourse. I'm not sure what the whoop was. Somewhere between a gasp of surprise and a cheer of delight. The Rathgar Beau connections beside us were unsurprisingly responsible for the lion's share of the latter.

My heart sank. I couldn't believe it. Moscow had been beaten. He took a false step and jinked a little. Maybe it was the cheer that startled him, or maybe he knew that he was number four. Brian and I exchanged glances. Oh well. Eamonn smiled. Barry smiled. What could we do? It had to happen some time. He had only gone down by a short head. He had lost hardly anything in defeat. I was delighted for Rathgar Beau. He deserved to win a Grade 1 race. And I was delighted for Shay Barry. And especially for Dusty Sheehy. I genuinely was. He is a top trainer who deserved this success fully. Both he and his horse were breaking their Grade 1 duck.

I am not usually one for post-mortems, but I did have a look at the photo finish print later. Then I realised why it had taken them so long to call a result. There are lots of anomalies. There is no reverse image. You can only see the print from one side. Most racecourses have a mirror positioned on the line so that you can see the print from both sides. This usually removes any doubt about the result. But Punchestown racecourse is so wide, apparently, that a mirror won't work. On looking at the print from one angle, it is impossible to say which horse's nose is the one on the line. There is a very strong case for saying that it is Moscow's nose that is on the line, and that Rathgar's nose ends just before the line. The two noses actually blend into each other, but you can just about make out the shadow of Rathgar's nose on the near side. Also, wherever Moscow's nose ends, it certainly doesn't end where they have drawn the line marked '2nd'. That is drawn just below his noseband. It cannot possibly be there. If it were there, it would mean that his noseband was on the tip of his nose. It wasn't. It never is, and it couldn't have been. In the print, Barry's head is in front of Shay's head. Moscow's ears are in front of Rathgar's ears. I suspect that if we had a reverse image we would see Moscow's nose on the line and Rathgar's just before it. But you couldn't tell for sure. Not without the reverse image.

A dead heat would unquestionably have been the correct result. The fact that it took eleven minutes for the result to be announced meant that even the judge had had a doubt. The print was inconclusive, and it remains so. I don't know what the judge was thinking. Why didn't he call a dead heat? It was the only result he could have called.

Over the next couple of days, many people asked me if I was going to object. The print had been published in a number of national newspapers and people had formed their own opinions. I wasn't. I never would. It would just be seen as sour grapes. Dusty's horse had been called the winner, and we would just leave it at that. When history is set you can't just change it so easily. It wouldn't have meant anything anyway as any amendment would have come weeks after the race. People had left the racecourse that day thinking that Moscow had been beaten. Let's just leave it at that. An amendment on an objection just wouldn't have been right. And I didn't want to take anything away from Dusty or his horse. I don't think Brian would have allowed me to object anyway. He was genuinely thrilled for Rathgar Beau.

He was thrilled with Moscow too, of course. We all were. He had done himself and us proud. He had just completed another extraordinary season. At the age of eleven. Probably the best of his career. A Tingle Creek Chase, a Champion Chase and a Melling Chase all in the same season. And all for a second time.

They were calling him an old-timer now. A veteran. It was hard to think of Moscow Flyer as a veteran, but I suppose he was. The thing about this veteran, however, was that he was still the fastest two-mile chaser in the business.

CHAPTER TWENTY-FOUR

A HERO'S LEGACY

We put Moscow into the field behind Eamonn's house for the summer of 2005. He likes it there, and Eamonn likes having him there. They can keep an eye on each other. Each can make sure the other comes to no harm.

During that summer, Brian, Eamonn and I picked up a number of awards on Moscow's behalf. We were at the National Hunt Awards again. Best two-mile chaser, best two-and-a-half-mile chaser, and this time BHB Horse of the Year as well. Dessie Hughes picked up the award for the best two-mile hurdler, Hardy Eustace, and Tom Taaffe for the best three-mile chaser, Kicking King. It was a good day. In fact, it had been an incredible season for Irish horses. Moscow had won the Champion Chase, Hardy Eustace had won the Champion Hurdle, Kicking King had won the Gold Cup, and then Hedgehunter, trained by Willie Mullins, went and won the Grand National. It was the first time ever that

Irish-trained horses had won the four top National Hunt races in the UK in the same season. It was fantastic to be a part of that. The Irish government hosted a very nice dinner for us in Farmleigh in the Phoenix Park to celebrate the achievement. That was a special occasion for all of us. An Taoiseach, Bertie Ahern, presented the awards. We also received a very nice presentation from the Moone-Timolin Council.

Moscow was voted Horse of the Year by Channel 4 viewers. Brian went to dinner in England on the last day of the National Hunt season to collect that award. The silks Barry wore when he won the Champion Chase were sold at a charity auction for £2,500. I wasn't allowed to wash them or anything. They had to have the Cheltenham dirt on them. Eddie Joyce got breeders' awards. Barry got riding awards. I think we all had to invest in new sideboards. And it was all thanks to Moscow Flyer.

Moscow, for his own part, just frolicked around his field for the summer. That is, if you can frolic at the age of eleven. Moscow can. If there was an award going for frolicking, he would win that as well. Still belying his years.

When you come towards the end of a journey, it is easy to look back and think, 'Well, if I hadn't turned right there, or if I hadn't gone straight on there, I wouldn't have ended up where I am now.' And it is true. Wherever you are in your life, you wouldn't have got there if you hadn't made the decisions you made. Many independent factors conspired to give us Moscow Flyer, and many unlikely events came to pass in order to allow the Moscow Flyer story to happen.

At its very base level, if Eddie Joyce's father-in-law had not liked the stallion Moscow Society, there would have been no Moscow Society foal out of the Duky mare Meelick Lady. If Eddie had sold the young horse privately before the 1998 Derby Sale, we would never have had the chance to buy him. If Eddie had not asked Jim Mernagh to prepare his horse for that sale, we probably wouldn't even have seen him. Moscow was the first horse Eddie sold at public auction. He could have asked anyone to consign him.

It was only because of Moscow's family history that he asked Jim. If Jim had not continually badgered Johnny about his four-year-old gelding, we wouldn't have gone to look at him. There were so many horses, and his pedigree did not stand out. If Shean Town had not won that day at Leopardstown, Brian Kearney would not have asked me to get a horse for him. If we had managed to buy one of the first two horses on which we bid for Brian – and we would have had they not been so expensive – we probably wouldn't have bought Lot 432. Even at that, if Bryan Murphy had bid two more bids, he would have had him. If things had worked out differently for me in England I would never have started training racehorses. If I hadn't married Johnny second time around . . . if he and Eamonn hadn't been training a few horses already when I arrived . . . The list goes on.

It may be that it wouldn't have mattered who had owned or trained Moscow Flyer. It may be that he would have turned out to be Moscow Flyer, champion two-mile chaser, in any case. But you just don't know. Obviously the training regime we have at Commonstown suits Moscow. He thrives on it. Another trainer might have trained him differently or campaigned him differently, and he might not have done so well. But you just never know. If Moscow had won a bumper, we might have geared him differently. If he had gone to Cheltenham in 2001 and won, or run well in, the Champion Hurdle, he might never have jumped a fence. If he hadn't almost killed himself on his first run over fences, he might never have learnt to jump so well. If Barry Geraghty hadn't ridden him . . . if Eamonn Leigh hadn't looked after him . . . Well, that's just ridiculous.

And standing here in the field, looking at him now, you wonder. What makes him different? Four legs, one in each corner. A head, a neck, a body, a tail. Check. The same as every other horse. But he is different. What you can't see is what's inside. His head and his heart. There's the difference. He wends his way over now, head outstretched. He knows he will get a tug on his ear and a pat on the neck. White blob on the middle of his forehead, white streak all the way down his face. Still there. Right where they have been since the day he was born.

When this horse came into my life in June 1998 – an ungainly adolescent, completely lacking in worldly wisdom – I could never have known the impact that he would have on it. I could never have known the places to which he would take me. The pinnacles he would scale for me. This beast has changed my life irrevocably. He has changed all our lives. This animal who lowers his head in front of me now. The one who seeks nothing more than a stroke on the neck. That's him. That's his character. Give everything, and seek hardly anything in return.

He will tell us when he doesn't enjoy his racing any more. When he has had enough. He'll let us know. And it won't matter if he doesn't win the 2006 Champion Chase at the age of twelve. Not a jot. He has nothing left to prove. Not to us, not to himself, not to anyone else. He has done it all. And then he has come back and done it all again.

You are forever looking forward in this game. Always looking to the next race, the next big day, the next big target. But at some stage there comes a time when you have to stop and take stock of what you have. Take the time to look back on the goals that have been reached. Appreciate all that has been achieved.

For Moscow Flyer, that time is now.

MOSCOW FLYER: COMPLETE RACING RECORD

Date	Position		Jockey	Course	Distance	Type	Class	Weight	OR	RR	Spd	SP	No of	Winning
30-Jan-1999	6	14.25	Mr P Fahey	FAIRYHOUSE	2m	NHF		11-05		89	0	9-1	28	£2,916
20-Feb-1999	3	3	Mr P Fahey	GOWRAN PARK	2m 1f	NHF		11-06		100	0	7-4	16	£3,683
5-Apr-1999	4	5.2	A Ross	FAIRYHOUSE	2m	NHF		11-08		105	0	8-1	27	£6,138
24-Apr-1999	3	9	Mr P Fahey	NAVAN	2m 2f	NHF		11-08		90	0	3-1	27	£2,916
31-Oct-1999	1		B J Geraghty	PUNCHESTOWN	2m	HDL		11-06		117	38	13-2	11	£3,696
6-Nov-1999	1		B J Geraghty	DOWN ROYAL	2m	HDL		11-00		121	44	5-2	4	£8,705
28-Nov-1999	1		B J Geraghty	FAIRYHOUSE	2m	HDL		12-00		133	30	7-2	4	£26,116
23-Apr-2000	8	46.95	B J Geraghty	FAIRYHOUSE	2m 4f	HDL		11-13			31	6-1	9	£9,360
2-May-2000	1		B J Geraghty	PUNCHESTOWN	2m	HDL		12-00		150		10-1	7	£24,800
21-Oct-2000	3	1.25	B J Geraghty	CORK	2m	HDL		11-11		152		9-2	8	£31,200
18-Nov-2000	1		P Moloney	PUNCHESTOWN	2m	HDL		11-13	143	151		2-5	5	£10,400
3-Dec-2000	2	3.5	B J Geraghty	FAIRYHOUSE	2m 4f	HDL		11-12	143	160		6-4	7	£23,400
31-Dec-2000	1		B J Geraghty	LEOPARDSTOWN	2m	HDL		12-00	144	165		5-1	7	£15,600
21-Jan-2001	F		B J Geraghty	LEOPARDSTOWN	2m	HDL		11-10	151	165		7-1	7	£53,629
18-Apr-2001	2	4.5	B J Geraghty	GOWRAN PARK	2m 2f	HDL		12-00	151	160		4-5	10	£8,911
27-Apr-2001	1		B J Geraghty	LEOPARDSTOWN	2m	HDL		12-00	151	170		6-1	7	£55,645
24-Oct-2001	F		B J Geraghty	FAIRYHOUSE	2m 2f	CHS		12-00				4-9	15	£7,790
9-Nov-2001	1		B J Geraghty	DOWN ROYAL	2m	CHS		12-00		123		2-5	17	£7,234
17-Nov-2001	1		B J Geraghty	PUNCHESTOWN	2m	CHS		11-02		151	120	4-6	4	£13,105
26-Dec-2001	1		B J Geraghty	LEOPARDSTOWN	2m 1f	CHS		11-12		151	120	5-4	8	£39,315
27-Jan-2002	F		P Moloney	LEOPARDSTOWN	2m 1f	CHS		11-12				4-6	7	£31,902
12-Mar-2002	1		B J Geraghty	CHELTENHAM	2m	CHS	A	11-08		167	118	11-2	12	£72,500

Date	Position	Jockey	Course	Distance	Type	Class	Weight	OR	RR	Spd	SP	No of	Winning
25-Apr-2002	1	B J Geraghty	PUNCHESTOWN	2m	CHS		11-12		155	116	2-5	6	£32,331
9-Nov-2002	1	B J Geraghty	DOWN ROYAL	2m 2f	CHS		12-00	159	168		4-11	3	£21,166
7-Dec-2002	U	B J Geraghty	SANDOWN	2m	CHS	A	11-07				2-1	6	£59,500
29-Dec-2002	1	B J Geraghty	LEOPARDSTOWN	2m 1f	CHS		11-12	159	162	118	4-9	6	£17,945
2-Feb-2003	1	B J Geraghty	PUNCHESTOWN	2m	CHS		12-00	160	163	112	2-7	5	£16,883
12-Mar-2003	1	B J Geraghty	CHELTENHAM	2m	CHS	A	12-00		174	112	7-4	11	£145,000
29-Apr-2003	U	B J Geraghty	PUNCHESTOWN	2m	CHS		12-00	170	165		4-11	7	£48,481
9-Nov-2003	1	B J Geraghty	NAVAN	2m	CHS		12-00	170	152	118	30-100	4	£21,104
6-Dec-2003	1	B J Geraghty	SANDOWN	2m	CHS	A	11-07	0	176	121	6-4	7	£58,000
27-Dec-2003	1	B J Geraghty	LEOPARDSTOWN	2m 1f	CHS		11-12	174	166	114	2-7	6	£21,104
17-Mar-2004	U	B J Geraghty	CHELTENHAM	2m	CHS	A	11-10				5-6	8	£145,000
2-Apr-2004	1	B J Geraghty	AINTREE	2m 4f	CHS	A	11-10		176	110	Evens	7	£89,250
27-Apr-2004	1	B J Geraghty	PUNCHESTOWN	2m	CHS		11-12	174	165	115	4-11	7	£65,493
7-Nov-2004	1	B J Geraghty	NAVAN	2m	CHS		11-12	174	167		30-100	5	£22,923
4-Dec-2004	1	B J Geraghty	SANDOWN	2m	CHS	A	11-07		179	125	2-1	7	£72,500
30-Jan-2005	1	B J Geraghty	PUNCHESTOWN	2m	CHS		12-00	178	166	113	2-11	5	£18,468
16-Mar-2005	1	B J Geraghty	CHELTENHAM	2m	CHS	A	11-10		182	117	6-4	8	£145,000
8-Apr-2005	1	B J Geraghty	AINTREE	2m 4f	CHS		11-10		180	118	4-9	6	£89,250
26-Apr-2005	2 0.1	B J Geraghty	PUNCHESTOWN	2m	CHS		11-12	180	166	118	1-4	7	£79,149
													£1,627,508

THE RACE VICTORIES:
ENTRIES FROM THE FORM BOOK

1999

[1142]PUNCHESTOWN (R-H)
Sunday, October 31

OFFICIAL GOING: Yielding

1269a	SHAMROCK CLASSIC MAIDEN HURDLE	2m
	3:45 (3:50) 4-Y-O+ £3,696 (£857; £375; £214)	

				RPR
1		Moscow Flyer (IRE)[190] [4262] 5-11-6 .... BJGeraghty		117
		(Mrs John Harrington, Ire) *led & disp ld: led 3rd: rdn after 2 out: styd on*	13/2[2]	
2	3	Young Buck (IRE)[280] [2803] 5-12-0 .... PCarberry		122
		(Noel Meade, Ire) *hld up: mstke 4th: hdwy 3 out: rdn to go 2nd st: chsd wnr: no imp u.p appr last: kpt on same pce*	8/13[1]	
3	10	Enterprising (IRE)[120] [86] 4-11-4 .... JRBarry		102
		(Mrs John Harrington, Ire) *hld up in rr: hdwy appr 3 out: mod 5th appr 2 out: 3rd nr last: styd on flat*	9/1	
4	8	Shawalan (IRE)[10] [1144] 5-11-6 .... KPGaule		96
		(John Joseph Murphy, Ire) *mod 3rd whn mstke 2nd: lft 4th at 6th: mstke 3 out: 4th, rdn & no imp between last 2: one pce*	33/1	
5	10	Why Bother (IRE)[14] [1066] 6-11-1 .... CFSwan		81
		(Stephen Ryan, Ire) *in tch: wnt 3rd at 5th: 2nd bef next: chsd wnr: 3rd & rdn early st: one pce & no imp appr last*	20/1	
6	5 ½	Clever Consul (IRE)[15] [603] 4-11-9 .... DTEvans		84
		(D K Weld, Ire) *hld up: lft 7th at 6th: mod 5th appr 2 out: no imp between last 2*	7/1[3]	
7	2 ½	Moll Hackabout (IRE)[18] [1048] 5-11-1 .... CO'Dwyer		73
		(Patrick Prendergast, Ire) *hld up towards rr: hdwy 5th: lft 3rd next: rdn & wkng 3 out: no imp appr next*	25/1	
8	shd	Winter Wishes (IRE)[91] [412] 5-11-6 .... GCotter		78
		(D T Hughes, Ire) *hld up: 7th at 4th & 3 out: no imp whn slt mstke 2 out: one pce*	9/1	
9	25	Chu Culainn (IRE)[42] [3229] 5-11-9 ....(t) KAKelly[(5)]		61
		(J F Bailey-Jun, Ire) *hld up: mod 6th at 4th: lft 8th & sltly hmpd 6th: n.d after next: t.o*	33/1	
10	9	Secret Native (IRE)[165] [4641] 4-11-4 .... JFTitley		42
		(T J Taaffe, Ire) *towards rr: 8th at 4th: lft 6th at 6th: wknd bef next: n.d: t.o*	10/1	
F		Belene Boy (IRE)[147] [46] 6-11-6 92.................................... DJCasey		—
		(A Kavanagh, Ire) *led & disp ld: hdd whn mstke 3rd: rn 2nd: cl 3rd whn fell 6th*	33/1	

4m 4.90s (14.90) **Going Correction** +99.99s/f
WFA 4 from 5yo+ 13lb   **11 Ran   SP% 134.3**
Speed ratings: **38,30,40,38,43 35,43,38,30,40 38** CSF £11.31 TOTE £7.20: £1.50, £1.40, £2.10; DF 2.80.
Owner Brian Kearney **Bred** Edward Joyce **Trained** Stud Moone, Co Kildare

[1392]DOWN ROYAL (R-H)
Saturday, November 6

OFFICIAL GOING: Soft

1399a	TATTERSALLS HURDLE			2m
	2:15 (2:15) 5-Y-O+		£8,705 (£2,544; £1,205; £401)	

					RPR
1		**Moscow Flyer (IRE)**[6] [1269] 5-11-0	BJGeraghty		121+
		(Mrs John Harrington, Ire) *mde all: clr after 3 out: easily*		**5/2**[2]	
2	15	**Greenstead (USA)**[118] [100] 6-11-4 [128]................................	PCarberry		110
		(Noel Meade, Ire) *m 2nd: trckd wnr: rdn & nt qckn after 3 out*		**1/3**[1]	
3	4 ½	**Celtic Project (IRE)**[502] [22] 6-11-0 [89].................................	KWhelan		101
		(Edward C Sexton, Ire) *m 3rd: no imp fr 3 out*		**33/1**	
4	3 ½	**Dainty Daisy (IRE)**[7] [1260] 6-10-9	CO'Dwyer		93
		(F Flood, Ire) *a same pl: no imp fr 3 out*		**16/1**[3]	

Going Correction +99.99s/f   4 Ran   SP% **112.4**
Speed ratings: **44,40,44,49** CSF £3.73.
Owner Brian Kearney **Bred** Edward Joyce **Trained** Stud Moone, Co Kildare

[1794]FAIRYHOUSE (R-H)
Sunday, November 28

OFFICIAL GOING: Soft

1805a	PEMBROKE ELECTRICAL ROYAL BOND NOVICE HURDLE (GRADE 1)			
	(9 hdls)			2m
	2:35 (2:35) 4-Y-O+		£26,116 (£7,633; £3,616; £1,205)	

					RPR
1		**Moscow Flyer (IRE)**[22] [1399] 5-12-0	BJGeraghty		133+
		(Mrs John Harrington, Ire) *mde all: rdn bef 2 out: jnd briefly flat: styd on u.p*		**7/2**[2]	
2	3	**Stage Affair (USA)**[36] [1149] 5-12-0	APMcCoy		130+
		(D K Weld, Ire) *hld up: rdn to chal appr last: jnd wnr flat: no ex last 150y*		**4/11**[1]	
3	5	**Vanilla Man (IRE)**[28] [1264] 6-12-0 [107].................................	TPTreacy		122+
		(P Mullins, Ire) *m 2nd tl mstke 2nd: cl 4th 3 out: kpt on same pce*		**6/1**[3]	
4	dist	**Moscow Retreat (IRE)**[34] [1245] 6-12-0	PGHourigan		—
		(Michael Hourigan, Ire) *hld up: mstke 3rd: rdn & lost tch appr 2 out*		**16/1**	

4m 9.60s (27.60) **Going Correction** +99.99s/f   4 Ran   SP% **115.7**
Speed ratings: **30,30,30,30** CSF £5.40 TOTE £3.80; DF 1.50.
Owner Brian Kearney **Bred** Edward Joyce **Trained** Stud Moone, Co Kildare

2000

PUNCHESTOWN (R-H)
Tuesday, May 2

OFFICIAL GOING: Yielding

137a	**EVENING HERALD CHAMPION NOVICE HURDLE (GRADE 1)**	**2m**
	5:00 (5:00) 5-Y-O+ £24,800 (£7,600; £3,600; £1,200; £800)	

				RPR
1		**Moscow Flyer (IRE)**[9] 4142 6-12-0 .... BJGeraghty		150+
		(Mrs John Harrington, Ire) *trckd lders in 3rd, prog 3 out, led 2 out, sn rdn clr, eased nr finish, impressive*	**10/1**	
2	13	**Aldino (GER)**[26] 3885 6-12-0 118.................................. NWilliamson		137
		(Ronald O'Leary, Ire) *hld up in rr, prog after 4 out, 3rd and rdn 2 out, styd on to go mod 2nd fr last*	**8/1**[3]	
3	4	**Sausalito Bay**[49] 3522 6-12-0 .... PCarberry		135+
		(Noel Meade, Ire) *led, hded bef 4th, led again after next, rdn and hdd 2 out, kpt on one pced until no ex fr last*	**4/7**[1]	
4	10	**Docklands Limo**[12] 4019 7-12-0 .... CLlewellyn		125+
		(N A Twiston-Davies) *prom, led bef 4th, mstke and hded 5th, slt mistake 4 out, wknd after 3 out*	**11/1**	
5	12	**Hang'Em High**[44] 3683 6-12-0 .... APMcCoy		114+
		(A P O'Brien, Ire) *hld up, prog into 4th after 4 out, no ex after 3 out*	**16/1**	
6	dist	**Teknash (FR)**[19] 2531 5-11-13 83..................................(t) RWalsh		—
		(Niall Madden, Ire) *a bhd, lost tch halfway, t.o fr 4 out*	**100/1**	
P		**Minella Hotel (IRE)**[8] 30 8-12-0 116................................... CFSwan		—
		(John J Nallen, Ire) *tracked leaders in 4th, pushed along after halfway, ridden and no impression from 3 out, pulled up before last*	**9/2**[2]	

3m 47.2s (-2.80) **Going Correction** +99.99s/f 　　　 **7** Ran 　 **SP% 117.2**
CSF £77.01 TOTE £7.30: £3.00, £3.60; DF 70.00.
Owner Brian Kearney **Bred** Edward Joyce **Trained** Stud Moone, Co Kildare

---

1898 PUNCHESTOWN (R-H)
Saturday, November 18

OFFICIAL GOING: Soft

2147a	**MORGIANA HURDLE (GRADE 2)**	**2m**
	1:15 (1:16) 4-Y-O+ £10,400 (£3,040; £1,440; £480)	

				RPR
1		**Moscow Flyer (IRE)**[28] 1685 6-11-13 143................................. PMoloney		151+
		(Mrs John Harrington, Ire) *led & disp ld: hit 2nd: rdn clr after 2 out: slt mstke last: kpt on*	**2/5**[1]	
2	3 ½	**Samapour (IRE)**[7] 2024 6-11-4 122.. JRBarry		134
		(Thomas Foley, Ire) *2nd & disp ld: 3rd & nt qckn st: 2nd early flat: kpt on: nt trble wnr*	**16/1**	
3	½	**Commanche Court (IRE)**[199] 142 7-11-4 .... GCotter		133
		(T M Walsh, Ire) *rn 3rd: rdn & lost tch appr 2 out: 4th & no imp over last: kpt on flat*	**8/1**[3]	
4	3 ½	**Balla Sola (IRE)**[237] 3524 5-11-10 137.................................. CFSwan		136
		(W P Mullins, Ire) *hld up in rr: hdwy 3 out: wnt 2nd st: rdn & no imp appr last: mstke: one pce*	**4/1**[2]	
5	3	**Hill Society (IRE)**[6] 4026 8-11-4 123..(t) TPRudd		127
		(Noel Meade, Ire) *hld up: 3rd, rdn & chsd ldrs whn slt mstke 2 out: no imp appr last*	**10/1**	

4m 25.3s (35.30) **Going Correction** +99.99s/f 　　 **6** Ran 　 **SP% 117.5**
CSF £8.03 TOTE £1.40: £1.10, £5.80; DF 8.80.
Owner Brian Kearney **Bred** Edward Joyce **Trained** Stud Moone, Co Kildare

[2795]LEOPARDSTOWN (L-H)
Sunday, December 31

OFFICIAL GOING: Heavy

2878a	A.I.B. AGRI-BUSINESS DECEMBER FESTIVAL HURDLE (GRADE 2) (8 hdls)	2m
	12:20 (12:22) 4-Y-O+	£15,600 (£4,560; £2,160; £720)

			RPR
1		**Moscow Flyer (IRE)**[28] [2420] 6-12-0 144................................ BJGeraghty	165
		(Mrs John Harrington, Ire) *trckd ldrs in 3rd: impr into 2nd 4 out: chald*	
		approaching 2 out: 4th u.pure before last: rallied to ld flat: styd on wl **5/1**[2]	
2	2	**Stage Affair (USA)**[240] [157] 6-11-11 146.........................(t) RWalsh	160
		(D K Weld, Ire) *hld up in tch: headway 2 out: led approaching last: ridden*	
		and headed flat: kept on u.pure **6/1**[3]	
3	3	**Mantles Prince**[57] [1892] 6-11-7 143................................ NWilliamson	153
		(P Hughes, Ire) *hld up: progress 4 out: disputed ld 2 out: ridden and*	
		headed when mistake last: one paced flat **10/1**	
4	15	**Sadr (NZ)**[211] 7-11-3 .... JLCullen	134
		(Mrs S A Bramall, Ire) *always behind: lost tch when halfway* **25/1**	
5	7	**Topacio**[62] [1878] 4-11-9 126.. JFTitley	133
		(P Hughes, Ire) *led: ridden after 3 out: headed and weakened 2 out* **20/1**	
P		**Aerleon Pete (IRE)**[51] [1940] 6-11-3 119.............................. FMBerry	—
		(C Roche, Ire) *close up in 2nd: weakened from 4 out: pulled up before 2*	
		out **33/1**	
F		**Istabraq (IRE)**[292] [3524] 8-12-0 176............................... CFSwan	162
		(A P O'Brien, Ire) *trckd ldrs in 4th: bad mistake 4 out: progress on inner*	
		2 out: sn ridden to chal: close 3rd when fell last **1/4**[1]	

4m 24.8s
WFA 4 from 6yo+ 10lb   **8 Ran   SP% 131.6**
CSF £34.12 TOTE £5.60: £1.90, £2.00; DF 33.90.
Owner Brian Kearney **Bred** Edward Joyce **Trained** Stud Moone, Co Kildare

2001

[3501]LEOPARDSTOWN (L-H)
Friday, April 27

OFFICIAL GOING: Soft to heavy

4747a	SHELL CHAMPION HURDLE (GRADE 1) (8 hdls)	2m
	3:20 (3:21) 5-Y-O+	
		£55,645 (£17,620; £8,346; £2,782; £1,854; £927)

			RPR
1		**Moscow Flyer (IRE)**[9] [4636] 7-12-0 151.................................. BJGeraghty	170
		(Mrs John Harrington, Ire) *disp ld: led 4 out: rdn and hdd ent st: 2nd and*	
		no imp whn lft clr fr last **6/1**[2]	
2	7	**Colonel Yeager (IRE)**[9] [4636] 7-12-0 144................................ RWalsh	163
		(T M Walsh, Ire) *trckd ldrs in 5th: prog into 4th appr 2 out: mod 3rd and*	
		no imp st: lft 2nd and sltly hmpd last **7/1**[3]	
3	4 ½	**Mantles Prince**[9] [4636] 7-12-0 142............................... GCotter	158
		(P Hughes, Ire) *trckd ldrs in 4th: prog into 3rd after 3 out: rdn and no imp*	
		bef 2 out **16/1**	
4	dist	**Sungazer (IRE)**[11] [2958] 5-11-13 123........................... PCarberry	—
		(Noel Meade, Ire) *a bhd: no ex fr 2 out: t.o* **40/1**	
5	7	**Penny Rich (IRE)**[75] [3619] 7-12-0 128.............................. DJCasey	—
		(T Hogan, Ire) *a bhd: wknd 3 out: t.o* **25/1**	
6	dist	**Aerleon Pete (IRE)**[69] [3732] 7-12-0 118.......................... CO'Dwyer	—
		(C Roche, Ire) *disp ld: hdd 4 out: sn rdn: wknd qckly after 3 out* **100/1**	
F		**Istabraq (IRE)**[96] [3263] 9-12-0 176.............................. CFSwan	173+
		(A P O'Brien, Ire) *trckd ldrs in 3rd: smooth hdwy after 3 out: led travelling*	
		easily ent st: fell last **2/7**[1]	

3m 56.9s   **7 Ran   SP% 117.7**
CSF £41.00 TOTE £6.30: £1.60, £1.80; DF 16.60.
Owner Brian Kearney **Bred** Edward Joyce **Trained** Stud Moone, Co Kildare

1457DOWN ROYAL (R-H)

Friday, November 9

OFFICIAL GOING: Yielding (good to yielding in places)

2087a	SEACAT BEGINNERS CHASE		2m
	3:00 (3:02) 4-Y-O+	£7,233 (£1,677; £733; £419)	

			RPR
1			

1 **Moscow Flyer (IRE)**[16] 1866 7-12-0 .... BJGeraghty 123+
(Mrs John Harrington, Ire) *a.p: j.w: 2nd 2 out: led last: drew clr flat: nt extended* **2/5**[1]

2 4 **Royal Jake (IRE)**[205] 4638 7-12-0 .... PCarberry 108
(Noel Meade, Ire) *trckd ldrs: 5th 5 out: hdwy after 3 out: rdn to ld 2 out: hdd last: no ch w wnr* **8/1**[3]

3 4½ **Tuesday (IRE)**[12] 1884 6-12-0 .... DJCasey 104
(W P Mullins, Ire) *hld up in tch: 8th after 3 out: 5th after 2 out: kpt on fr last* **11/2**[2]

4 2 **Monitor**[16] 1866 7-12-0 ....(t) CO'Dwyer 102
(G M Lyons, Ire) *hld up: 8th 3 out: prog next: mod 3rd at last: rdn and one pced* **8/1**[3]

5 3½ **Mr Flowers (IRE)**[16] 1869 9-12-0 75.. TPRudd 98
(Miss S Barkley, Ire) *cl up in 2nd: led fr 6th: rdn and hdd after 3 out: kpt on one pced* **25/1**

6 1½ **Amptina (IRE)**[20] 1781 6-12-0 60.. PMoloney 97
(C A McBratney, Ire) *trckd ldrs in 3rd: 2nd 5 out: rdn to ld briefly after 3 out: one pced fr next* **25/1**

7 1 **Definition (IRE)**[16] 1866 6-12-0 .... PACarberry 96
(Michael McElhone, Ire) *prom: 4th 3 out: sn rdn and no imp: no ex and eased bef last* **50/1**

8 25 **Atomic (IRE)**[356] 2142 7-11-11 .... SMMcGovern(3) 71
(S J Mahon, Ire) *hld up: 10th 1/2-way: no imp fr 3 out* **16/1**

9 **Aura About Him (IRE)**[28] 1705 7-11-11 .... MrPPO'Brien(3) —
(Michael Cunningham, Ire) *mid-div: prog into 6th 5 out: no ex fr 3 out* **16/1**

10 **Indiana Journey (IRE)**[30] 1695 6-11-9 .... KWhelan —
(A J Martin, Ire) *s.i.s and nvr a factor* **10/1**

11 **Native Glen (IRE)**[328] 2640 7-12-0 ....(t) GTormey —
(Gerard Farrell, Ire) *a bhd* **20/1**

12 **Victor Boy (IRE)**[6] 1979 8-11-11 ....(t) SPMcCann(3) —
(Gerard Keane, Ire) *s.i.s and bhd: hdwy into 8th 5 out: no ex fr 3 out* **10/1**

13 **Kergaul (IRE)**[28] 1704 7-11-7 .... IJPower(7) —
(Noel Meade, Ire) *a bhd* **20/1**

14 **Victor Meldrew (IRE)**[11] 1365 6-11-9 .... JPElliott(5) —
(S J Mahon, Ire) *a bhd* **25/1**

15 **Rovet (IRE)**[169] 526 11-12-0 ....(b) JLCullen —
(W Newman, Ire) *led: hdd 6th: sn wknd: t.o* **25/1**

P **Ocean Sunset (IRE)**[433] 1193 6-12-0 .... KPGaule —
(T Hogan, Ire) *mid-div: wknd 5 out: p.u bef 3 out* **25/1**

P **Jack The General (IRE)**[28] 1704 8-11-11 .... NPMulholland(3) —
(C A McBratney, Ire) *bhd whn p.u 1/2-way* **25/1**

4m 20.5s **17** Ran SP% **173.5**
CSF £8.08.

Owner Brian Kearney **Bred** Edward Joyce **Trained** Stud Moone, Co Kildare

1981 PUNCHESTOWN (R-H)
Saturday, November 17

OFFICIAL GOING: Soft

2238a	CRADDOCKSTOWN NOVICE CHASE (GRADE 3)		2m
	1:15 (1:15) 4-Y-0+	£13,104 (£3,830; £1,814; £604)	

				RPR
1		**Moscow Flyer (IRE)**[8] 2087 7-11-2 .... BJGeraghty		151+
		(Mrs John Harrington, Ire) *nt fluent early: disp ld 5 out: led bef next: drew clr bef 2 out: unchal*	**4/6**[1]	
2	4	**Masalarian (IRE)**[40] 5301 6-11-2 .... CO'Dwyer		139
		(A L T Moore, Ire) *hld up in tch: wnt 2nd bef 3 out: sn rdn: no imp fr 2 out: kpt on*	**4/1**[3]	
3	8	**Grimes**[30] 1774 8-11-12 141.................................... PCarberry		141
		(C Roche, Ire) *led: hdd 4th: reminders next: last and drvn along 4 out: 3rd whn mstke 3 out: rdn and no imp: mstke last*	**10/3**[2]	
4	dist	**Penny Native (IRE)**[20] 1884 9-11-2 105.......................... BMCash		—
		(A L T Moore, Ire) *cl up: led fr 4th: jnd 5 out: pushed along and hdd bef next: wknd 3 out: t.o*	**14/1**	

4m 19.6s **Going Correction** +0.35s/f (Yiel)   **4 Ran SP% 109.7**
Speed ratings: 120,118,114,— CSF £3.87 TOTE £1.90; DF 3.60.
Owner Brian Kearney **Bred** Edward Joyce **Trained** Stud Moone, Co Kildare

---

LEOPARDSTOWN (L-H)
Wednesday, December 26

OFFICIAL GOING: Yielding

3031a	DENNY GOLD MEDAL NOVICE CHASE (GRADE 1) (11 fncs)		2m 1f
	2:40 (2:40) 4-Y-0+	£39,314 (£11,491; £5,443; £1,814)	

				RPR
1		**Moscow Flyer (IRE)**[39] 2238 7-11-12 .... BJGeraghty		151+
		(Mrs John Harrington, Ire) *cl up in 2nd: led after 3 out: clr after last: styd on wl: comf*	**5/4**[1]	
2	2	**Youlneverwalkalone (IRE)**[25] 2497 7-11-12 .... PMoloney		147+
		(C Roche, Ire) *hld up in rr: slow 2nd and 4 out: 5th 2 out: impr into 2nd appr last: kpt on wl wout troubling wnr*	**3/1**[2]	
3	4	**Colonel Yeager (IRE)**[32] 2375 7-11-12 .... RWalsh		143
		(T M Walsh, Ire) *trckd ldrs in 4th: pckd 4th: 5th 4 out: rdn fr 2 out: 3rd and no imp fr last*	**6/1**	
4	1½	**Just Our Job (IRE)**[18] 2619 6-11-12 .... KAKelly		144+
		(D T Hughes, Ire) *hld up: hdwy into 3rd 5 out: 2nd and rdn after 2 out: no imp whn bad mstke last*	**14/1**	
5	6	**Masalarian (IRE)**[39] 2238 6-11-12 .... CO'Dwyer		136
		(A L T Moore, Ire) *hld up in tch: 6th 3 out: no imp fr next*	**10/1**	
6	hd	**Michael Mor (IRE)**[52] 1985 7-11-12 .... PCarberry		—
		(Noel Meade, Ire) *hld up in tch: 7th appr 2 out: rdn and no imp*	**10/1**	
7	dist	**Over The First (IRE)**[34] 2370 6-11-12 116....................... GCotter		—
		(C F Swan, Ire) *led: slow 2nd: hdd after 3 out: slt mstke 2 out: sn rdn and wknd*	**14/1**	
P		**Golden Storm (IRE)**[34] 2368 4-11-1 .... JRBarry		—
		(Ms F M Crowley, Ire) *settled 3rd: lost pl 5 out: bhd fr 3 out: eased 2 out: t.o*	**11/2**[3]	

4m 25.7s **Going Correction** +0.175s/f (Yiel)   **9 Ran SP% 130.6**
WFA 4 from 6yo+ 10lb
Speed ratings: 120,119,117,116,113 113,—,— CSF £6.72 TOTE £2.30: £1.30, £1.60, £1.90; DF 6.30.
Owner Brian Kearney **Bred** Edward Joyce **Trained** Stud Moone, Co Kildare

2002

3483 CHELTENHAM (L-H)

Tuesday, March 12

OFFICIAL GOING: Good to soft (good in places)
Weather: overcast

4189	IRISH INDEPENDENT ARKLE CHALLENGE TROPHY CHASE GRADE

1 (12 fncs) 2m

2:35 (2:36) Class A 5-Y-O+

£72,500 (£27,500; £13,750; £6,250; £3,125; £1,875)

Form						RPR
11F/	**1**		**Moscow Flyer (IRE)**[44] 3532 8-11-8 .... BJGeraghty			167+
			(Mrs John Harrington, Ire) *lw: hld up in rr: hdwy 6th: chsd ldrs 4 out: wnt cl 2nd 3 out: led next: drvn clr run-in: readily*		**11/2**	
111/	**2**	4	**Seebald (GER)**[59] 3259 7-11-8 152... APMcCoy			160
			(M C Pipe) *lw: bhd: pushed along 6th: hdwy 8th: styd on wl to press ldrs 3 out: chsd wnr after next: kpt on but no imp run-in*		**5/2**[1]	
211/	**3**	13	**Armaturk (FR)**[24] 3796 5-11-3 .... TJMurphy			144+
			(P F Nicholls) *lw: trckd ldr: chal 5th: led next: narrowly hdd and blnd 2 out: kpt on same pce u.p*		**8/1**	
112/	**4**	¾	**Truckers Tavern (IRE)**[30] 3732 7-11-8 .... JPMcNamara			146
			(Ferdy Murphy) *dropped rr 3rd: rdn and outpcd 3 out: rallied u.p fr 2 out: kpt on run-in but nt a danger*		**11/1**	
P11/	**5**	5	**Fondmort (FR)**[75] 2890 6-11-8 143.................................... MAFitzgerald			142+
			(N J Henderson) *in tch: chsd ldrs fr 8th: rdn 3 out: wknd after 2 out: fin lame*		**4/1**[2]	
115/	**6**	2	**Assessed (IRE)**[30] 3732 8-11-8 .... RWalsh			142+
			(W P Mullins, Ire) *bhd: blnd 5th and 7th: sme hdwy fr 3 out: styng but nt a danger whn mstke last: kpt on again cl home*		**25/1**	
111/	**7**	9	**Barton**[59] 3254 9-11-8 .... ADobbin			133+
			(T D Easterby) *in tch: chsd ldrs fr 4th: rdn after 4 out: wknd next*		**9/2**[3]	
P11/	**8**	2½	**Kadarann (IRE)**[19] 3881 5-11-3 134.. JTizzard			123
			(P F Nicholls) *chsd ldrs: hit 4th: wnt 2nd 8th: rdn 4 out:sn wknd*		**16/1**	
246/	**9**	18	**Ei Ei**[11] 3997 7-11-8 120.. WWorthington			110
			(M C Chapman) *chsd ldrs: chal 3rd: styd prom tl wknd 8th*		**100/1**	
132/	**10**	½	**Youlneverwalkalone (IRE)**[16] 3960 8-11-8 .... CO'Dwyer			130+
			(C Roche, Ire) *lw: hld up in rr: hmpd bnd after 8th: rdn next and sn wknd*		**10/1**	
111/	**P**		**Il'Athou (FR)**[59] 3248 6-11-8 133... HOliver			—
			(S E H Sherwood) *swtg: led to 6th: wknd 8th: t.o whn p.u bef last*		**20/1**	
P3/	**F**		**Jardin De Beaulieu (FR)**[10] 4026 5-11-3 .... DRDennis			—
			(Ian Williams) *hit 2nd: bhd whn blnd 7th: t.o whn fell 2 out*		**100/1**	

3m 50.5s (-8.90) **Going Correction** -0.10s/f (Good)

WFA 5 from 6yo+ 4lb **12** Ran SP% **127.1**

Speed ratings: **118,116,109,109,106 105,101,99,90,90** —,— CSF £21.55 CT £117.09 TOTE £6.20: £1.80, £1.70, £2.20; EX 24.30 Trifecta £285.90 Pool £6,122.50 - 15.20 winning units..

Owner Brian Kearney **Bred** Edward Joyce **Trained** Stud Moone, Co Kildare

FOCUS
This was a fast run race.

[4943]PUNCHESTOWN (R-H)
Thursday, April 25

OFFICIAL GOING: Good

4953a	**SWORDLESTOWN CUP NOVICE CHASE (GRADE 1)**		**2m**
	3:50 (3:50) 5-Y-O+ £32,331 (£9,907; £4,693; £1,564; £1,042)		

			RPR
1		**Moscow Flyer (IRE)**[44] [4189] 8-11-12 .... BJGeraghty	155+
		(Mrs John Harrington, Ire) *cl up: disp ld fr 5 out: led bef next: clr after 3 out: nt extended* **2/5**[1]	
2	7	**Mantles Prince**[46] [4227] 8-11-12 .... JLCullen	140
		(P Hughes, Ire) *trckd ldrs in 4th: 2nd 4 out: rdn after 2 out: no imp: kpt on u.p* **7/1**[3]	
3	hd	**Assessed (IRE)**[44] [4189] 8-11-12 135.................................... RWalsh	140
		(W P Mullins, Ire) *led and disp: mstke 6 out: 4th and rdn 3 out: no imp fr next: kpt on u.p* **11/2**[2]	
4	8	**Michael Mor (IRE)**[15] [4792] 8-11-12 126................................ PCarberry	132
		(Noel Meade, Ire) *hld up in tch: 5th and rdn after 3 out: 3rd and no imp 2 out: j.lft and almost uns rdr last* **10/1**	
5	25	**Winter Garden**[24] [4707] 8-11-12 ....(b[1]) CO'Dwyer	107
		(A L T Moore, Ire) *hld up in tch: slt mstke 2nd: no imp fr 4 out: trailing fr next* **50/1**	
F		**Dantes Bank (IRE)**[12] [4802] 10-11-12 119..............................(t) KPGaule	—
		(Annette McMahon, Ire) *led and disp: hdd bef 4 out: no imp whn fell 2 out* **20/1**	

3m 59.5s **Going Correction** -0.275s/f (Good)   **6** Ran   **SP% 115.1**
Speed ratings: 116,112,112,108,95 — CSF £4.45 TOTE £1.40: £1.20, £2.60; DF 4.40.
Owner Brian Kearney **Bred** Edward Joyce **Trained** Stud Moone, Co Kildare

[1856]DOWN ROYAL (R-H)
Saturday, November 9

OFFICIAL GOING: Chase: soft; hurdle: heavy

1878a	**KILLULTAGH PROPERTIES LTD CHASE (GRADE 3)**		**2m 2f**
	2:35 (2:35) 5-Y-O+ £21,165 (£5,828; £2,760)		

			RPR
1		**Moscow Flyer (IRE)**[198] [4953] 8-12-0 159.............................. BJGeraghty	168+
		(Mrs John Harrington, Ire) *settled 3rd: slt mstke 4th: led 7th: drew clr fr 3 out: easily* **4/11**[1]	
2	20	**Kadarann (IRE)**[182] [197] 5-11-6 .... RWalsh	145
		(P F Nicholls) *2nd early: led bef 4th: hdd 7th: pushed along 4 out: no imp fr next* **5/2**[2]	
3	dist	**Fiery Ring (IRE)**[27] [1515] 7-11-2 118.................................... RGeraghty	116
		(J R H Fowler, Ire) *led tl hdd bef 4th: sn trailing: t.o bef 7th: one pced* **8/1**[3]	

4m 45.9s   **3** Ran   **SP% 113.0**
CSF £1.91.
Owner Brian Kearney **Bred** Edward Joyce **Trained** Stud Moone, Co Kildare

[2809]LEOPARDSTOWN (L-H)
Sunday, December 29

OFFICIAL GOING: Heavy

2826a	**PADDY POWER DIAL-A-BET CHASE (GRADE 2)** (11 fncs)	**2m 1f**
	1:30 (1:32) 5-Y-O+ £17,944 (£5,245; £2,484; £828)	

RPR

1   **Moscow Flyer (IRE)**[22] [2369] 8-11-12 159............................ BJGeraghty   162+
(Mrs John Harrington, Ire) *a cl up: disp ld 4th: cl 2nd fr 4 out: led*
travelling wl after 2 out: drew clr bef last: rdn and one pced cl home 4/9[1]

2   5   **Knife Edge (USA)**[42] [2018] 7-11-12 149.................................. RWalsh   152
(M J P O'Brien, Ire) *cl up in 4th: led 4 out: rdn and hdd after 2 out: outpcd*
bef last: kpt on u.p: flat 8/1[2]

3   5   **Go Roger Go (IRE)**[750] [2475] 10-11-10 .... NWilliamson   145
(E J O'Grady, Ire) *bhd: prog into mod 4th 3 out: 3rd and kpt on fr next* 20/1

4   2½   **Copernicus**[14] [2536] 7-11-7 136.. JLCullen   140
(P Hughes, Ire) *chsd ldrs in 5th: rdn and outpcd bef 1/2-way: last 3 out:*
kpt on under pressrue fr next 12/1

5   dist   **Arctic Copper (IRE)**[42] [2022] 8-11-7 136............................(b) PCarberry   —
(Noel Meade, Ire) *cl up in 2nd: dropped to 4th 1/2-way: rdn and wknd fr 4*
out: t.o 10/1[3]

P   **Alcapone (IRE)**[21] [2408] 8-11-12 144................................... DJCasey
(M F Morris, Ire) *led: jnd 4th: hdd & wknd 4 out: mstke 3 out: t.o whn p.u*
after 2 out 8/1[2]

4m 41.1s **Going Correction** +1.05s/f (Soft)   **6 Ran**   SP% **113.0**
Speed ratings: **118,115,113,112,**,— CSF £5.09 TOTE £1.50: £1.40, £2.20; DF 3.60.
Owner Brian Kearney **Bred** Edward Joyce **Trained** Stud Moone, Co Kildare

---

2003

[3413]PUNCHESTOWN (R-H)
Sunday, February 2

OFFICIAL GOING: Soft to heavy

3422a	**BYRNE GROUP PLC TIED COTTAGE CHASE (GRADE 3)**	**2m**
	2:30 (2:30) 5-Y-O+ £16,883 (£4,935; £2,337; £779)	

RPR

1   **Moscow Flyer (IRE)**[35] [2826] 9-12-0 160............................... BJGeraghty   163+
(Mrs John Harrington, Ire) *settled 3rd: 2nd 6 out: led 5 out: clr fr 3 out:*
mstke last: rdn and kpt on flat 2/7[1]

2   9   **Copernicus**[35] [2826] 8-11-10 135... PCarberry   147
(P Hughes, Ire) *a.p: led 6 out: hdd next: 2nd and lost tch 3 out: sn rdn:*
kpt on one pced 12/1

3   4   **Commanche Court (IRE)**[307] [4705] 10-12-0 166...................... RWalsh   147+
(T M Walsh, Ire) *hld up: mod 4th and rdn 4 out: 3rd 2 out: kpt on one*
pced 7/1[2]

4   3½   **Killultagh Storm (IRE)**[14] [3198] 9-11-7 136............................. DJCasey   137
(W P Mullins, Ire) *hld up in rr: slt mstke 5th: bad mstke 6th: sn lost tch:*
kpt on one pcede fr 3 out 8/1[3]

5   13   **Fiery Ring (IRE)**[63] [2281] 8-11-4 120................................... RGeraghty[(3)]   124
(J R H Fowler, Ire) *led: clr early: mstke and hdd 6 out: mod 3rd and rdn 4*
out: wknd fr next 25/1

4m 35.2s **Going Correction** +1.125s/f (Heavy)   **5 Ran**   SP% **112.9**
Speed ratings: **112,107,105,103,97** CSF £5.07 TOTE £1.20: £1.10, £2.10; DF 3.50.
Owner Brian Kearney **Bred** Edward Joyce **Trained** Stud Moone, Co Kildare

[4097] CHELTENHAM (L-H)
Wednesday, March 12

OFFICIAL GOING: Good (good to soft in places)
Weather: overcast & chilly

4111	QUEEN MOTHER CHAMPION CHASE GRADE 1 (12 fncs)	2m
	3:15 (3:15) Class A 5-Y-O+	
	£145,000 (£55,000; £27,500; £12,500; £6,250; £3,750)	

Form				RPR
U11/	**1**		**Moscow Flyer (IRE)**[38] [3422] 9-12-0 .... BJGeraghty	174+
			(Mrs John Harrington, Ire) lw: hld up in tch: trckd ldrs fr 5th: hit 4 out: chalng and gng wl whn lft clr 2 out: drvn clr run-in **7/4**[1]	
151/	**2**	7	**Native Upmanship (IRE)**[41] [3372] 10-12-0 .... CO'Dwyer	165+
			(A L T Moore, Ire) bhd:pushed along fr 8th: hdwy and gng wl 3 out:chsng ldrs and hmpd whn lft 2nd 2 out: kpt on but no imp on wnr **12/1**	
112/	**3**	3	**Cenkos (FR)**[32] [3524] 9-12-0 169 .... RWalsh	164+
			(P F Nicholls) chsd ldrs: rdn and outpcd 3 out: lft 3rd and hmpd 2 out: styd on same pce **7/1**[3]	
312/	**4**	5	**Geos (FR)**[25] [3628] 8-12-0 153.................................. MAFitzgerald	159+
			(N J Henderson) lw: bhd: pushed along 4th: hit 8th: nvr gng pce to rch ldrs: no ch whn hmpd 2 out: styd on fr last **25/1**	
24P/	**5**	5	**Flagship Uberalles (IRE)**[76] [2685] 9-12-0 169 ....(b) RJohnson	151+
			(P J Hobbs) lw: bhd: hdwy 5th: chsd ldrs and rdn 4 out: wknd fr next **12/1**	
211/	**6**	2½	**Edredon Bleu (FR)**[53] [3186] 11-12-0 171 ....(t) JCulloty	148
			(Miss H C Knight) led tl narrowly hdd 8th: styd pressing for ld tl wknd 3 out **12/1**	
211/	**7**	1¼	**Kadarann (IRE)**[32] [3524] 6-12-0 167 .... JTizzard	151+
			(P F Nicholls) a bhd: blnd 2nd: nt fluent 7th: no ch whn hit 4 out **9/1**	
44P/	**8**	10	**Florida Pearl (IRE)**[31] [3540] 11-12-0 .... PCarberry	138+
			(W P Mullins, Ire) lw: hit 2nd: a struggling to go pce and bhd **12/1**	
421/	**F**		**Tiutchev**[25] [3628] 10-12-0 167.................................. APMcCoy	—
			(M C Pipe) lw: trckd ldrs tl fell 5th **5/1**[2]	
550/	**F**		**Latalomne (USA)**[89] [2468] 9-12-0 150 .... VTKeane	163
			(B Ellison) pressed ldrs: chal fr 7th tl led 4 out: stl slt advantage and gng wl whn fell 2 out **25/1**	
222/	**F**		**Seebald (GER)**[53] [3179] 8-12-0 162 .... NWilliamson	163
			(M C Pipe) lw: sn in tch: trckd ldrs 5th: chal fr 7th: slt ld next: narrowly hdd but ev ch 4 out: upsides and rdn whn fell 2 out **14/1**	

3m 53.7s (-5.60) **Going Correction** -0.05s/f (Good)   **11 Ran**   SP% **120.7**
Speed ratings: **112,108,107,104,102 100,100,95,—,— —** CSF £25.24 CT £122.64 TOTE £2.50: £1.60, £3.70, £2.50; EX 36.90 Trifecta £196.20 Pool of £10,143.80 - 36.70 winning units.
Owner Brian Kearney **Bred** Edward Joyce **Trained** Stud Moone, Co Kildare

FOCUS
A fast pace as one would expect and a worthy winner after plenty of grief at the second last.

[842]NAVAN (L-H)
Sunday, November 9

OFFICIAL GOING: Good to firm

		BALLYMORE HOMES FORTRIA CHASE (GRADE 2)		2m
2047a		1:30 (1:30) 5-Y-0+	£21,103 (£6,168; £2,922; £974)	

				RPR
1		**Moscow Flyer (IRE)**[194] [23] 9-12-0 170................................ BJGeraghty		152+
		(Mrs John Harrington, Ire) *mde all: drvn along after 2 out: styd on wl fr last*		
2	5	**Glenelly Gale (IRE)**[1] [2023] 9-12-0 128................................ CO'Dwyer	30/100[1]	145+
		(A L T Moore, Ire) *hld up in rr: hdwy to go 2nd appr 3 out: drvn along to chse ldr after 2 out: no ex fr last: eased cl home*		
3	6	**Rathgar Beau (IRE)**[192] [65] 7-11-6 .... JLCullen	11/2[3]	133
		(E Sheehy, Ire) *settled 3rd: 2nd fr 3rd: mstke 5 out: drvn along after 3 out: rdn and kpt no ex fr 2 out*		
4	dist	**Fiery Ring (IRE)**[8] [1888] 8-11-3 123................................ RGeraghty	3/1[2]	—
		(J R H Fowler, Ire) *trckd ldr in 2nd: slt mstke and dropped to 3rd fr 3rd: drvn along appr st: sn in rr: t.o*		

4m 3.80s **Going Correction** -0.55s/f (Firm)   14/1

     4 Ran   **SP% 124.0**

Speed ratings: 118,115,112,— CSF £3.54 TOTE £1.30; DF 2.80.
Owner Brian Kearney **Bred** Edward Joyce **Trained** Stud Moone, Co Kildare

---

[2571]SANDOWN (R-H)
Saturday, December 6

OFFICIAL GOING: Chase course - good; hurdle course - good to soft (goingstick: chase 8.1; hurdles: 7.4)

	WILLIAM HILL - TINGLE CREEK TROPHY CHASE SHOWCASE RACE		
2593	GRADE 1 (13 fncs)		
	2:20 (2:23) Class A 5-Y-0+		2m

			£58,000 (£22,000; £11,000; £5,000; £2,500; £1,500)	

Form				RPR
1U1/	**1**		**Moscow Flyer (IRE)**[27] [2047] 9-11-7 .... BJGeraghty	176+
			(Mrs John Harrington, Ire) *trckd ldr: led 8th: mde rest: in command 2 out: rdn out flat*	
11U/	**2**	4	**Azertyuiop (FR)**[32] [1934] 6-11-7 161................................ RWalsh	6/4[1] · 172
			(P F Nicholls) *t.k.h: hld up in tch: effrt 3 out: rdn to chse wnr 2 out: no imp*	
P51/	**3**	7	**Flagship Uberalles (IRE)**[221] [23] 9-11-7 165............... RJohnson	2/1[2] · 166+
			(P J Hobbs) *settled last of main gp: prog 6th: chsd wnr bef 3 out: sn rdn and no imp: wknd last*	
112/	**4**	3½	**Le Roi Miguel (FR)**[14] [2298] 5-11-7 159................................ MAFitzgerald	16/1 · 162
			(P F Nicholls) *cl up: effrt 8th: chsd wnr 4 out tl bef next: sn lost pl u.p*	
161/	**5**	¾	**Cenkos (FR)**[22] [2133] 9-11-7 168................................ TJMurphy	11/2[3] · 164+
			(P F Nicholls) *led to 8th: steadily lost pl fr 4 out: wl btn whn mstke last*	
214/	**6**	11	**Seebald (GER)**[32] [1934] 8-11-7 161................................ APMcCoy	8/1 · 153+
			(M C Pipe) *cl up: nt fluent 5th: mstkes 8th and 4 out: nvr on terms w ldrs after*	
1P5/	**7**	dist	**Eskleybrook**[210] [208] 10-11-7 149................................ RBiddlecombe	14/1 · —
			(N A Twiston-Davies) *rel to r and lft 20l: nvr able to regain grnd: mstke 3rd: t.o after 4 out*	

3m 55.8s (-7.40) **Going Correction** +0.075s/f (Yiel)   100/1

     7 Ran   **SP% 113.4**

Speed ratings: 121,119,115,113,113 107,— CSF £4.99 TOTE £2.20: £1.70, £2.20; EX 5.80.
Owner Brian Kearney **Bred** Edward Joyce **Trained** Stud Moone, Co Kildare

FOCUS

As good a renewal of the Tingle Creek as you could wish to see. The winning time was over two seconds faster than the Henry VIII won by Thisthatandtother.

[2966]LEOPARDSTOWN (L-H)
Saturday, December 27

OFFICIAL GOING: Soft

3009a	PADDY POWER DIAL-A-BET CHASE (GRADE 2) (11 fncs)	2m 1f
	2:00 (2:02) 5-Y-O+	£21,103 (£6,168; £2,922; £974)

				RPR
1		**Moscow Flyer (IRE)**[21] [2593] 9-11-12 174.............................BJGeraghty		166+
		(Mrs John Harrington, Ire) cl up in 2nd: led fr 6 out: rdn after 2 out: styd on wl u.p	**2/7**[1]	
2	5	**Native Scout (IRE)**[27] [2490] 7-11-7 141......................(t) PCarberry		151
		(Donal Hassett, Ire) hld up: prog 6 out: 2nd next: rdn to chal after 2 out: no imp last: kpt on wl	**8/1**[2]	
3	6	**Knife Edge (USA)**[13] [2752] 8-11-12 148.........................(p) LCooper		150
		(M J P O'Brien, Ire) trckd ldrs: 5th 6 out: 3rd next: 4th 3 out: sn rdn: 3rd and kpt on fr next	**14/1**[3]	
4	1	**Killultagh Storm (IRE)**[13] [2752] 9-11-7 143.......................(p) DJCasey		144
		(W P Mullins, Ire) hld up: 5th 2 out: lft 4th last: kpt on	**16/1**	
5	dist	**No Need For Alarm**[252] [4638] 8-11-2 135....................MrDerekO'Connor		—
		(K J Burke) led: slt mstke 1st: hdd whn slt mstke 6 out: sn wknd: t.o	**20/1**	
F		**Rathgar Beau (IRE)**[13] [2752] 7-11-7 149.........................(b) JRBarry		144
		(E Sheehy, Ire) settled 3rd: mstke 5th: effrt whn mstke 3 out: 4th and no ex 2 out: fell last	**8/1**[2]	

4m 18.5s **Going Correction** +0.20s/f (Yiel)   **6 Ran**   SP% 117.3
Speed ratings: 114,111,108,108,— CSF £4.13 TOTE £1.50: £1.20, £2.30; DF 3.40.
Owner Brian Kearney **Bred** Edward Joyce **Trained** Stud Moone, Co Kildare

---

2004

[4623]AINTREE (L-H)
Friday, April 2

OFFICIAL GOING: Good
The ground was described as 'on the easy side of good'.
Weather: fine

4639	MARTELL COGNAC MELLING CHASE GRADE 1 (16 fncs)	2m 4f
	3:10 (3:14) Class A 5-Y-O+	£89,250 (£33,000; £16,500; £7,500; £3,750)

Form					RPR
11U/	1		**Moscow Flyer (IRE)**[16] [4396] 10-11-10 ....BJGeraghty		176+
			(Mrs John Harrington, Ire) trckd ldrs: led 2 out: shkn up and r.o wl after last: readily	**1/1**[1]	
511/	2	6	**Isio (FR)**[27] [4196] 8-11-10 164............................MAFitzgerald	**4/1**[2]	167+
			(N J Henderson) chsd ldr: hit 6th: led 9th to 2 out: nt qckn appr last		
513/	3	13	**Native Upmanship (IRE)**[40] [3970] 11-11-10 ....CO'Dwyer		153
			(A L T Moore, Ire) hld up: hdwy 9th: outpcd whn hit 12th: one pce fr 3 out	**5/1**[3]	
544/	4	1¼	**Cenkos (FR)**[16] [4396] 10-11-10 165............................JTizzard		153+
			(P F Nicholls) led: hit 5th: hdd 9th: outpcd fr 13th	**33/1**	
151/	5	dist	**Strong Magic (IRE)**[9] [4536] 12-11-10 93......................ARoss		—
			(J R Cornwall) outpcd and bhd whn mstke 9th: sn t.o	**200/1**	
4F4/	F		**Le Roi Miguel (FR)**[62] [3591] 6-11-10 158.......................RWalsh		—
			(P F Nicholls) hld up: hdwy 9th: 5th and in tch whn fell 12th	**6/1**	
322/	P		**Flagship Uberalles (IRE)**[16] [4396] 10-11-10 164.................RJohnson		—
			(P J Hobbs) mstkes: blnd 4th: outpcd and bhd 9th: blnd 11th: sn t.o: p.u bef 13th	**16/1**	

5m 2.40s (-4.90) **Going Correction** +0.025s/f (Yiel)   **7 Ran**   SP% 110.3
Speed ratings: 110,107,102,101,— —, CSF £5.18 TOTE £1.90: £1.70, £2.00; EX 4.60.
Owner Brian Kearney **Bred** Edward Joyce **Trained** Stud Moone, Co Kildare
FOCUS
A strong line-up but just a steady pace.

PUNCHESTOWN (R-H)
Tuesday, April 27
OFFICIAL GOING: Good to yielding

38a | **BETDAQ.COM CHAMPION CHASE (GRADE 1)** | **2m**
3:15 (3:15) 5-Y-O+   £65,492 (£20,070; £9,507; £3,169; £2,112)

			RPR
1		**Moscow Flyer (IRE)**[25] 4639 10-11-12 174.............................. BJGeraghty	165+
		(Mrs John Harrington, Ire) *a cl up: led 4 out: rdn and kpt on wl fr 2 out: comf*	
			4/11[1]
2	2	**Rathgar Beau (IRE)**[16] 4769 8-11-12 145................................. JRBarry	158
		(E Sheehy, Ire) *settled 5th: 4th and hdwy 4 out: 3rd after slt mstke next: 2nd travelling wl 2 out: sn rdn and no imp: kpt on fr last*	
			12/1
3	6	**Strong Run (IRE)**[31] 4580 11-11-12 145..........................(t) PCarberry	153+
		(Noel Meade, Ire) *led: drvn along and hdd after 5 out: 2nd 3 out: 3rd and no ex next*	
			8/1[3]
4	8	**Native Upmanship (IRE)**[25] 4639 11-11-12 160.................... CO'Dwyer	146+
		(A L T Moore, Ire) *cl up in 2nd: led after 5 out: mstke and hdd 4 out: 4th and no ex fr next*	
			7/1[2]
5	3½	**Killultagh Storm (IRE)**[16] 4769 10-11-12 140........................(p) RWalsh	141
		(W P Mullins, Ire) *bhd: kpt on one pced fr 2 out*	
			33/1
6	12	**Alcapone (IRE)**[24] 4647 10-11-12 148.. JCulloty	129
		(M F Morris, Ire) *prom early: 5th 4 out: sn wknd*	
			16/1
U		**Native Scout (IRE)**[16] 4769 8-11-12 149.............................(t) DNRussell	—
		(Donal Hassett, Ire) *bhd: last 4 out: mod 5th and no imp whn uns rdr last*	

4m 6.90s **Going Correction** -0.50s/f (Good)   7 Ran   SP% **122.5**
Speed ratings: 115,114,111,107,105 99,— CSF £7.52 TOTE £1.50: £1.30, £5.90; DF 13.30.
Owner Brian Kearney **Bred** Edward Joyce **Trained** Stud Moone, Co Kildare

---

[787]NAVAN (L-H)
Sunday, November 7
OFFICIAL GOING: Soft

2090a | **BALLYMORE PROPERTIES FORTRIA CHASE (GRADE 2)** | **2m**
3:20 (3:20) 5-Y-O+   £22,922 (£6,725; £3,204; £1,091)

			RPR
1		**Moscow Flyer (IRE)**[194] 38 10-11-12 174........................ BJGeraghty	167+
		(Mrs John Harrington, Ire) *settled 2nd: impr to ld at 4th: edgd 3 l clr 4 out: rdn and styd on wl fr 2 out: lft wl clr fr last*	
			30/100[1]
2	25	**Arctic Copper (IRE)**[21] 1761 10-11-10 140......................(p) PCarberry	138+
		(Noel Meade, Ire) *led: hdd 4th: remained cl up: reminders 6th: 3rd and drvn along 4 out: sn lost tch: lft remote 2nd fr last*	
			20/1
3	4	**Fiery Ring (IRE)**[21] 1757 9-11-7 130.. DJCasey	131
		(J R H Fowler, Ire) *trckd ldrs: 4th whn slt mstke 5th: trailing fr bef 4 out*	
			25/1
4	7	**Fadoudal Du Cochet (FR)**[210] 4769 11-11-10 143................. BMCash	127
		(A L T Moore, Ire) *hld up: 4th 5 out: lost tch bef next: no ex fr 3 out* **14/1**[3]	
U		**Rathgar Beau (IRE)**[30] 1646 8-11-7 149.................................... JRBarry	158
		(E Sheehy, Ire) *sn trckd ldrs in 3rd: impr into 2nd 4 out: impr to chal after 3 out: rdn and no imp next: mstke and uns rdr last*	
			10/3[2]

4m 5.70s   6 Ran   SP% **38.4**
CSF £7.59 TOTE £1.30: £1.50, £2.80; DF 7.20.
Owner Brian Kearney **Bred** Edward Joyce **Trained** Stud Moone, Co Kildare
FOCUS
A good reappearance win by former Champion Chaser Moscow Flyer who now has the Tingle Creek and King George on his agenda.

[2610]SANDOWN (R-H)

Saturday, December 4

OFFICIAL GOING: Chase course - good to soft (good in places); hurdle course - good to soft (soft in places)

2633	WILLIAM HILL - TINGLE CREEK TROPHY CHASE GRADE 1 (13 fncs)		2m
	2:35 (2:36) Class A 5-Y-O+		

£72,500 (£27,500; £13,750; £6,250; £3,125; £1,875)

Form					RPR
/11-	**1**		**Moscow Flyer (IRE)**[27] [2090] 10-11-7 .... BJGeraghty		181+
			(Mrs John Harrington, Ire) *trckd ldr: hit 9th: led after next: kpt on gamely: rdn out*	**2/1**[2]	
1/1-	**2**	1 ½	**Azertyuiop (FR)**[32] [1969] 7-11-7 177... RWalsh		179+
			(P F Nicholls) *t.k.h: trckd ldrs: trckd wnr appr 3 out: nt fluent 2 out: sn rdn: kpt on but no imp on wnr fr last*	**5/6**[1]	
1/2-	**3**	shd	**Well Chief (GER)**[22] [2168] 5-11-7 157.................................... TJMurphy		178
			(M C Pipe) *h.d.w: hld up bhd ldrs: tk clsr order after 4 out: chsd wnr 2 out: sn rdn: kpt on but no imp on wnr run-in*	**6/1**[3]	
/1U-	**4**	25	**Cenkos (FR)**[22] [2168] 10-11-7 162...................................... RJohnson		158+
			(P F Nicholls) *led: hit 9th: hdd after next: sn rdn: outpcd appr 2 out*	**25/1**	
/45-	**5**	11	**Upgrade**[14] [2344] 10-11-7 150.. TScudamore		142
			(M C Pipe) *chsd ldrs: lost tch fr 4 out*	**80/1**	
/50-	**6**	dist	**Blazing Batman**[22] [2167] 11-11-7 100................................ DrPPritchard		—
			(Dr P Pritchard) *sn bhd: t.o whn blnd 4 out*	**300/1**	
06P-	**7**	shd	**Blackchurch Mist (IRE)**[16] [2305] 7-11-0 106..........................(t) CMStudd		—
			(B W Duke) *sn bhd: t.o*	**300/1**	

3m 52.2s (-11.00) **Going Correction** -0.05s/f (Good)　　　　**7** Ran　SP% **107.9**
Speed ratings: **125,124,124,111,106** —,— CSF £3.75 TOTE £2.50: £1.40, £1.40; EX 4.80.
Owner Brian Kearney **Bred** Edward Joyce **Trained** Stud Moone, Co Kildare
FOCUS
A magnificent race in which the mouth-watering rematch between brilliant two-milers Moscow Flyer and Azertyuiop, the last two winners of the Queen Mother Champion Chase, was enhanced still further by the confirmation that last season's top two-mile novice Well Chief is yet another potential champion. The pace was very strong and the winning time, four seconds faster than that of Contraband, was most impressive, even for a Grade One contest. Outstanding form.

2005

[3375]PUNCHESTOWN (R-H)

Sunday, January 30

OFFICIAL GOING: Hurdle course - soft to heavy (heavy in places); chase course - heavy

3608a	BYRNE GROUP PLC TIED COTTAGE CHASE (GRADE 3)		2m
	2:30 (2:30)　5-Y-O+	**£18,468** (£5,418; £2,581; £879)	

					RPR
	1		**Moscow Flyer (IRE)**[57] [2633] 11-12-0 178............................... BJGeraghty		171
			(Mrs John Harrington, Ire) *mde all: drew clr 4 out: reduced advantage after 2 out: rdn to assert after last: easily*	**2/11**[1]	
	2	2 ½	**Steel Band**[7] [3502] 7-11-3 120... GTHutchinson		138
			(Paul A Roche, Ire) *hld up in tch: 4th 3 out: 3rd and rdn next: 2nd and clsng whn mstke last: kpt on u.p wout threatening wnr*	**33/1**	
	3	3	**Hi Cloy (IRE)**[8] [3496] 8-12-0 150... TJMurphy		156
			(Michael Hourigan, Ire) *settled 2nd: 3rd and outpcd 4 out: 2nd next: 3rd and kpt on fr last*	**13/2**[2]	
	4	11	**Glenelly Gale (IRE)**[14] [3383] 11-12-0 142............................... CO'Dwyer		135
			(A L T Moore, Ire) *hld up in tch: 5th 3 out: sn rdn and no imp*	**14/1**[3]	
	5	shd	**Fiery Ring (IRE)**[14] [3383] 10-11-10 128.................................. RGeraghty		130
			(J R H Fowler, Ire) *chsd ldrs: 3rd 1/2-way: mod 2nd 4 out: 3rd next: sn no ex*	**33/1**	

4m 14.8s **Going Correction** -0.05s/f (Good)　　　　**5** Ran　SP% **110.5**
Speed ratings: **113,111,110,104,104** CSF £7.58 TOTE £1.20: £1.10, £6.50; DF 8.40.
Owner Brian Kearney **Bred** Edward Joyce **Trained** Stud Moone, Co Kildare

[4381]CHELTENHAM (L-H)
Wednesday, March 16

OFFICIAL GOING: Good changing to good (good to soft in places) after race 3 (3.15)

Wind: Moderate, against Weather: Steady rain most of meeting

4396	QUEEN MOTHER CHAMPION CHASE GRADE 1 (12 fncs)	2m
	3:15 (3:16) Class A 5-Y-O+	

£145,000 (£55,000; £27,500; £12,500; £6,250; £3,750)

Form				RPR
111-	**1**		**Moscow Flyer (IRE)**[45] [3608] 11-11-10 .... BJGeraghty	182+
			(Mrs John Harrington, Ire) *lw: sn trcking ldrs: wnt 2nd 7th:chal and nt fluent 4 out: slt ld appr next: hrd drvn appr last and styd on strly* **6/4**[1]	
F12-	**2**	*2*	**Well Chief (GER)**[32] [3808] 6-11-10 [177].................................... TJMurphy	179
			(M C Pipe) *lw: hld up rr but in tch: hdwy 5th: wnt 3rd 8th: trckd wnr after 3 out: rdn and styd on wl appr last but no imp on wnr* **7/2**[3]	
231-	**3**	*13*	**Azertyuiop (FR)**[32] [3808] 8-11-10 [178].. RWalsh	172+
			(P F Nicholls) *lw: sn trcking ldrs: 2l 4th whn blnd 6th (water) and lost pl: nt rcvr but rdn and effrt fr 3 out: nvr in contention* **2/1**[2]	
111-	**4**	*7*	**Oneway (IRE)**[39] [3698] 8-11-10 [149].. GLee	161+
			(M G Rimell) *lw: held up rr: hit 4th: drvn and effrt 4 out: nvr gng pce to get nr ldrs and no ch whn hit 3 out* **16/1**	
235-	**5**	*7*	**Kadarann (IRE)**[32] [3808] 8-11-10 [154].................................... PJBrennan	154+
			(P F Nicholls) *led to 4th: rdn 7th: hit 8th and sn btn* **100/1**	
121-	**6**	*4*	**Central House**[24] [3982] 8-11-10 ....(b) PCarberry	148
			(D T Hughes, Ire) *trckd ldr: slt ld fr 4th: hdd appr 3 out: wknd sn after* **25/1**	
30P-	**7**	*1½*	**Venn Ottery**[11] [4190] 10-11-10 [145]..(t) JEMoore	147
			(M C Pipe) *a in rr* **50/1**	
605-	**P**		**Cenkos (FR)**[39] [3698] 11-11-10 [153].. JTizzard	—
			(P F Nicholls) *hit 1st: bhd: no ch whn blnd 8th: p.u bef 4 out* **100/1**	

3m 54.3s (-5.00) **Going Correction** +0.125s/f (Yiel) **8** Ran SP% **109.2**
Speed ratings: **117,116,109,106,102 100,99,—** CSF £6.63 CT £8.54 TOTE £2.20: £1.30, £1.60, £1.40; EX 4.60 Trifecta £5.70 Pool: £17,264.60 - 2,116.67 winning units..
Owner Brian Kearney **Bred** Edward Joyce **Trained** Stud Moone, Co Kildare

FOCUS
A classic renewal of this contest - arguably the best race of the entire meeting - and Moscow Flyer confirmed himself the best chaser since Desert Orchid with another superb display. The winning time was quite acceptable for a race of this quality in the conditions, despite being slower than the Arkle the previous day.

[4747]AINTREE (L-H)

Friday, April 8

OFFICIAL GOING: Grand national course - good to soft; mildmay course - good; hurdle course - good (good to soft in places)

Wind: Fresh 1/2 behind. Weather: Fine but blustery and cold.

4763	**JOHN SMITH'S MELLING CHASE GRADE 1** (16 fncs)	**2m 4f**
	3:10 (3:14) Class A 5-Y-O+ **£89,250** (£33,000; £16,500; £7,500; £3,750)	

Form						RPR
111-	**1**		**Moscow Flyer (IRE)**[23] [4396] 11-11-10 .... BJGeraghty			180+
			(Mrs John Harrington, Ire) *lw: t.k.h early: lft 2nd 6th: led on bit 12th: wnt clr between last 2: impressive*		**4/9**[1]	
145-	**2**	16	**Le Roi Miguel (FR)**[22] [4408] 7-11-10 158.................................... RWalsh			162+
			(P F Nicholls) *lw: hld up: hdwy 8th: wnt prom 11th: 2nd whn hit 13th: rdn next: no ch w wnr*		**9/2**[2]	
020-	**3**	28	**Therealbandit (IRE)**[21] [4435] 8-11-10 155..........................(v[1]) TJMurphy			132
			(M C Pipe) *lw: led and qcknd pce after 4th: hdd 12th: wkng whn hit next: t.o whn hit 2 out: eased*		**9/1**[3]	
355-	**4**	dist	**Kadarann (IRE)**[23] [4396] 8-11-10 150................................. PJBrennan			—
			(P F Nicholls) *led tl after 4th: 2nd whn blnd 6th: drvn along and lost pl 9th: t.o 13th*		**40/1**	
010-	**5**	17	**Davoski**[21] [4437] 11-11-10 116................................. JAMcCarthy			—
			(Dr P Pritchard) *sn detached in last: t.o fr 5th*		**200/1**	
124-	**F**		**Mister McGoldrick**[55] [3808] 8-11-10 159................................ DElsworth			—
			(Mrs S J Smith) *chsd ldrs: fell 3rd*		**11/1**	

5m 1.40s (-5.90) **Going Correction** +0.175s/f (Yiel)   **6** Ran   SP% **108.7**
Speed ratings: **118,111,100,—,—** — CSF £2.83 TOTE £1.40: £1.30, £1.90; EX 2.70.
Owner Brian Kearney **Bred** Edward Joyce **Trained** Stud Moone, Co Kildare

FOCUS
Worthy opposition was in short supply and the peerless Moscow Flyer made it 19 wins from 19 completed starts over fences, including this Grade 1 prize for the last two years.

INDEX